DAGGERS
DRAWN

'We believe, as did the ancient Greeks, who originated the word 'aristocracy', that every man with the right attitude and talents, regardless of birth and riches, has a capacity in his own lifetime of reaching that status in its true sense.

In fact, in our SAS context, an individual soldier might prefer to go on serving as an NCO rather than leave the Regiment in order to obtain an officer's commission.

All ranks in the SAS are of "one company" in which a sense of class is both alien and ludicrous.'

David Stirling, founder of the SAS

This book is dedicated to Lt Col Paddy Mayne DSO and three bars of the SAS and Maj Anders Lassen VC, MC and two bars of the SBS, two of the most courageous soldiers of the Second World War.

It is also a respectful tribute to the bravery of all the behind-the-lines raiders of the wartime SAS/SBS who took such risks to inflict such colossal damage on the enemy in so many theatres of war on the long road to victory.

DAGGERS DRAWN

REAL HEROES OF THE
SAS & SBS

MIKE MORGAN

SUTTON PUBLISHING

This book was first published in 2000 by
Sutton Publishing Limited · Phoenix Mill
Thrupp · Stroud · Gloucestershire · GL5 2BU

This new revised edition first published in 2003

British Library Cataloguing in Publication Data
A catalogue record for this book is available from the
British Library

ISBN 0 7509 3058 6

Typeset in 10/11pt Photina.
Typesetting and origination by
Sutton Publishing Limited.
Printed and bound in Great Britain by
J.H. Haynes & Co. Ltd, Sparkford.

Contents

Foreword
By Major Roy Farran, DSO, MC and two bars   vii

Preface   ix

Acknowledgements   xi

Introduction
How the SAS was Born   1

The Fearless Legends
David Stirling, Paddy Mayne, Anders Lassen VC,
Roy Farran   23

Demons of the Desert
Jock Lewes, Fitzroy Maclean, Bob Lilley, John Sillito,
Johnny Cooper   94

Blistering Action – France and Germany
Derrick Harrison, Chalky White, Ian Fenwick,
Bill Fraser   137

Three Great SBS Commanders
George Jellicoe, David Sutherland, John Lapraik   161

The Hell that was Italy
George 'Bebe' Daniels, Philip Pinckney, Reg Seekings   170

Leading from the Front
  Brian Franks, Bill Stirling, Eric Barkworth 187

Unsung Heroes
  Denis Bell 215

Appendix I
  Maps 225

Appendix II
  *Official Citations: Lt Col Robert Blair Mayne
  and Maj Anders Lassen* 230

Bibliography 235

Index 237

Foreword

*By Major Roy Farran DSO, MC and two bars
Former 2nd SAS Operational Commander*

A personal appreciation of the Special Air Service Regiment and its most famous fighting son, Lt Col Paddy Mayne DSO and three bars.

'Although I was a late arrival and fought in the Western Desert and Crete with my own parent regiment, the 3rd The King's Own Hussars, I am very proud that I was recruited later into the Second SAS by Sandy Scratchley in North Africa. It is an invidious distinction to single out different SAS characters for praise – that is apart from the obvious stars like David Stirling himself, Blair (Paddy) Mayne, and George Jellicoe etc., and I cannot do it. I admire and am proud of them all. Indeed I am very proud to have been associated with such a band of heroes of all ranks. I also feel that those who have served in the SAS since the Second World War have been worthy successors of the originals. Honour and praise to them all!

Paddy Mayne was a great friend of mine and I have stayed in his home at Newtownards – a neat white house kept in immaculate shape by his mother. Blair Mayne was a very strong man and played rugby football for Ireland, one of the few areas where north and south combined for a united team. He was an Orangeman but knew the words of all the Irish rebel songs as well as 'The Sash Me Father Wore'. So did I, and once in his company I began to sing 'The Foggy Dew' in a pub in Belfast. Paddy was horrified and sprang to my defence when hostile Orangemen took umbrage. He was strong enough to bend an iron bar or a nail in his bare hands. Yet, except in his cups, he was very gentle. Of course, in action he was like a Viking who runs berserk and I can quite well imagine his pulling the dashboard out of a Messerschmitt when his party had run out of explosives and ammunition, as he actually did in an early desert raid. He was fearless when his blood was up.

David Stirling had recruited him in Cairo when he was in trouble for banging together the heads of two military policeman who objected to his pulling trees out by their roots along a main boulevard. When he had been drinking he was a holy terror, but brave as a lion. His officers and men adored him, even though they were terrified of him when he was taken with drink. He was a great soldier with good tactical sense and his men would follow him anywhere. I only fought alongside him once – at Termoli – and was most impressed by him and his raiding force.

Paddy was quite well read and had a very soft voice on most occasions. He did not get along with women – I think he was frightened of them in some way, although he was neither a homosexual nor misogynist. Towards the end of his life he did become very attached to a girl who knew how to handle him. He was not a bigoted Ulsterman either and one of his best friends was Ambrose McGonigal, ex-SAS, Roman Catholic and a judge after the war. Some accounts leave the impression that Paddy Mayne was an alcoholic and drunk most of the time. That is just not true although he enjoyed a party. Most of the time, he did not drink at all.

Mayne was a fascinating character and reminded one of some Celtic warrior of ancient times who could mow down his opponents with a double-edged claymore that no one else could even lift.

Preface

This book has been written to emphasise the extraordinary courage and outstanding deeds of valour carried out by members of the Special Air Service and Special Boat Service during the Second World War. Its purpose is to bring together in one exciting volume some of the best-known characters involved and the amazing true stories of their hair-raising action behind enemy lines, together with some brand new ones. As we forge ahead into a new millennium, the likelihood is that the world will never again see such a terrible, protracted land war as the Second World War, or such a proliferation of colourful, die-hard Special Forces soldiers. Their superhuman deeds, often accomplished hundreds of miles behind enemy lines with little more than small arms, knives and delayed action bombs with which to defend themselves, are now passing into legend.

The successors to the wartime originals, the current SAS and SBS, have embraced modern technology and highly sophisticated techniques to become the envy of the world, in roles often very different from those of their forefathers, including counter-terrorism and hostage-busting. When called upon, however, they have shown that they are capable of similar acts of daring and brave ferocity in hand-to-hand firefights all over the globe, as events have proved in the Gulf, Kosovo, Afghanistan and many other hot spots.

It must be stressed that this compilation of tales of these outstanding individuals does not pretend to record the full extent of the bravery shown by the SAS and SBS during the Second World War. Many incredible feats of courage went unwitnessed or unrecorded and so have not passed into the public domain. Many experts would argue, in any event, that *all* the hand-picked veterans of the SAS and SBS were heroes in their own right, and that the factual records and personal experiences related by many veterans almost always bear this out.

Previous books about the SAS and SBS, some now out of print, have tended to concentrate on the history of the units and provide a detailed chronological record of great interest to military scholars. *Daggers Drawn* unashamedly concentrates on the all-action individual heroics of a band of men the like of which we may never see again. However, readers can still gain a good idea of the history of the units from the authentic stories recounted here. Once the appetite is whetted, the bibliography contains books that will provide further information about the elite soldiers of these extraordinary wartime forces.

Meanwhile, extensive research of material already in the public domain, including records and accounts by serving veterans, has thrown up many new connections and fascinating insights on famous events and the larger-than-life personalities and actions. It is plain to see that these men were special in every sense of the word and, in this latest format, one can almost taste the heady danger and wild excitement of behind-the-lines Second World War action.

Acknowledgements

I would like to thank the many SAS veterans of the Second World War who have helped with key information and advice for this book regarding Regimental matters and history, especially Maj Roy Farran, one of the outstanding commanders of the wartime SAS, for his friendship over many years, his informative correspondence, advice and encouragement.

Also, I am especially grateful for his permission to quote at length from his classic wartime book *Winged Dagger*.

The extensive selection of authentic photographs, many rare and previously unpublished, have been provided from the collections of wartime veterans of the SAS, the Imperial War Museum and my own sources.

I am grateful to all veterans and their families who have played a part including Denis Bell, George Daniels, Gary Hull, Arthur Huntbach, Tom Robinson, Mark Rhodes, Steve and Kevin James, Jan Weekes and family and also the Blair Mayne Association of Northern Ireland.

There have been many more supporters, both individuals and past and present members of the Regiment too numerous to name. My thanks to all.

Finally, I would like to acknowledge the debt I owe to the SAS soldier who inspired me to become interested in the history of the Regiment in the first place - my late father Cpl Jack Morgan. An original wartime veteran of the 2nd SAS Regiment, he later served in Italy working on the intelligence of Maj Farran's famous missions, the secret planning for the major behind-the-lines SAS drops in support of the D-Day invasion of Europe and the liberation of Norway.

My memories of his skill, determination and steadfast resolve provided the motivation and inspiration to write this book.

Introduction

How the SAS was Born

The Special Air Service is, without question, the most famous and accomplished of all the world's Special Forces, with a track record of achievements second to none. Many countries from various continents and with differing political backgrounds have attempted to emulate the success of Lt Col David Stirling's stunning concept of behind-the-lines raiding. However, none have so far bettered the tough standards laid down by the widely respected – and feared - British force, hand-picked from the cream of the finest recruits in the British Army.

From the Second World War, through Malaya and a multitude of hot spots to the Falklands, the Gulf War, Northern Ireland to Kosovo and the ongoing tragedy of the Balkans and the Iraq crisis, the SAS and its sister unit the Special Boat Service have constantly been at the forefront of the action. In recent times in the deadly mountains of Afghanistan they have operated fearlessly and heroically against the Taliban and Al Qaeda terrorists. Soldiers and officers of the SAS and SBS have always taken on the most difficult and dangerous covert assignments from behind-the-lines sabotage and surveillance, to counter terrorism and siege busting.

The SAS Regiment rocketed to fame in May 1980 with the spectacular storming of the Iranian Embassy in London when a highly trained counter-terrorist team halted the murder by terrorists of twenty-one hostages, the drama being transmitted by television cameras to millions worldwide. But popular fascination and admiration of this intensity is a relatively modern phenomenon. The current prestige of the Regiment, and the familiarity with which the general public perceives it, is demonstrably at an all time high. It is therefore sometimes diffcult to grasp that before the Second World War the SAS and SBS simply did not exist. The fact that the SAS grew, under Lt Col David Stirling's driving inspiration, into the world-leading force it is today is a lasting tribute to his unique foresight, courage and tenacity and of the calibre of the men and officers he recruited to join his fledgling team. However, recognition of the true value of such specialist, modern raiding forces took a long time to be fully acknowledged.

From 1941 to 1945, thousands of SAS and SBS raiders operated in campaigns in North Africa and other widely dispersed theatres, including Italy, the Mediterranean, the Aegean, France, Belgium, Holland and Germany, destroying hundreds of enemy aircraft, trains, troops, supplies, installations and communication facilities. But even so, few people at home in Britain at the time had even heard of the units. When the war ended, the SAS Regiment was declared to be surplus to requirements and summarily disbanded. It was thought by those in higher command to have been a wartime 'one-off' which would never be needed again in peacetime. However, as soon as the crisis in Malaya flared up in 1948, the SAS wartime veterans were urgently recalled for active service and won a brilliantly successful campaign against Communist terrorists. Subsequently, the Regiment has hardly been out of action ever since in numerous trouble spots all over the world.

It was not until years after the Second World War had ended that books started to be written by veterans and authors divulging the spell-binding contributions made by the SAS to the war effort against Hitler and Mussolini, giving a true inkling of their immense part in the victory. These early ground-breaking successes were achieved by troops operating in many cases hundreds of miles behind enemy lines using fighting knives, pistols, grenades, Tommy and Bren guns and machine-guns, and finding their way to the target on foot or in jeeps, using a compass, maps and gut instinct. Today's SAS and SBS have a bewildering and powerful array of modern weapons and high technology at their disposal, including hand-held satellite navigation systems which can tell soldiers precisely where they are anywhere in the world to within a matter of centimetres. They are versatile, highly trained specialists who can turn their hands to almost any military or covert task asked of them. One traditional link between the SAS of the Second World War and those of the present day remains, however, in the shape of the arduous SAS selection process. This tests physical and mental toughness to the limit to ensure that only the best recruits go through to gain the ultimate honour of wearing the famous Winged Dagger badge.

While the future of Britain's SAS Regiment seems assured for many years to come, never has it been more important to remember the Regiment's illustrious roots. It is also a near-certainty that never again will so many SAS and SBS soldiers go into action as they did in their thousands in the white hot cauldron of the Second World War – the time when the 'Who Dares Wins' heroes were born.

Origins

The Special Air Service was a development of the Commandos, whose daring raids took the war directly to the enemy, a form of warfare much favoured by pugnacious British war leader Winston Churchill, especially after things went so badly for Britain early in the war. After Britain's forces were ejected from Europe by the all-conquering German Army in 1940, Churchill was desperate to hit back at the enemy by any means available, in the air, via the sea and on land. Therefore, when Lt Col Dudley Clarke prepared a report suggesting the formation of a mobile, highly trained fighting force which could strike suddenly at widely dispersed targets on land or by sea, Churchill eagerly approved the scheme for a so-called Commando force. Churchill's 'leopards', as he termed them were, like the SAS who followed them, recruited from existing units of the British

Army and were equipped with the finest weaponry imported from America, including the trademark Tommy guns and razor sharp Commando knives for silent killing of sentries.

By the end of June of that year, almost 200 officers and men formed the first Commando unit, which began the soon-to-be-familiar intensive training programme. Many more were to follow in this unit's wake. However, though early cross-Channel raids were relatively successful, later larger scale operations in Syria, Crete and North Africa by Layforce Commando Brigade were not. This was because large seaborne formations made it almost impossible to surprise the enemy; the situation was compounded by a chronic shortage of suitable ships. The desperately brave but unsuccessful raid to kill or capture Rommel led by Lt Col Geoffrey Keyes, who won a posthumous VC in the vain attempt in November 1941, was the last operation true to the original concept. For the rest of the war, the Commandos were largely used as a hard-hitting shock assault force going in first in large-scale landings or operations.

Significantly for the birth of the SAS, a highly important event occurred earlier in 1941 when a consignment of parachutes bound for the 2nd Parachute Brigade in India found their way into the hands of Lt Jock Lewes, of No. 8 Commando, based at Alexandria, North Africa. Lewes was a very intelligent, determined and adventurous officer who was also, coincidentally, a close friend of David Stirling, a Commando officer himself and the man who was to make the SAS dream a reality. Lewes obtained Maj Gen Sir Robert Laycock's permission to experiment with the parachutes. Stirling joined the risky venture and with a handful of fellow Commandos jumped from an obsolete Valencia bomber – but things went wrong. Stirling badly damaged his spine in a heavy landing and was temporarily paralysed. However, being the productive genius he undoubtedly was, he put an enforced spell in the Scottish Military Hospital in Alexandria to excellent use.

Stirling wrote a lucid report on airborne raiding

operations, arguing that current Commando raids were too large and that groups of about sixty men divided into four-man patrols should be used instead to strike at enemy airfields on the vulnerable coastal plain. Other existing forces were well aware of the possibilities posed by the long and wide-open desert flank, which stretched for many hundreds of miles. Using Lewes' skill with compact bomb making, the raiders would strike swiftly and silently at their targets using special charges and then simply melt away into the darkness to rendezvous with the Long Range Desert Group who would bring them back by truck to British lines.

The daring plan required a minimum of men and resources and seemed feasible. So, after being discharged from hospital in July, Stirling, in a famous incident, wangled his way into the office of the deputy commander Gen Ritchie by a mixture of cunning and sheer good luck to try to get top-level backing for his scheme. Fortunately, his plan appealed to Ritchie and the commander-in-chief, Gen Auchinleck. At this time, Auchinleck was under intense pressure from Churchill to mount a new offensive and believed special operations such as the scheme put forward by Stirling would help the success of his general attack. He was building up a mass of men and resources and hoping to knock Rommel out of the desert war for good. The Layforce group of Commando units, coincidentally, was earmarked for disbandment and so a rich pool of crack, highly trained soldiers was available in the Middle East, ripe for picking. The man destined to reap the harvest was the young Lt Stirling, soon to lead the newly formed SAS.

Stirling was itching to unleash his bold raiding plan, using small patrols of men to strike deep behind enemy lines, causing untold mayhem and confusion. The redundant Commandos were just the troops he needed to do the job. They were, after all, presently unemployed and trained in all the necessary close fighting and demolition skills. Thus, at the end of July 1941, the Special Air Service

was formed. The choice of name coincidentally involved
Dudley Clarke, now a brigadier, and formerly the founder of
the Commandos. He was trying to deceive the Axis forces
about the size, strength and composition of British
formations in North Africa by cunning subterfuge,
including dummy gliders designed to fool enemy spotter
planes into believing Allied positions were far stronger at
certain points than they actually were.

Formation of L Detachment

Dudley Clarke developed bogus units, one of which was
called 1st Special Air Service Brigade and, when he heard
of the formation of Stirling's parachute unit, suggested
Stirling's real raiding unit be similarly named to reinforce
credibility in his deception schemes. Stirling readily agreed
to calling his force L Detachment, Special Air Service
Brigade . . . and a legend was born.

By August, Stirling had been authorised by Auchinleck
to recruit sixty-six Commandos from Layforce. He
established L Detachment at Kabrit, a desolate area in the
Canal Zone about 100 miles from Cairo. The area was
barren when his men arrived to set up camp and they had
to beg, steal or borrow tents and equipment from wherever
they could find them. The men improvised, as SAS soldiers
the world over have ever since. The clock was ticking with
just three months to go before Auchinleck's long awaited
November offensive and the SAS's inaugural mission.
Stirling's original officers were Fraser, Lewes, Thomas,
Bonnington, McGonigal and Mayne. Stirling recruited
Mayne even though he was under arrest for striking his
commanding officer. He recognised that as he was such a
fine, aggressive soldier he would make a valuable recruit to
the SAS. As future events unfolded, Stirling's faith in the tall,
powerful, courageous Irishman was repaid a thousandfold,
especially after he took command when Stirling was later
disastrously captured.

Intensive training began and all recruits were trained in

a high level of skill in explosives, navigation and night movement. Expert handling of all Allied and Axis weapons was a priority, with troops continually stripping and reassembling weapons, sometimes blindfold. In fact, some of the German weapons such as the Schmeisser machine pistol were far superior to the British versions and were often used in combat. It became a trademark of the SAS that a mixture of weapons was used – sometimes American, sometimes British, sometimes German – whichever was judged to be the best at any particular point in time. Parachute training was greatly improvised. Stirling and his men performed hair-raising backward rolls off the back of a 3-ton lorry at 30 to 50mph and many back, leg and ankle injuries resulted! But Stirling allowed no let up. No proper parachute training facilities were available at first, although later towers of varying height were built out of scaffolding with impressive ingenuity for more realistic practice.

Nothing could, however, substitute for the real thing. Several appeals to the parachute training school at Ringway, near Manchester, for advice on equipment and procedure fell on deaf ears and this had a direct bearing on the tragic deaths of two troopers when the SAS made their first jumps from an RAF Bristol Bombay. The two men were killed when the static line clips on their chutes failed – an accident that the personnel at Ringway already had experience of. An immediate strengthening of the clips solved the problem and Stirling was first to jump next day, sensibly leaving his men little time to dwell on the disaster.

At about this time, the L Detachment raiders became the target of ribbing from certain members of headquarters' staff who had a derisory opinion of irregular units such as the SAS. One senior RAF officer took Stirling to task on this point. Rising to the challenge, the SAS commander bet him his men could get into Heliopolis, the main RAF airbase outside Cairo, without being spotted. Stirling gauged it would also be useful practice for his imminent groundbreaking SAS raids against German and Italian air bases. The SAS men set out across the desert by various routes, reaching the guarded British base undetected. They broke in through the perimeter and stuck labels on most of the aircraft there. Some had several labels plastered all over them, veterans of the time recall. Then the raiders silently melted away into the darkness. The SAS had won the bet hands down, to the embarrassment of the RAF!

As Auchinleck's November offensive approached, Stirling and Jock Lewes and their men were trained to a high peak of readiness. Countless hours were spent poring over intelligence reports, checking maps, weapons and explosives. Everyone felt it was now or never for the Special Air Service. The plan was to parachute in to attack a group of German frontline airfields which housed some of the best of the Luftwaffe's aeroplanes, including fighters. Lewes had perfected his famous 'sticky bomb' which was specially designed to wreck aircraft with a deadly combined incendiary and blast charge made of thermite and plastic explosive. It was this secret weapon that the SAS planned to unleash on the unsuspecting Germans.

The First SAS Raid

Tragically, blistering desert winds – the worst for years - turned the SAS's first mission on 16 November 1941 into a disastrous nightmare. More than sixty SAS officers and men in five groups were dropped from Bristol Bombay aircraft, but the vicious gale-force winds scattered the raiders all over the desert. Some were severely injured on landing and many more were literally blown away into the desert, never to be seen again. Only twenty-two officers and men returned from the raid. Fortunately, the key men, Stirling, Lewes and Mayne, were among those who lived to fight another day, but all the containers, bombs and most of the weapons were lost in the mayhem and so none of the chosen airfields could be attacked.

The LRDG met the group as arranged to ferry the disconsolate survivors back to Allied lines. Stirling immediately realised he had to abandon the idea of parachuting into the desert. Less-determined men would have called it a day after this débâcle but, after talking over the matter with LRDG commander David Lloyd Owen, Stirling decided that in future the raiders would be dropped off and picked up near their targets by the LRDG. This simple change of plan was to be the crucial key to success for the fledgling SAS force.

The LRDG, brainchild of Ralph Bagnold, was formed in June 1940 as an intelligence-gathering unit. Its soldiers travelled in specially modified Chevrolet and Ford trucks, defended by heavy machine-guns. But as the war progressed, the LRDG diversified its method of operations, raiding bases and airfields in its own right. Patrols took British agents to and from their destinations, patrolled very deeply behind enemy lines, gathered valuable intelligence and found new routes for larger forces. They also operated their famous clandestine road watches to observe and count the strength and composition of enemy convoys and other forces. Now they became the 'taxi force' that the SAS desperately needed to survive.

Gen Ritchie, now commander-in-chief of the Eighth Army, ordered L Detachment to Jalo oasis, which it shared with a unit of the LRDG. It was soon to become a happy hunting ground for both units. Stirling struck swiftly to eliminate all memory of the failure of the first SAS raid and to spike the guns of the gathering group of GHQ and other doubters. In December 1941, SAS squads simultaneously attacked three enemy airfields at Sirte, Agheila and Agedabia. These raids brought an astonishing success and the SAS was credited with destroying over sixty enemy aircraft and thirty vehicles with their Lewes bombs. Then, just before Christmas, another raid was mounted with Stirling and Paddy Mayne attacking airfields at Tamet and Sirte, while Lewes and others targeted a similar site at Nofilia. While Mayne's charmed Irish luck held again,

Lewes was tragically killed during the return trip, when his column of vehicles was strafed by an enemy plane and he was hit, dying almost immediately. His loss was keenly felt by the SAS as he was one of the unit's leading strategists and Stirling's right-hand man. Lewes was also the SAS's training supremo, cunningly schooling his men in the intricacies of behind-the-lines desert raiding.

The Famous Badge and Wings

The raiders were by now sporting their famous insignia of a flaming sword of Damocles over the legendary motto 'Who Dares Wins'. Though the debate continues to this day over the actual origins of the world-famous badge, it was allegedly originally made up by a Cairo tailor and many believe it was for this reason that the flaming sword came out looking more like a dagger with wings! The colours of dark and light blue represented the Oxford and Cambridge University rowing background of Oxbridge officers, including Lewes. Parachute wings in white and two-tone blue were proudly worn on the right upper arm of troopers after five or more jumps. Officers wore them on the left breast and, after a period of operational service, other ranks were allowed to follow suit. These wings became more highly prized to the SAS than virtually any award for bravery.

Free French Swell the Ranks

Stirling was promoted major in January 1942 and, as the score of enemy aircraft destroyed climbed steadily, he was encouraged to enlarge his unit with new recruits. This, of course, was just what Stirling wanted and had planned for. Among these recruits was a company of Free French paratroopers under Capt Berge. This unit became the French Squadron of the SAS and was later to distinguish itself on returning to its home country after D-Day.

In the earliest days, distinctive white berets were originally worn to complement the SAS insignia, but these drew scorn from other units and caused fights in the bars in Cairo. A sand-coloured beret soon replaced the embarrassing white versions and these became the unit's distinctive headgear. Although, as will be seen later, after 2nd SAS was officially formed in 1943, they wore a maroon version. In January 1944, when the SAS Brigade was formed under the 1st Airborne Division, red berets were supposed to be worn by all SAS units. Though these continued to be accepted by 2nd SAS and the foreign SAS squadrons, many of the later re-named 1st SAS and SBS veterans stubbornly refused to obey orders to replace their beige berets with maroon. One of the foremost to stick to his guns on this issue of pride and tradition was the fearsome Lt Col Paddy Mayne. A similar beige beret is worn by the modern equivalents today.

The SBS Join the Fray

Backtracking to the desert, Stirling's ceaseless determination to widen the role of his raiding force led to the absorption into the SAS of the men of the Special Boat Section of No. 8 Commando. A joint raid on shipping in Bouerat harbour followed in January 1942. This original SBS unit, which was in fact a separate Commando entity, is easily confused with the later SAS Special Boat Squadron and, ultimately, the Special Boat Service which also came under the SAS umbrella. The combined SAS and Commando SBS raiders on Bouerat were again transported to the target by truck and the unerring accuracy of the ace navigators of the LRDG, but unfortunately the canoe that was to be used in the raid was damaged en route. Even so, a great deal of damage was done to the harbour facilities, stores and petrol tankers were devastated by the raiders' bombs. In March of the same year, Stirling tried a similar attack on Benghazi harbour, but again the boat being carried was damaged, although Paddy Mayne destroyed about fifteen aircraft at Berka.

The Greek Sacred Squadron

At about this time, the Greek Sacred Squadron joined
Stirling's flourishing SAS L Detachment. This unit was
commanded by Col Kristodoulus Tsigantes, who later served
in the Aegean, winning the DSO. The squadron comprised
former officers and men of the Greek Army who had
bravely escaped German occupation of their homeland. The
French Squadron of the SAS had just completed their SAS
training and now it was the turn of the Greeks to be put
through their paces. They passed with flying colours.
Having witnessed the crushing of their home country by
the Nazi invaders, these men were desperately keen to get
to grips with the enemy. They were hell bent on revenge,
having witnessed countless atrocities against their families
and countrymen. In truth, they were a bloodthirsty bunch
and little quarter was asked or given.

The SAS received top-priority orders to stop the Luftwaffe
from sinking a vital convoy bound for Malta. Several
groups of raiders were ordered to attack aircraft on airfields
at Benghazi, Barce, Derna and Heraklion on Crete. The
Crete raiders, led by Capt Berge and comprising British and
Free French SAS, were decimated after successfully
damaging the enemy airfield. Earl Jellicoe, later commander
of the Special Boat Service, managed to escape to safety
along with a Greek guide. The rest of the party were either
killed or taken prisoner and shot – the fallen unfortunately
included the courageous Berge.

The Arrival of the Famed SAS Jeeps

In June 1942 a consignment of jeeps arrived from the USA
and Stirling immediately realised that not only would these
be ideal for desert raiding and could carry heavy weaponry,
but would give the SAS independence from the LRDG. Their
radiators were fitted with simple but highly effective
condensers, which enabled the vehicles to cope with the
fierce desert temperatures. Water expanded into the

condensers in the same way that expansion bottles work on modern motor cars. As a result, the vehicles did not overheat and when the radiators cooled, the water simply drained back into them without loss of precious coolant.

By chance, while looking for suitable machine-guns, Stirling came across some RAF Vickers K drum-fed weapons which used to be fitted to now obsolete aircraft and were on their way for scrap. Not only did these have a phenomenally high rate of fire at more than a thousand rounds a minute, but they were principally designed to shoot up and set ablaze aircraft in air-to-air combat, having a deadly mixture of tracer, armour-piercing and explosive bullets. These simple and highly effective weapons could be mounted in pairs and so twin sets of machine-guns were fixed front and rear on the jeeps which, with extra jerrycans strapped on to the rear and bonnet, had an extended range of several hundred miles. Browning .5-inch heavy machine-guns were placed on some of the jeeps in anti-aircraft mountings to give further range and firepower.

In due course, what was to become one of the legendary missions in SAS history took place thanks to the arrival of a further batch of twenty brand new four-wheel-drive jeeps.

The Big Jeep Raid

The target selected for a massive, co-ordinated jeep raid was Sidi Haneish, a landing ground in the Fuka area that housed a large number of Ju 52 transport planes. These were, at this crucial stage of the desert war, in short supply and were a vital part of Rommel's stretched supply lines. Stirling hatched a daring plan to destroy as many planes as possible in one devastating raid made in the light of the full moon. Surprise and overwhelming strength were the keywords. Eighteen jeeps drove at the base in line abreast, allowing a clear field of fire to knock out the perimeter defences. Then, once on the field, a green Very light was fired and the jeeps changed formation to an arrowhead, headed by Stirling's jeep with a co-ordinating navigator's jeep in the front centre behind. The SAS drove straight on to the airfield between the rows of planes. Almost seventy machine-guns opened up simultaneously with devastating results, blasting everything in their path on either side. Planes were set ablaze or literally shot to pieces.

To ensure pinpoint precision, the SAS had practised the manoeuvre in the desert beforehand, including live firing sessions. Nothing was left to chance as Stirling realised that this was one ploy that could be used once and once only on this grand scale, as counter measures were bound to be taken by a furious enemy. To the raiders' delight, there were not only Ju 52s but also Messerschmitts and Stukas on the airfield. The SAS just could not miss from less than 50 yds and the deafening roar of their machine-guns was joined by the dull thuds of exploding petrol tanks as plane after plane was blown sky high. The heat was so intense some of the British men's hair and eyebrows were singed and panic-stricken German troops could be seen running about in the distance, silhouetted by the flames.

Stirling's jeep was hit by a stray burst of fire and put out of action, but he signalled for another jeep to pick up him and his crew. A heavy enemy machine-gun returned fire and caused the only SAS casualty of the action – Sandy Scratchley's front gunner was hit and killed outright. However, concentrated fire from the jeeps soon silenced all opposition. Stirling ordered his men to destroy some remaining planes temptingly sited on the edge of the airfield and then the raiders roared away into the desert. As a parting gesture, the irrepressible Paddy Mayne was seen running from his jeep to place a bomb on the wing of an undamaged plane and then rushing back to his jeep. The airfield and its planes were a scene of total devastation.

The jeeps drove off into the desert, split up into groups and independently made their way to a pre-determined rendezvous. One group got lost, driving on to a flat stretch of stony desert with absolutely no cover from the enemy aircraft that would be sent out to look for them. Luckily, an early mist cleared and they found a large depression cut by deep wadis, with thick scrub – a perfect hiding place. Soon all the jeeps were hidden and it was only then that the tension that had built up during the high drama of the attack could be released. The dead soldier was buried with simple dignity with the men briefly paying their last respects.

This one big raid, together with a smaller one nearby, had accounted for up to 50 enemy aircraft, bringing the running total after a year's operations to about 250 destroyed. An impressive number by any standards. Afterwards, however, it was a case of once bitten, twice shy as far as the Germans were concerned and the number of sentries posted was increased dramatically. Jeep raids were mounted in future many times, but never on this awesome scale. It was a magnificent one-off, so typical of Stirling's flamboyant daring and improvisation, which he repeated time and again throughout the desert war.

Evolution of the Special Boat Squadron

In August 1942, the Special Boat Section of Middle East Commando came under SAS control. Earl Jellicoe and Fitzroy Maclean organised units within the overall SAS unit, which would later emerge as the SAS Special Boat Squadron. The SBS were equivalent members of the SAS, entitled to wear the coveted wings and sand-coloured beret. Maclean was given command of M Detachment and trained for operations behind enemy lines in case Germany invaded Persia and Iraq. When this threat failed to materialise, Maclean was parachuted into Yugoslavia as Churchill's personal representative to Tito's partisans, playing a vital part in ultimate victory in that country and the tying up of countless German forces. His detachment was taken over by Ian Lapraik and Langton and Sutherland commanded other units. In September 1942, the SBS attacked the island of Rhodes, destroying aircraft and stores.

Formation of 1st SAS

Meanwhile, Stirling's L Detachment dropped its title and became the 1st Special Air Service, a regiment in its own right with a strength of about 400. The disbandment of Middle East Commando allowed Stirling to recruit 10 more valuable and highly trained officers and 100 extra men. Stirling's command now comprised almost 800 men, including 1st SAS, French SAS Squadron, Greek Sacred Squadron and Special Boat Section men. A 2nd SAS Regiment now began to be formed under Stirling's brother William. It began training with the US 1st Army which landed in Africa during the Operation Torch invasion in November 1942.

Stirling's Capture

In January 1943 disaster struck when Stirling was captured by a German counter-SAS unit in the Gabes area of Tunisia while attempting to link up with American forces for the first time. Despite several escape attempts, he was eventually incarcerated at Colditz Castle, where he spent the rest of the war. Paddy Mayne took over as commander of 1st SAS. At the end of the war in North Africa, the SAS had destroyed more than 400 of the enemy's best fighters and bombers - a phenomenal and decisive contribution to the overall victory.

The French Squadron returned to Britain and was strengthened and retrained while 1st SAS was split in two with 250 men under Earl Jellicoe becoming the Special Boat Squadron, absorbing the Special Boat Section and the Small Scale Raiding Force. This highly specialised unit had seen action off the coast of France and Africa, before becoming part of the Commandos.

Anders Lassen VC

The SBS made a base near Haifa and linked up with the Greek Sacred Squadron to raid enemy occupied Mediterranean and Aegean islands and the Adriatic. The SBS was later retitled the Special Boat Service and Anders Lassen became its most famous son, winning a magnificent VC posthumously with the end of the war almost in sight by knocking out a series of heavily defended strong points at Lake Comacchio, in northern Italy.

The Formation of the 2nd SAS

The 2nd SAS was officially formed in May 1943 at Philippeville in Algeria. It raided Sardinia, Sicily and the Italian mainland, but Lt Col William Stirling soon had the first of several fierce arguments with his superiors, believing his men would be more effectively used in small sabotage groups parachuted far behind enemy lines than in a Commando-type role.

Assault on Sicily and Italy

Paddy Mayne's 1st SAS was temporarily renamed the Special Raiding Squadron and led the assault on Sicily, operating for the next few months on Commando lines, landing by sea against well-defended enemy positions on mainland Italy. One of the toughest SAS engagements of the war was at Termoli in October 1943 when 1st SAS, with Commando units and a contingent of 2nd SAS, repulsed a series of attacks by the crack German 1st Parachute Division despite being heavily outgunned and outnumbered. Serious losses were sustained, however, including an entire SAS section wiped out by a single shell blast. At the end of 1943, SRS reverted to 1st SAS once again and was placed under the command of 1st Airborne Division.

Preparations for D-Day

In early 1944, it was decided to form a full SAS Brigade and
in March, after further action in Italy, 1st and 2nd SAS were
ordered back to Britain to retrain for Overlord, the long-
awaited invasion of Europe. At about this time Lt Col William
Stirling, commanding officer of the 2nd SAS, resigned. Some
senior staff members at Army headquarters wanted the SAS
to be parachuted into France to operate as the filling in a
sandwich between the invasion beach area forces and the
Panzer reserve divisions deeper inland, waiting ready to move
towards the coast and crush the invaders. Stirling rightly
argued that such a deployment would not only be a total
misuse of his highly trained SAS men, but would also be
suicidal and lead to the annihilation of the SAS.

Stirling won his argument but overstepped the subtle
line of Army protocol and was forced to resign. An
extremely able commander was lost who was much missed
by the SAS. He was succeeded by another equally able
commander, Lt Col Brian Franks, who led his men to glory
in France right up to the very borders of Germany itself.

The SAS brigade, now some 2,000 strong, was formed in
Ayrshire in January 1944 consisting of 1st and 2nd British
and Commonwealth SAS, 3rd and 4th French SAS, the
Belgian SAS Squadron and F Squadron HQ signals and
communications, otherwise known as Phantom. This
intelligence, signals and reconnaissance unit gathered
information in forward areas behind enemy lines, radioing
the vital data back to GHQ. One of its most famous
members was the Hollywood film actor David Niven.
Shoulder titles were now issued for the SAS units in the
airborne colours of pale blue on maroon.

Hitler's Infamous Execution Order

In behind-the-lines missions on a mainland Europe teeming
with enemy forces, SS and Gestapo units, the SAS were to
face greater dangers than ever before. Hitler had issued his

infamous Commando Order in retaliation for earlier Commando and SAS raids. Its orders were that all SAS and Commandos were to be handed over to the Gestapo to be interrogated and executed. Several veterans recall that units were called out on parade and informed of the order and its consequences should they be captured in France or elsewhere in Europe. They were told they could return to their units with no honour lost if they chose to leave. But as far as is known, no one did.

As D-Day, 6 June 1944, dawned, British SAS troops parachuted into enemy occupied France in unprecedented force, operating in clandestine groups all the way across central and northern France. Other units went into Belgium to prepare resistance there ready for the approach of the main invasion force. The codenames of the operations were to become milestones in SAS history – Kipling, Loyton, Wallace, Bulbasket, Hardy, Houndsworth and Haggard. In the case of Loyton, the very borders of Germany itself were reached, but at a tragically high cost. The full story of what happened to many of the missing men was not known until after the war when the brilliant 2nd SAS intelligence officer Maj Eric Barkworth tracked down and brought to the hangman's noose those responsible for unspeakable atrocities.

Behind the Lines in France

Carefully hidden bases were set up in the forests of France. These were supplied by air with ammunition, explosives and rations and after completion of the initial phase, the famous heavily armed jeeps were parachuted in, now fitted with armour-plate shields and bullet-proof windscreens for additional protection. Overall, a massive amount of damage was done to enemy communications, trains, fuel supplies, railway lines, troop convoys and enemy headquarters.

Casualties inflicted on the enemy in these lightning raids were, as usual, totally out of proportion to the numbers of SAS employed. However, owing to the large quantities of

SAS troops deployed overall and the much larger numbers of ruthless SS troops and Gestapo throughout the various areas of operations, SAS casualties were sometimes very heavy indeed. Many were, however, only captured after fierce firefights against vastly superior enemy forces when all ammunition was exhausted. The elite British fighters even tried to battle their way out with their bare fists as a last resort in some cases and a few managed miraculous escapes in amazingly difficult circumstances.

Crucially, the constant, harrying attacks and self-sacrifice of the SAS caused a major paralysis of the enemy communication network, especially among the main railway lines around the Paris, Lyons and Dijon area which were continually cut, preventing reinforcements and supplies getting through to the invasion area. Movement of the decisive Panzer divisions was slowed and restricted.

High Price Paid by SAS and the Resistance

Inevitably, the price of success was high with many SAS officers and men brutally tortured and executed after capture. Even though their deaths were avenged ten times over in the final reckoning, it was difficult for comrades to bear the loss of close friends, some of whom had been with the Regiment from its earliest days in the desert.

Roughly 150 men of the French SAS corps operated with about 3,000 Maquis fighters in Operation Dingson, near Vannes. But the large and obtrusive base was, not unsurprisingly, surrounded and heavily attacked by the Germans and though the defenders gave a good account of themselves it was clear that the group could not fight on indefinitely. Members were forced to disperse, with the SAS breaking up into smaller units to continue operating with success in Brittany. SS reprisals on civilians in areas where the SAS were working were savage, with countless men, women and sometimes children executed with terrifying savagery.

Final Victory in Italy and Germany

As the advancing Allied armies caught up with the behind-the-lines men, the SAS moved further forward, working with resistance groups in Belgium and Holland, finally driving into Germany itself. In late 1944, members of 2nd SAS, commanded by Major Roy Farran, parachuted into Italy in the famous Operation Tombola mission, working with Italian partisans and causing mayhem in that region until Italy was finally liberated.

In March 1945 Brig McLeod, the officer then commanding the SAS, was posted to India and his replacement was the famous Chindit brigadier 'Mad Mike' Calvert, an exceedingly brave officer who had seen extensive action behind Japanese lines in Burma. Calvert seemed a natural choice for the SAS as he was an acknowledged expert on guerrilla warfare and long-range penetration behind enemy lines.

The Belgian Squadron became 5th SAS as more recruits enabled units to sweep through liberated Belgium en route for Holland and Germany itself. Squadrons operated with the Canadian Army in a reconnaissance role in northern Holland and Germany and, later, the Belgian SAS were involved in counter-intelligence work in Denmark and Germany as the final and total defeat of Nazi Germany approached at last. When the war ended in Europe on 8 May 1945 about 330 casualties had been sustained by the SAS Brigade, which in return had killed or seriously wounded a staggering total of almost 8,000 of the enemy and had assisted in the capture of a further 23,000.

Norwegian Interlude

Both 1st and 2nd SAS were sent to Norway to supervise the surrender of 300,000 German troops who had been 'sitting out' the war there on Scandinavia's long and vulnerable coastline waiting for a British invasion that never came. The all-conquering SAS were fêted as heroes by the brave Norwegians who had withstood the Nazis stubbornly with a thriving resistance network for five long years. Lasting ties were cemented and a grateful King Olav rewarded members of the SAS with a personally signed scroll to commemorate the liberation and the unique part the SAS had played.

Stirling Plans Attacks on Japanese Empire

David Stirling was freed from Colditz prison and, with Japan still far from beaten, returned to the SAS with plans to launch operations against the Japanese along the Manchurian railway. The use of the vastly experienced SAS was considered an essential factor in the final defeat of the Empire of the Rising Sun. However, when the world's first atomic bombs were dropped on Hiroshima and Nagasaki in August 1945, the unconditional surrender of the Japanese made these plans unnecessary.

In only four years, the SAS had grown from a germ of an idea in Stirling's fertile imagination to a full-scale brigade in the British Army. Its members had achieved, at proportionately little cost, decisive damage where it hurt most and inflicted casualties on the enemy forces that far exceeded all expectations.

Shock of Disbandment

When the SAS returned from Germany and Norway to their base at Wivenhoe in Britain as conquering heroes after four long years of war, it is little wonder that they were shocked and dismayed at the bombshell news that the Regiment was to be disbanded and they were to be returned unceremoniously to their parent regiments, or back to civilian life. The High Command had decided, in its wisdom and, many veterans feel, thinly disguised envy, that there was no place in post-war forces for specialist elite units like the SAS, and by October the Regiment had ceased to exist. How very wrong those chair-borne soldiers were, as world events were shortly to prove in Malaya and numerous operations ever since.

The Fearless Legends

David Stirling, Paddy Mayne,
Anders Lassen VC, Roy Farran

SIR DAVID STIRLING DSO – SLAYER OF GOLIATHS

David Stirling's groundbreaking special force, the Special Air Service, is today the envy of the world. Many experts would agree that the brilliant Scot who created such a potent mix of skill, daring and subterfuge during the Second World War ranks alongside Hannibal and Wellington as one of the most extraordinarily gifted and original military thinkers of all time. The SAS that the modest Special Forces maestro created six decades ago is as vital a part of Britain's twenty-first century military forces today as it was in the arid North African desert back in 1941.

Paradoxically, it is widely accepted that the brave, enigmatic, lanky Scot with the disarmingly polite manner and rock-steady gaze was not the most obedient soldier in the British Army during the Second World War by a long way, as he was the first to admit. In a regular regimental role, he would never have made a front-line general of the breathtaking ability of Rommel or awesome discipline of Montgomery. In fact, his almost pathological disdain for red tape and obsession with risky, imaginative schemes meant that if his behind-the-lines unit, the SAS, had not exploded into being in the searing heat of the desert, he might never have risen above the rank of captain in a conventional military unit and would now be unrecognised and long forgotten.

Doubters Defeated

Stirling was no ordinary man as even the doubting, egotistical Field Marshal Montgomery, British high commander of the all-conquering Eighth Army and not an early admirer of Stirling's unconventional tactics and requirements, had eventually to concede. Though fearless at the sharp end in countless danger-charged SAS raids in the Western Desert, Stirling was head and shoulders above the rest of his generation in terms of Special Forces tactical innovation, employing unrivalled imagination, improvisation and determination. It is these qualities, and his own powerful and fiercely private personality, that set him apart from the rest. His story is essentially a battle royal, not only with the enemy but a continuous fight against doubters in high places on his own side, a classic David and Goliath contest he almost always won.

Stirling's story, as told here, is presented to show his achievements as a unique and historic military leader. It has been stripped of most of the danger-fraught raiding missions that are regaled in the following tales from his finest fellow officers and troopers. History remembers him for his inspired creation of the SAS by a stupendous force of will, but Stirling had many key advantages to complement his bravery, consummate military skills and natural vision.

Stirling was born into one of the most important families in Scotland, part of the aristocracy, and his father was a general with an impressive military background. Consequently, from the outset, Stirling had connections at the highest level both politically and militarily, and he was commissioned into one of the elite units in the British Army, the Scots Guards. Sometimes he rode roughshod over officialdom to get what he wanted, sometimes he used diplomacy, subtle persuasion and his key contacts to achieve the same result. But the deadly formula he conceived for his desert raiding force proved to be not the flash-in-the-pan success that many predicted, but a cast-iron winner that could be modified and applied to virtually any campaign, at any time, in any era. Consequently, the chameleon-like complexity of Stirling's military mind has bequeathed to the present day a simple, unshakeable fact: a small force of well-trained, well-armed, determined men operating deep behind enemy lines can achieve damage and destruction totally out of proportion to its size. This concept remains as true today as it was then. Stirling created an original combat unit, much copied but never equalled – the feared and envied Special Air Service.

A True World Beater

Stirling's simple and yet highly effective concept was as successful in the Falklands, the Gulf and Kosovo as in the war-torn Western Desert, Italy, France and Germany two generations ago. Britain still leads the way in this deadly Special Forces game of Russian roulette. Twenty-first-century technology in the form of satellite navigation, hi-tech communications and weaponry has, however, increased the power of the SAS phenomenally. In marked contrast, in the Second World War in the desert Stirling's SAS attacked on foot with small arms, combat knives and time bombs and found their way to and from the target by compass or the stars and, later, by trucks and jeeps bristling with machine-guns.

After transferring to the Middle East Commando from his regiment, Stirling plotted his great raiding enterprise. He predicted with unerring accuracy that the German and Italian forces strung out along the North African coast were vulnerable to attack by small groups of well-trained, determined saboteurs. The swashbuckling way he went about achieving his famed tilt at glory is now part of military folklore.

It largely came about because Jock Lewes, a highly methodical and adventurous officer in the Welsh Guards, who had also come out to the Western Desert with No. 8 Commando, had by pure chance stumbled across some parachutes destined for India. The 'liberated' consignment of fifty parachutes fell into his hands and he began to experiment with them, despite the fact that there were no instructors, manuals or training facilities. Parachuting was then in its infancy and could be a decidedly risky business in unqualified hands. However, Stirling, knowing that this method of attack would be perfect for raiding behind enemy lines, joined the enterprise with alacrity, even though the static lines had to be fixed to the legs of the seats of the ancient aircraft they were using and there was a high chance of the chutes snagging on the fuselage or tail of the aircraft on exiting. This is precisely what happened to Stirling on one of his early practice jumps. Because his damaged parachute spilled out air far more quickly than it should have done after catching against the tail in the slipstream, he hit the stoney ground very hard, severely injuring his back, so badly in fact, that his legs were temporarily paralysed and he had to spend several weeks convalescing in hospital. During this enforced spell of confinement, he penned his historic plan for the formation of a desert raiding force, the unit that was to become the Special Air Service.

Going Straight to the Top

How Stirling ensured that his scheme was read by the most senior officer possible is now a legendary part of history. In his mind, there was only one person to approach. That person was the Commander-in-Chief, Gen Auchinleck. Stirling knew very well that he had no chance of gaining an interview with Auchinleck if he applied through the normal, official channels and so with typical verve he decided to 'gatecrash' the general's headquarters without any pass or permission.

Still on crutches after his parachuting accident, he arrived unannounced at the headquarters of Middle East Command and cheekily tried to bluff the sentry into letting him in, predictably without success. However, when the sentry's attention was distracted momentarily by the arrival of a staff car, Stirling took his chance and simply hobbled in, soon finding himself lost in a maze of corridors. The first door he opened contained a major who, almost disastrously, remembered him from his early days with the Scots Guards when the officer had lectured him in the complexities of combat. Stirling recalled with embarrassment that he had found the lectures so tedious, he had often fallen asleep! Consequently, the major was highly annoyed with this 'upstart's' sudden intrusion. Stirling mumbled an apology, saluted smartly and beat a hasty retreat. It looked as though Stirling was certain to be defeated at the first hurdle in his audacious scheme, but before leaving the building he opened one last door and found himself face to face with the Deputy Commander Middle East, Gen Ritchie. Rapidly apologising for his interruption, Stirling blurted out the reason for his visit and handed over his plan for Gen Auchinleck's attention.

Far from being angry, Ritchie studied the proposal intently and then, to Stirling's surprise, said he would discuss the idea with the C-in-C at a suitable juncture. Stirling would be summoned back to a conference at a future date once the details had been digested. He had been incredibly lucky and he knew it. In fact, he could not believe his good fortune in even having his scheme assessed. However, at this stage of the war, a sabotage force of the type proposed by Stirling was just the sort of initiative that might help alter the balance in favour of Britain and her allies. The desert war was precariously poised on a knife-edge and could swing either way. Gen Auchinleck had succeeded Gen Wavell as Commander-in-Chief the previous July when the entire Middle Eastern Army was on the defensive. There was a great deal of pressure for a major offensive to be mounted to drive the Axis out of North Africa, but resources were scarce.

Auchinleck's Big Gamble

The canny Auchinleck saw there was the possibility of great gain for little expenditure in Stirling's bold enterprise and so invited him back for interview. The result was that Stirling was promoted captain and given permission to recruit a force of sixty-six men from Layforce Middle East Commando. His unit, under the direct authority of the C-in-C, would include seven officers and many well-trained NCOs with, exactly as Stirling suggested, raiding groups based on four-man squads attacking enemy aircraft on the ground with time bombs. The go-ahead was given to set up a training camp in the Canal Zone at Kabrit. Stirling was given operational command, with permission to acquire any supplies necessary. The first objective would be to attack German airfields the night before Auchinleck's major November offensive. Known as L Detachment, Special Air Service Brigade, this newly formed unit gave Stirling an independent command beyond his wildest dreams. In practice the 'brigade' only existed on paper, but Middle East headquarters wanted the Germans to be fooled into believing it was real as soon as they got wind of it, which they invariably did through their efficient spy network.

Jealousy Spawned

Stirling had achieved the near-impossible, but the official blessing from Auckinleck given so readily to such a junior, relatively unproven officer caused considerable resentment among other units. Many more similar and unfounded jealousies sprang up concerning the SAS during the rest of the war.

Stirling showed great personal courage and sound leadership while training for the first momentous SAS mission when two men plunged to their deaths on an early training parachute jump in the desert due to defective harness clips. He had the problem sorted and then made sure he was first out of the aircraft the next day to prove the point that all was well. It was a brave gesture much appreciated by his troops who were waiting to jump in dread. From the outset, he set an unwavering example to his fellow officers that they should never expect their men to do anything that they were not prepared to do themselves. Many veterans remember this as one of Stirling's finest qualities.

Drop into Windswept Hell

L Detachment's first mission was an unmitigated disaster, as detailed in Jock Lewes's tragic story recounted later in this book. The parachutists were dropped in a howling gale and the men scattered over a wide area. Many of the party were killed or lost and never seen again. None of the allocated airfields could be attacked as the bombs and weapons' containers were also scattered beyond reach of those who survived the jump. Though there were initial fears that this first raid would be the last for the fledgling SAS, the high command kept faith and persevered with the unit despite the overwhelming disappointment. Fortunately, success soon came and was spectacular. This came with the decision to abandon parachuting until later in the war and to introduce the experienced Long Range Desert Group to transport the SAS raiders to and from their targets by truck.

Although Stirling could easily have sent other officers in his place, he personally led many of the famous early desert raids, displaying great bravery and determination. He also showed an uncanny ability to conceive and plan a bewildering number of complex operations which were carried out by various raiding patrols under his command, details of which were largely carried in his own head. He was mentioned in despatches several times, but many feel his brilliance should have been rewarded with the highest honour, the VC. Later, he developed the efficient method of using mobile teams in heavily armed jeeps, combining the devastating firepower of Vickers K machine-guns with 'sticky bomb' sabotage, destroying a colossal total of more than 400 of the enemy's best fighters and bombers in the desert alone, as well as countless ammunition dumps, petrol supplies, trains and enemy forces on the ground.

The Big Jeep Raid

There was no bolder example of Stirling's innovative approach in the desert than the massed jeep raid on Sidi Haneish, near Fuka in 1942. Stirling had taken delivery of twenty brand-new jeeps when reconnaissance reported that the airfield at Sidi Haneish was jam-packed with aircraft, especially the precious transport carriers that the enemy was very short of.

Stirling took a calculated gamble. He proposed to catch the Germans by surprise by driving directly on to the airfield in full moonlight in a mass jeep attack. But first he ensured that his SAS raiders practised the complex manoeuvre in the desert until they had it drilled to perfection. There would be no room for mistakes with more than sixty machine-guns firing at once in such close formation. Eighteen jeeps would approach the perimeter defences at speed and, on a signal from Stirling, open up with their machine-guns to shatter the defences. Once on the field, a green Very light would be sent up to change the jeep formation into a huge, moving arrowhead. This grouping would then file between the parked rows of planes blasting them with 1,000 rounds a minute from the deadly Vickers K machine-guns. The effect would be devastating.

However, as the SAS approached the airfield, they got the shock of their lives. It was suddenly brilliantly lit by floodlights! Stirling thought at first they had been rumbled, but then heard an enemy plane coming into land. Stirling, in the lead, quickly opened fire and the rest followed. Messerschmitts, Stukas, Heinkels and Junkers were set ablaze or blown apart in a cacophony of ear-shattering noise. In the classic book *The Phantom Major*, Virginia Cowles says: 'David's jeep was hit by a splinter. No one was hurt but the vehicle was put out of action. The whole movement came to a standstill. He shouted to the gunners to concentrate on the Breda [machine-gun] post and signalled one of the jeeps farther down the line to move forward and pick up himself and his crew.' He and his crew then calmly transferred to the other vehicle.

More planes on the perimeter were spotted and destroyed, one last one claimed by a Lewes bomb planted on foot by Paddy Mayne. The jeeps then roared off into the desert. The only casualty was one of the SAS gunners who was apparently hit by a mortar fragment and killed instantly. The great gamble had come off spectacularly, but was never repeated on this scale as it was appreciated that the Germans were unlikely to be caught cold in such fashion again. Stirling's example encouraged many others to rise to the challenge of destroying enemy aircraft and disrupting the supply chain to help defeat Rommel and achieve Britain's first victory over the Germans at El Alamein, the turning point of the war for the Allies.

Man of Vision

The effectiveness of Stirling's L Detachment SAS raiders was vindicated time and again in countless raids in the North African desert until his untimely capture in Tunisia in 1943. Key damage was consistently caused out of all proportion to the amount of men and resources deployed. Stirling's vision enabled the creation of a unique force, the like of which had never been seen before. Incarceration in the daunting Colditz Castle was a crushing blow for Stirling and the SAS, but not a fatal one, as by this time the unit had grown to such a size that it had attracted a large number of very able officers who were well schooled in Stirling's ways and the unit's future was assured. However, there is no doubt that Stirling's absence changed the course of future SAS operations for the rest of the war. It is tantalising to speculate what glories might have been achieved if Stirling had remained in charge, but it is equally certain that no one could have made a finer successor than the redoubtable Paddy Mayne.

Following his release from captivity at the end of the war, Stirling, always seeking new challenges, left the Army to pursue different goals. His long spell of imprisonment in Colditz, the forbidding 'escape-proof' fortress for special prisoners, was not idly spent as he planned in minute detail how he could best serve his country in the turbulent post-war years. This lead to a myriad schemes of national and international importance, all with Britain's interests firmly at heart. These far-sighted initiatives included formation of the Capricorn Africa Society, which brought together representatives of numerous nations to fight to abolish racial discrimination in Africa by establishing a common citizenship. Also, the Better Britain Society with the aim of establishing a code of morality for everyone in the country. Throughout the 1950s until his death in November 1990, he remained a guiding influence on the SAS, dispensing his invaluable wisdom discreetly from the sidelines. Only now, years after his death, is Britain beginning to realise the full debt it owes to this many faceted man who drew such similarly brave men towards his leadership.

Daring Heroes

There were soldiers who talked their way through enemy roadblocks in full British uniform and tore a strip off the guard for neglecting to check their papers! Veterans who, though outnumbered fifty to one, killed a quarter of the opposition by blazing their way out to safety from a seemingly inescapable SS death trap in a bullet-scoured jeep in occupied France – and lived to tell the tale! This is the story of how it all began, told through Stirling's larger-than-life heroes of the Second World War – the vibrant tales of the toughest nuts and the most cunning brains of the 1st and 2nd SAS and the highly trained specialists of the Special Boat Service. This is the true story of the finest of those who dared.

PADDY MAYNE – THE BRAVEST SAS SOLDIER
OF THEM ALL

Lt Col Robert Blair Mayne, known to everyone as Paddy, was one of the Allied forces' most decorated soldiers in the Second World War winning no less than four DSOs and numerous other honours. A giant of an Irishman, both in height and sheer physical size, he possessed phenomenal strength, was a crack shot and yet could also move swiftly and strike silently with the knife, if required. Paddy was ferocious and personally attacked the enemy at every opportunity with Tommy gun, Bren light machine-gun, grenades and deadly Lewes bombs, amassing a huge personal total of enemy aircraft, troops, vehicles and installations destroyed.

Mayne possessed an uncanny ability to quickly assess situations and always carefully measured his responses and avoided taking suicidal risks. He was also, undoubtedly, blessed with more than his share of the legendary luck of the Irish. Many times in the Western Desert, Paddy's men returned to base with tales of great destruction wreaked on enemy airfields and installations when other SAS raiding parties inexplicably drew a blank. While he revelled in the adrenaline rush of action and relished eliminating the enemy, he was not a sadist and his treatment of prisoners was humane. If any of the wartime SAS veterans are asked who was the Regiment's most outstanding man of action, the reply will be without hesitation 'Paddy Mayne'. When Mayne became involved in critical or even hopeless situations, the effect was like *magic*, they said. It is this word that is most often used in conjunction with Mayne, and spoken with immense pride.

Deadly Shot

Paddy would fearlessly – and without hesitation – sort a problem out, often with acts of great personal gallantry, sometimes using his great strength to fire a hefty Bren gun from the shoulder like a rifle in trademark staccato bursts. He was also an ace shot with the pistol and Tommy gun. In fact, he and his close friend Eoin McGonigal were in charge of the Commando shooting courses while on their four-month training exercise on the Isle of Arran in Scotland before being shipped out to the Middle East and later joining the SAS.

Tragically, McGonigal was one of the many casualties on the first disastrous desert operation by L Detachment.

On one of Paddy's subsequent raids on an enemy airfield in the desert, he found that he had run out of explosives with which to destroy one of the remaining aircraft. Without delay, Mayne ripped out the instrument panel with his bare hands, rendering the plane inoperable – an amazing feat of brute strength.

L/Cpl Denis Bell, who served with Mayne throughout the war in the 11th Scottish Commandos, 1st SAS and SRS, said: 'Paddy was *the* man. He wasn't frightened of anything, nothing at all. If he decided to attack, he would quickly weigh everything up making the best use of circumstances and the lie of the land and then act. He wouldn't take any silly risks, but would rely on boldness, deadly accurate firepower and speed of action.'

Paddy's Roots

To understand fully Paddy Mayne's prowess as a senior officer in the world's first true Special Forces raiding unit, it is helpful to look at his origins and the influences that helped to forge his character. He was born into a well-to-do Protestant family in Newtownards, Northern Ireland, on 11 January 1915, one of six children. Paddy was named after a cousin of his mother, Capt Robert Blair, of the 5th Battalion, The Border Regiment, an officer who was killed during the First World War in the act of winning a valiant DSO. Young Blair had a boisterous and happy childhood and displayed a precocious strength and quiet self-confidence, captaining his school rugby team. He had developed such power by the age of thirteen that he was able to drive a golf ball further than most of the adult players at a nearby golf course.

After leaving school, Mayne decided to follow a career in law and was apprenticed to a local solicitor. At eighteen, he was captain of Newtownards rugby team, but it was while attending Queen's University, Belfast, that Paddy really began to stand out as an international sportsman of true class. At the age of twenty-one he became the Irish universities' heavyweight boxing champion, and, even more notably, Paddy was picked for Ireland as a second-row rugby forward in the years leading up to the Second World War. He won six full caps for his country and toured South Africa with the British Lions in 1938, but his international career was brought prematurely to an end by the approach of worldwide conflict. Mayne was regarded as almost indestructible on the rugby pitch, a fair but hard player. He was not known as an instigator of violent situations, however, if attacked he would retaliate with such ferocity that he often left several of the opposing scrum in a dazed heap on the ground. The toughness of the sport and the responsibility of playing with sportsmen of high calibre and ability instilled the qualities of durability, team work, stamina and leadership in Paddy which were to become so evident in his later SAS career.

Born Leader

A natural and inspirational leader in wartime, Paddy also possessed a razor-sharp tactical sense and in action was decisive and always prepared to lead from the front if required, especially if his men's lives were under threat. Later in the war, his fierce protective instinct to guard his men's well-being at all costs became even more apparent. Several times on the run up to D-Day he mysteriously disappeared from the camp in Gloucestershire where the SAS forces were confined, with security at a premium. It was later revealed that, under cover of darkness and in strict secrecy, he had parachuted into France to meet British agents, returning a few days later via small boats to be picked up off the coast of Brittany by submarine.

From some quarters there was fierce opposition to these risky reconnaissance trips, on the basis that Mayne was too valuable to lose and knew too much as senior commander of 1st SAS about the forthcoming SAS post-D-Day operations in France. However, Paddy refused to be dissuaded. He not only wanted to vet the landing site options in the various proposed areas of operation, but to assure himself of the loyalty of the assorted French Resistance (Maquis) groups with which the SAS would be closely working. It was well know that treachery and jealous in-fighting were rife in some areas among rival bands, creating a potentially lethal cocktail. Paddy's over-riding priority was to ensure, as far as humanly possible, that his men would not be betrayed to the Germans.

It was this burning loyalty and his consistently outstanding leadership skills that led many veterans who served under him to say they would have followed him to the very ends of the earth, into hell itself, if necessary – and in practice they were almost required to do just that while participating in some of the toughest engagements of the war. Many veterans, however, also freely admit that they greatly feared Paddy's dark moods and irrational, often violent outbursts, which inevitably followed prolonged drinking binges away from the action. Woe betide any man who crossed the giant SAS commander when he was under the influence of alcohol. On one famous occasion while on leave in Cairo, a group of burly, 6-ft-tall Red Cap military policemen unwisely tried to arrest a truculent Mayne, who was out celebrating. Paddy's reaction was to knock them out cold one by one.

Most of the time, however, Paddy did not drink at all, but when he did he went on roller-coaster benders with trusted comrades during which he did not eat or sleep for days. Alcohol seemed to unlock the ferocious side to his nature, which he struggled to control. When the SRS (Special Raiding Squadron) went to Molfetta, north of Bari, during their Italian campaign to rest and enjoy some serious drinking, Paddy virtually destroyed the mess. According to Roy Bradford and Martin Dillon's *Rogue Warrior of the SAS*, he ripped out iron railings from a balcony and threw Phil Gunn, the unit's 6-ft-tall medical officer, whom he was fond of, against a wall, damaging his shoulder badly. Capt

Johnny Wiseman, quoted in *Rogue Warrior of the SAS*: 'In action he was superb, out of action we were terrified of him. He was completely unpredictable, particularly when we were hanging around. It wasn't a blind fury. He just became destructive, especially after several days' solid drinking without a single bit of food.' By contrast during the heat of action, his aggressive fearlessness became his greatest asset and he was supremely in command.

Courage Worthy of the VC

It is widely accepted by many military analysts that Paddy Mayne and David Stirling should both have had their outstanding achievements in the Western Desert rewarded with the ultimate honour of a VC. These exceptional SAS leaders had, after all, masterminded and supervised the destruction of more than 400 of the enemy's best fighters and bombers using a mere handful of SAS raiders to complete a task that had a vital bearing on the outcome of the desert war. Mayne's squadrons later tore through the heart of Sicily, Italy, France, Belgium, Holland and Germany, killing hundreds of enemy troops, capturing thousands and causing havoc behind the lines, destroying enemy communications, supply dumps, trains, vehicles, heavy guns and headquarters.

Both Mayne and Stirling had seen more face-to-face action in a few raids than some frontline soldiers would in their entire careers and had founded and nurtured the SAS from being a simple idea in Stirling's brilliant military mind to one of the most formidable and feared Special Forces in the world. The fact that neither was honoured to the degree they deserved is an indictment of the petty jealousy shown by some of those in high command who mistrusted the fledgling SAS, believing wars should be fought and won by regular Army units, steeped in battle honours and tradition. Many openly despised the success of the various 'private armies' that the desert war had spawned so readily among the Allied ranks. But others admired and appreciated the skill and daring of the SAS and did all in their power to make the force grow and prosper. Clearly the legendary exploits of Mayne and Stirling are undiminished by any honours that were omitted, however much deserved. Their reputations, particularly Stirling's, have grown in stature since the war, as the enormity of what they accomplished with sheer guts and such limited resources has come to be fully appreciated.

True Hero

Few soldiers throughout the ages, however, have been so outstandingly heroic as Paddy Mayne, while Stirling ranks among the greatest military brains of all time as a uniquely innovative, tactical genius. Maj Gen David Lloyd Owen, whose LRDG patrols often took Stirling and Mayne to and from their early raids on the desert airfields, ports and installations, had a tremendous respect for both men, as he related to John Strawson in his *History of the SAS Regiment*. Paddy Mayne, Lloyd Owen said, had: 'All the colour, dash and attraction of a great buccaneer. He was the "perfect instrument in the hands of David Stirling's genius".' Lloyd Owen was convinced that Mayne would have won far higher honours than his four DSOs if some of his more remarkable feats had not been achieved in single combat and had been more comprehensively witnessed. On Stirling, Lloyd Owen added: 'I know full well that David knew what fear was. He could recognise the symptoms and did not like them. But he could control that fear, which was very real to him and that is the measure of true courage and supreme self-confidence. David had both. I know of no other man who did more to deserve the Victoria Cross and who was so inadequately decorated for his exploits.'

Even though Paddy Mayne later went on to distinguish himself in command of the SAS after Stirling's capture in Tunisia in 1943, and was consistently at the centre of numerous hard-fought engagements all the way through to the final surrender in Germany in May 1945, his greatest tangible reward was to receive yet another bar to his original DSO. It seemed to many to be a grossly inadequate form of recognition and that a VC would have been appropriate. The occasion of the winning of his fourth and final DSO was considered by many to be one of his most memorable feats of courage, but Mayne never voiced any public criticism for the apparent oversight regarding the supreme award. At the time, however, many knowledgeable veterans and senior officers were shocked and dismayed at the snub and said so. Maj Gen Sir Robert Laycock wrote to Paddy shortly after the war saying that while his achievement in winning four DSOs was only equalled by one other 'superman' in the RAF in the whole of the British forces during the Second World War (Gp Capt J.B. 'Willie' Tait, who won four DSOs for bombing missions), the top brass should nevertheless have given him a VC.

Robbed by the Faceless Men

David Stirling was also furious that Mayne did not receive the highest honour, bitterly castigating the 'faceless men who didn't want Mayne and the SAS to be given the distinction'. The frustration bubbling beneath the surface was hinted at when Paddy told his family he would have preferred to receive a Military Cross rather than a third bar to his DSO. While it is widely believed that Mayne was clearly robbed of the supreme award, it can also be argued that the disillusionment he felt at the dearth of interest in the SAS at the end of the war – felt and shared by many of his comrades – may have contributed to his loss of drive, heavier drinking and eventually his untimely early death behind the wheel of his powerful car only ten years after the end of the war. He was aged just thirty-nine. Despite the controversy, however, Mayne's amazing exploits are undiminished and stand out as some of the most couragous feats of human endeavour in the Second World War.

However, Paddy Mayne was demonstrably a flawed hero, a man who, like Stirling, scorned authority when it suited him and broke virtually every rule in the book. He did not, however, possess Stirling's effortless, cultured diplomacy and contacts in high places and had to learn the hard way how to get the best for his unit from those in higher authority who had not always the best interests of the SAS at heart. Later in the war, however, few fought so hard, or successfully, as Mayne to defend the SAS and maintain its existence. The responsibility of command brought out his finest attributes.

Baptism of Fire at Litani River

While serving with the 11th Scottish Commandos shortly before joining the SAS, Mayne was mentioned in despatches for his courage at the Battle of the Litani River, a seaborne landing carried out against Vichy French forces in Lebanon. Due to a navigational error, some of the British landing craft were put ashore in the thick of the enemy defences. The commanding officer Col Pedder, half the other officers and 120 men were killed, but Mayne was in his element, at the forefront of the action.

Not long after this engagement, Geoffrey Keyes, son of the famous British admiral, who also distinguished himself in the Litani action, was appointed the new CO of the 11th Scottish Commandos, and Mayne, under the influence of drink, chased everyone, including Keyes, out of the officers' mess with a rifle and fixed bayonet. This horrendous outburst, which was generously overlooked by Keyes, was followed by a much more serious incident when Mayne's volcanic temper again erupted without apparent provocation and he knocked Keyes completely out as he approached a chess game in the mess. Paddy was instantly placed under close arrest and all his friends feared his military career was finished.

Bid to Kill Rommel

The official reason for Mayne's violent attack has never been made public, but it was almost certainly connected with the fact that Keyes had not chosen Mayne to accompany him as one of his officers on the famous Rommel raid in 1941, an abortive attack on a headquarters that the brilliant German general sometimes used in Libya. The idea was to try and capture, or kill, the elusive 'Desert Fox'. If successful, the raid would have been a sensational success. In the event, Rommel was not in his lair when the Commandos attacked and Keyes was killed in the valiant attempt to storm the building, winning a posthumous VC to add to the MC he gained for his part in the Litani River action and the Croix de Guerre awarded him for service in Norway at the start of the war.

Mayne, meanwhile, was awaiting court martial for his actions and an abrupt, ignominious end to his war was looming fast when David Stirling rescued him by using his top-level contacts and influence to get Paddy out of the brig so he could join his L Detachment SAS force, then forming in the Western Desert. Stirling fully appreciated that Mayne was too valuable an asset to let slip through his – and the British Army's – fingers and promised Paddy he would be able to take on the enemy at every opportunity and see all the action his restless spirit craved. However, Stirling also made it perfectly clear to Mayne that he would not tolerate any repetition of the embarrassing physical attacks of the type that had floored Keyes. Paddy gave his solemn pledge for good conduct from now on – a promise he never broke as he had great respect for the SAS founder and never felt the need to challenge his authority, barring occasionally arguing his corner when the need arose.

The Raid that Ignited the SAS Legend

On 14 December 1941, during the first successful SAS raid on Tamet, one of Rommel's forward air bases on the coast road between Tripoli and El Agheila, Paddy showed a reckless disregard that amounted to aggressive bravado. He stealthily approached a wooden hut on the edge of the airfield from which sounds of laughter and horseplay could be heard. The building housed the officers' mess and contained about thirty off-duty German and Italian pilots who were relaxing, drinking and playing cards. They never expected to be attacked so far from the front line, or thought that within seconds so many of them would be dead, dying or seriously wounded. The airfield was 250 miles behind the lines and seemingly unassailable.

Suddenly, the door was booted open with a crash and the khaki-clad figure of Mayne was framed in the doorway, brandishing a deadly Thompson sub machine-gun with fifty rounds in the drum. It was the weapon American gangsters favoured for their bloody attacks of retribution on rival gangs. For a split second, nothing happened – and then all hell broke loose with Paddy spraying the room with burst after deadly burst of automatic fire. It was a bloodbath. A few of the enemy reacted to the shock of seeing Mayne and his Tommy gun blasting out its deadly message of death by diving for any available cover. As a parting gesture, Paddy shot the lights out and disappeared as suddenly as he had arrived into the desert night. Later, he dispassionately described the technique to employ in such circumstances was to shoot the first man to move and then let those closest have it. Few could escape his lightning reactions.

Sgt Reg Seekings, one of the five other men in the raiding party, waiting in trepidation nearby, said the result of Paddy's lethal foray was that the 'whole place went mad'. The panic-stricken enemy guards opened up with everything they had and the SAS men were lucky to get away with their lives as tracer bullets scythed across the darkened airfield, missing the fleeing raiders by inches. It was an uncharacteristic, impulsive incident which Mayne later admitted he regretted and never repeated, even though his prime objective had undoubtedly been to kill pilots, who were so valuable to the enemy forces, equally as valuable as their latest fighters and bombers in many cases. He realised that this spectacular one-man war with a

Tommy gun had drawn far too much unwanted attention and detracted from the main object of the exercise, which was to blow up enemy aircraft.

On Paddy's orders, the group returned to the airfield after an hour, reasoning that the enemy would not expect them to attack again so soon and would be off guard. Paddy's shrewd assumption was proved correct and the group of raiders was unmolested as they left their bombs on planes, supply dumps and other random targets. Seekings witnessed Paddy's memorable feat of ripping out one of the planes' instrument panels with his bare hands because he had run out of bombs. The raiders tensely waited to see the start of their deadly handiwork. Suddenly the sky was lit by flaming explosions as bomb after bomb went up. What a baptism for the SAS! In the confusion, some of the German and Italian guards even fired at each other. Fourteen aircraft were destroyed, with ten more aircraft damaged by having instrument panels wrecked, petrol and bomb dumps obliterated and several telegraph poles blown up. For his part in this spectacular inaugural success, Mayne received his first well-deserved DSO.

No Quarter Given

The calm and collected Stirling also shocked one of his senior NCOs not long after the first SAS raid when an SAS patrol came across a dozen or so Italian soldiers sleeping by their tents in the desert. Asked by his men what they should do, Stirling abruptly told them to open fire. They obeyed and wiped out the helpless enemy soldiers. Regimental Sgt Maj Bob Bennett, later to become one of the legendary stalwarts of the SAS and a close friend of Paddy Mayne, was among the group and was deeply troubled by the one-sided massacre. Later, he could no longer keep his feelings to himself and told Stirling of his misgivings. Stirling simply replied that the odds were stacked so heavily against the British and Commonwealth forces at that crucial stage of the war that the 'gloves were off' and the enemy was fair game, sometimes even in circumstances such as these. In order to maximise their pioneering behind-the-lines role, the SAS had to shake the enemy's confidence with random attacks such as this, which would help give the impression of greater SAS strength and invulnerability. Stirling added simply: 'It's against my nature to kill people, but it's got to be done.'

The SAS, operating behind the lines in this brutal, total war, often hand-to-hand against the enemy, had not the time, resources or means to debate the finer points. They simply had to kill or be killed using whatever methods were at hand. Sometimes this involved employing what many regular soldiers would regard as 'unsporting' tactics. This realistic and uncompromising attitude undoubtedly added fuel to the growing resentment emanating from certain sections of the established forces regarding the SAS.

Fortunately, not all other units were so narrow-minded. Many officers and men fully appreciated that this war was a grim and unglamorous struggle for the sheer survival of the British nation, not the death or glory quest of previous wars. Maj Gen David Lloyd Owen vividly remembers meeting Paddy at the pre-arranged desert rendezvous after the Fuka aerodrome raid. He asked Paddy how things had gone and the Irishman calmly replied that it had been difficult because the enemy had put a sentry on nearly every plane. This meant that he had had to knife them before he could place his Lewes bombs on them – the chilling total was about seventeen. While not glorying in the killing, both Mayne and Stirling realised full well that this was a brutal battle to the finish and that sometimes there was no time for qualms. However, in other respects, both behaved as British officers of any other unit would have done. For instance, prisoners taken were treated under the terms of the Hague Convention.

The Second DSO

A myriad raids were undertaken throughout the Western Desert by Stirling's unit, but Paddy did not win his next

DSO until the invasion of Sicily. On this occasion the temporarily renamed Special Raiding Squadron (1st SAS), commanded by Mayne, went into action to knock out key gun batteries on the Cape Murro di Porco, a prominent headland just south of Syracuse. A lightning assault from the sea was scheduled to take place on the night of 10/11 July 1943. After the stunning victory in North Africa, British and American forces were full of confidence and were to land side by side on a 75-mile front around the south-eastern corner of the island. The plan was to strike swiftly northwards, cutting Sicily in half, a move designed to trap the enemy forces and prevent as much of the Axis army from escaping to the mainland as possible.

The task that the SRS had been secretly training hard for was to capture and destroy the headland's coastal batteries to protect the main invasion force. Paddy's men went into action aboard assault landing craft. Mayne, like the rest of the SRS, was armed with a Colt automatic pistol, while many of the raiders were heavily armed with sub machine-guns and a variety of other weapons. These included captured German Schmeissers, which some preferred owing to their quality and accuracy and the fact that ammunition for the German weapon was lighter and more could be carried than for some Allied counterparts.

The SRS met little early opposition. They scaled steep cliffs using ladders, cut through the protective wire and swiftly attacked the first gun emplacement. Enemy fire opened up from all around the site. The Italian soldiers were in dugouts beneath the guns, but many lacked the will to put up sustained resistance. Paddy, oblivious to the danger, strode purposefully through the area chivvying his men to hurry up and clear the site as Royal Engineers were waiting, ready to blow the guns. Alex Muirhead, an officer who was later to distinguish himself in France after D-Day, urged his men on to drop 3-in mortar shells on a nearby barracks and command post. The late Reg Seekings said in Roy Bradford and Martin Dillon's biography on Mayne, *Rogue Warrior of the SAS*: 'We went in with the bayonet.

That was Paddy's idea – we had trained in the Guards drill specially for the op. Left, right, fire a volley in step, reload, left, right, fire! It could be bloody terrifying if you were at the wrong end. At one point we shot up a statue – thought it was an Eyetie! We were cleaning out places. There were these big underground bunkers and we could hear voices. We were just going in. The blood was running high and we were in a real killing mood.' A few civilians were mixed up with the action, together with some British troops from 4th Airborne who had been captured in the vicinity.

After the threat of grenades being thrown down their bunkers, the enemy defenders gave up and the battery had been taken by 5 a.m. and several 6-in guns, 20-mm anti-aircraft weapons and heavy machine-guns put out of action. Paddy gave the order to fire green rockets to signal to the waiting ships that the operation was successful. He then directed his men in clearing out pockets of enemy snipers and some nearby defended farmhouses and then the SRS set off hot foot for Syracuse, about 5 miles away, taking many prisoners along the way. To reinforce the view earlier expressed about Mayne's attitude to prisoners, Paddy gave a clear order that the enemy was to be given the chance to give themselves up before his men opened fire.

However, on approaching a second battery, the fighting got harder. Again the 3-in mortars of the SRS caused havoc, hitting an ammunition dump and an anti-aircraft site. Two troops of raiders then attacked against strong opposition and took the position, capturing a further five heavy anti-aircraft guns. Just as they were about to attack the main guns, Mayne's instinct took over. Ever on his guard and with an uncanny sixth sense for danger, Paddy had spotted an Italian shaping up to shoot Sgt Maj Rose, one of the SAS originals, in the back. In a flash, his pistol cracked twice, killing the Italian instantly. The raiders then destroyed the guns and continued on to join the advance party of the British 5th Division, reaching their intended destination of Syracuse the next day.

Amazingly, although almost 500 prisoners were taken and 200 to 300 of the enemy killed or wounded, only one SRS man died and two others were injured. They had brilliantly achieved their objective of knocking out two crucial batteries which could have wreaked slaughter on the main invading force. The daring success of the operation can be gauged by the number of medals showered on the SRS. Maj Harry Poat received the Military Cross, as did the pugnacious Lt Johnny Wiseman. Sgt Reg Seekings received a Military Medal to add to the DCM he had won earlier in the war. MMs were also won by L/Sgts A. Frame and John Sillito and Cpl C. Dalzell, L/Cpl T. Jones and Pts A. Skinner and J. Noble.

The second operation included in the award of the bar to Paddy's DSO was the capture and holding of the town of Augusta by the SRS just two days later on 12 July. This landing, again seaborne, was carried out in daylight and the Italians were driven from well-prepared positions and large amounts of stores and equipment saved from destruction by demolition. The citation states: 'He personally led his men from landing craft in the face of heavy machine-gun fire. By this action, he succeeded in forcing his way to ground where it was possible to form up and sum up the enemy's defences.' Mayne's bar to his DSO was just reward not only for his personal bravery, but also for his outstanding and inspirational leadership of these inaugural seaborne actions for the SRS/SAS.

Third DSO

The complex and dangerous campaign in France led to a third bar to Paddy's DSO for his continued impressive leadership. The official citation for this said:

> Lieutenant Colonel R.B. Mayne DSO has commanded 1st SAS Regiment throughout the period of operations in France. On 8th August 1944, he was dropped to Houndsworth base, located west of Dijon, in order to co-ordinate and take charge of the available

detachments of his Regiment and co-ordinate their activities with a major Airborne landing which was then envisaged near Paris.

He then proceeded in a jeep in daylight to motor to the Gain base making the complete journey in one day. On the approach of Allied forces, he passed through the lines in his jeep to contact the American forces and to lead back through the lines his detachment of twenty jeeps landed for Operation Wallace. During the next few weeks, he successfully penetrated the German and American lines on four occasions in order to lead parties of reinforcements. It was entirely due to Lt Colonel Mayne's fine leadership and example, and his utter disregard of danger, that the unit was able to achieve such striking success.

With Paris safely liberated, Mayne was awarded the Croix de Guerre by the grateful French, whose countrymen as part of the Resistance had greatly assisted the SAS campaigns behind the lines.

The Heroic Fourth DSO

This award, won in Germany during the final weeks of the Second World War, was for an act of supreme individual bravery by Mayne, who was instrumental in driving out dangerous, aggressive German forces from a strongly held village which was holding up the advance in the whole of his sector. It was a deed of such outstanding individual heroism and cool leadership that many afterwards considered it well worthy of the VC. Indeed, combined with Mayne's previous record, the supreme award for valour seemed to have been guaranteed at last.

On 9 April 1945 Mayne was ordered by the general commanding the Canadian 4th Armoured Division to lead his Regiment of armoured jeep squadrons through the German lines. The general direction of advance was north-east through the city of Oldenburg. Mayne's main task was to clear a path for advancing Canadian armoured cars and tanks whose objective was the U-boat base at Wilhelmshaven. He was also ordered to cause disruption behind the enemy lines, something he and the battle-hardened SAS regarded as routine after four long years of war.

The SAS had received intelligence reports that any opposition was likely to be weak, consisting mainly of Volksturm, the German equivalent of the Home Guard, and Hitler Youth. However, the SAS was warned that there were likely to be several fortified strong points on the route to Oldenburg and the ever-watchful Mayne cautioned his men to be careful. In the event, lying in wait undetected were elements of the crack German 1st Parachute Division, victors of Crete in 1941.

Crucially, Mayne's squadrons, which contained many seasoned veterans, also comprised a number of new inexperienced recruits. Consequently, some of the jeeps in the patrol became bunched up too close together, making it far easier for the enemy to launch a successful ambush. Tragedy struck when the leading squadron was hit by heavy enemy fire after only an hour's travel and the squadron commander, Maj Dick Bond, a close friend of Mayne's, was among those killed. The leading elements of the SAS were under fire from machine-guns and hand-held Panzerfaust anti-tank weapons and had to leave their jeeps with only pistols, Bren guns and Tommy guns with which to defend themselves against the fierce onslaught.

After receiving an urgent wireless message, Paddy, in one of his infamous silent rages, immediately sped off in his jeep to the scene. The official account said that from the time he arrived until the end of the action, Lt Col Mayne was in full view of the enemy and exposed to fire from small arms, machine-guns and sniper's rifles. Screeching to a halt, Paddy took the Bren from his jeep together with several magazines and entered the nearest of two houses flanking the ambush site, ensuring that the enemy there had withdrawn or been killed. His driver Billy Hull went

inside the same house to give further covering fire,
hammering several bursts towards the adjacent nearby
house and receiving a welter of bullets in reply.

Mayne, meanwhile, left the house and carefully began
to stalk the enemy, remaining in cover in the lee of the
first house and then boldly stepping from the corner of
the building to fire multiple, deadly accurate short bursts
into the second house, killing and wounding the enemy
there. He also raked the nearby woods, which were
occupied by other well-armed troops, with deadly bursts.
He then returned to the main column of SAS vehicles and
asked for a volunteer to accompany him on a jeep attack
on the strongest enemy positions. It was an intrepid plan,
but also exceedingly dangerous. In the circumstances it
was a calculated but risky gamble. John Scott bravely
volunteered to act as rear gunner on the twin Vickers
machine-guns. Without hesitation, Paddy blasted up the
road past the point where Maj Bond had been killed
shortly before to where the furthest section of jeeps was
halted, cut off by the intense and withering enemy fire.
SAS casualties lay trapped, helpless alongside their
pinned-down comrades. By this time, the SAS had lost
more men, killed and wounded, including Bond's driver
Tpr Lewis, who had courageously volunteered to try and
bypass the drainpipe obstruction in the ditch where Bond
had been scythed down earlier. Lewis was a smaller man
and thought he could wriggle past undetected and reach
the trapped men, but as he crawled down the ditch he too
fell victim to a sniper's deadly bullet.

Meanwhile, Paddy Mayne was in full furious flow,
speeding along the road urging Scott on, yelling orders as
to where best to engage the enemy with blistering fire
poured from the jeep. He turned the nimble vehicle around
and Scott leapt into the front seat getting in further deadly
bursts from the heavy Browning machine-gun all the way
along the road, concentrating on the woods. When they
reached the abandoned jeeps, Scott opened up again with
the Vickers, hosing bullets into the enemy troops. The main

threat, as Paddy quickly surmised, came from the trees to the side of the furthest house and the enemy were quickly silenced, or forced to flee, under the persistent hail of accurate, close-range fire. The daring jeep attack had almost completely subdued the enemy by this stage, allowing Paddy to get out of the vehicle and lift the wounded out of the ditch. In fact, the enemy had suffered heavy casualties and had begun to withdraw. Later, Scott, who had also performed courageously in the action, asked Paddy to gauge what their chances were of surviving the escapade. Mayne thought for a moment and calmly replied, 'About fifty-fifty.'

The Canadian armour, which was supposed to be following hard on the heels of the SAS, had not caught up with the jeep squadrons and so, with casualties needing urgent medical attention, Mayne decided to withdraw back to the British lines and make his report. Both Maj Blackman and Capt Harrison, who wrote up the citation outlining the incident within hours of its conclusion, and SAS Brig Mike Calvert, commanding officer of the SAS, were all convinced that Paddy had won a long overdue VC at last. It was beyond doubt that Mayne's individual heroism throughout the action, combined with his inspired leadership of Scott and others, had won the day.

Speculation remains rife to this day that the main reason why Mayne did not receive the VC was not that his superlative deeds of bravery were insufficient for the supreme honour, but simply that his buccaneer conduct had offended those in high places outside the SAS once too often. Memories of his earlier behaviour were slow to fade. There seems to be no other rational explanation. Whatever the truth of the matter, Calvert passed the report of the action on to the Canadians and it was then sent to higher authorities in London, who decided on a record-breaking fourth DSO instead. Paddy was now, VC or not, the most decorated soldier in the entire British Army.

Other Breathtaking Exploits

Various accounts, from official records and eyewitness testimonies, underline the amazing reactions and bravery of Lt Col Mayne. A few of the highlights from the latter half of the war are detailed here.

At Termoli, Italy, where the SRS supported various other Commando units in a desperate defence of the town against crack German forces, a single shell unluckily killed twenty-nine of Paddy's men in a truck. However, whenever the Lieutenant Colonel was in action, the record was usually set straight one way or another. Just before this tragic episode, on entering the town, veterans state that Paddy, who was in charge of Squadron headquarters, directed his men to engage a party of over forty Germans with mortars at a bend in a road, which led up a ravine. Suddenly, unnoticed by the others in the heat of the action, he disappeared. With his speed and cunning in making use of all available cover, he amazed his men by appearing suddenly above the enemy's flank. Tossing a grenade with unerring accuracy, as if he were merely lobbing a cricket ball, he wiped out a mortar crew. Then, using his favourite trick of using a Bren gun like a rifle, he killed or scattered the rest with repeated, deadly bursts of light machine-gun fire. Members of 40 Commando, who were operating with the SRS at Termoli, then helped round up and capture the survivors of the totally demoralised force. The engagement was a total success thanks to Mayne's instinctive quick thinking and uncanny tactical awareness. After the action, the bodies of no less than twelve Germans scythed down by Mayne were found at the scene.

In France at Houndsworth base, west of Dijon, after being parachuted in to coordinate the various detachments of the 1st SAS Regiment, Lt Col Mayne decided that on 1 September a jeep crew should go and collect a trailer from the Kipling base. Lt Monty Goddard volunteered to drive, with Paddy manning the twin Vickers in the front. It was almost as if he sensed that action was in the wind. There was little traffic on the road, but suddenly Mayne heard the rumbling of heavy vehicles in the distance and the pair quietly pulled into cover at the side of the road where to their surprise they discovered brave but lightly armed members of the Maquis French Resistance preparing an ambush for the approaching German patrol.

According to Bradford and Dillon's *Rogue Warrior*, Paddy told Goddard to drive the jeep out of sight and to quickly bring back the Bren gun and single Vickers and ammunition for both from the vehicle. The SAS men were determined to take on the convoy whether the Maquis decided to attack or not. Paddy strode up to one of the Frenchmen, depriving him of several grenades before returning to his chosen position, which had a clear view of the approaching Germans. The convoy rolled into sight, protected by a quick-firing vehicle with several trucks packed with soldiers following and a staff car at the rear. When the vehicles came within 50 yd Mayne signalled to Goddard to open fire, which he did, boldly advancing and firing the single Vickers from his hip. Soldiers leapt from the trucks and the 36-mm mobile quick firer at the head of the convoy burst into action. The enemy soldiers scattered into ditches on either side of the road and Mayne crept swiftly with his Bren to a patch of raised ground about 50 yd away, which gave him a clear view of the ditches and trucks.

Goddard shot the quick-firer crew, but having bravely advanced into a very exposed position was killed by cannon-fire that opened up from one of the trucks. Mayne immediately blasted a full magazine into the trucks killing all those inside. Mayne's own position was now coming under heavy fire from a machine-gun near one of the trucks, so he tossed several grenades into the ditch where the Germans were sheltering while reloading his Bren. Mayne fired one final burst from his Bren and took off into the woods. The Germans, floundering around in disarray, did not follow. Mayne's jeep had vanished, but he made his

way on foot with one of the Maquisards who had stopped
to help guide him. After commandeering a civilian car
they arrived back at camp where the Maquisard recounted
the bravery of Mayne and Goddard to everyone. Typically,
Paddy dismissed the fierce encounter as a 'minor scrap'.

A dramatic radio message tip-off that a motorised German
troop convoy was approaching near Oldenburg, Germany,
led to Mayne, his faithful driver Billy Hull and another
trooper carrying out an ambush at a site cunningly chosen
by Mayne, It left no less than seventy enemy dead. The rest
of Paddy's men were all out on offensive patrols, but this
was too good an opportunity to miss for the seasoned SAS
commander. With a glint in his eyes and an urgency in his
manner he told the remaining two troopers to stop brewing
tea and get into a jeep.

Paddy then raced off at break-neck speed to set up an
ambush. The SAS men got to their destination at a wooded
area with just enough time to site their weapons for
optimum effect. A handy S bend in particular would, it was
calculated, slow down the enemy vehicles temporarily and
cause them to bunch. Paddy manned the Browning heavy
machine-gun on the jeep, which was hidden in cover
nearby, and Hull sited a Bren gun on an adjacent rise,
which gave a superb field of fire. Williams carried a sub
machine-gun, a deadly weapon at short range, especially in
skilled hands. Within minutes, the rumble of German half-
tracks was clearly heard as the convoy approached, each
vehicle packed full with about thirty German soldiers.

As Patrick Marrinan in *Colonel Paddy* recorded: 'Paddy let
the leading one go past, then opened up and his two
companions followed suit. A tornado of screams and shouts
rose from the Germans. Their trucks began to blaze, bodies
were scattered everywhere. The ambush had thrown them
into an utter panic.' Mayne had timed the ambush to
perfection, picking his site and directing his men's fire so as
to cause the enemy vehicles to wedge up on the bend,
where they were abandoned by their drivers as the welter of

bullets poured down. However, the three SAS, being vastly outnumbered, realised they had already outstayed their welcome. Again, Paddy judged the perfect moment to depart before the superior German force recovered from the initial shock and reformed to attack and overwhelm them. Paddy's two comrades leapt aboard the wildly revving jeep and roared away from this scene of chaos. However, in order to withdraw, Paddy had to reverse at full speed down the narrow lane for more than 50 yd before he could turn around. By this time the Germans were returning fire wildly, but all three SAS men returned to base safely.

The next day, the SAS went back to the site to witness a scene of unbelievable devastation. Several half-tracks were burnt out and German corpses littered the area all around. In this one brief action, Paddy had added considerably to his enormous personal tally of enemy soldiers killed with his own hands.

A similar ambush was carried out by Mayne and Hull one late April afternoon towards the end of the war, with Paddy employing similarly effective tactics. Ever on the look-out for action, Mayne spotted the approach of a German convoy consisting mainly of horse-drawn carts packed with supplies and explosives and radioed for a jeep in the rear to come forward. But, racing off without waiting for it to arrive, he drove his jeep into cover at the side of the road and waited, safely camouflaged by the lush foliage.

Paddy again manned the Browning heavy machine-gun with Hull, his loyal sidekick, ready to add to the deluge of firepower on the quick-firing twin Vickers. The pair did not have long to wait and, as the ragged procession of carts and lorries drove past, they let rip. Hull described the bloody inferno in Bradford and Dillon's *Rogue Warrior of the SAS* in his typical staccato fashion: 'Carts and lorries were exploding. We ran out of ammunition. They didn't even have time to fire back. They were in disarray. They didn't know what had hit them. Big Mayne reversed the jeep out of the action and loaded up [with ammo], then went back for more.

The roadway was a shambles. Bodies all over the place. Other jeeps arrived and took over from us.'

Such deadly massacres were beginning to become a habit. On another occasion, Paddy, Hull and an SAS trooper were travelling along a seemingly quiet road when suddenly Paddy, who was driving, slammed the accelerator to the floor. In a ditch at the side of the road ahead was a German machine-gun with three soldiers gathered around it. Luckily, the Germans were taken by surprise by the vehicle roaring straight at them. Without hesitation, Mayne drove the jeep into the ditch right over the enemy soldiers. 'I felt the vibrations as the vehicle ploughed over the three Germans,' Hull said, as recorded in Bradford and Dillon's *Rogue Warrior*, 'Paddy reversed it, the Germans were writhing on the ground. He stopped the jeep, reached across, took hold of a Schmeisser [German machine-pistol] and fired several bursts into the wounded men. There wasn't much left.' Paddy then turned to his comrades and said, simply and reproachfully in his soft Irish brogue, 'In future, keep yer eyes open.' His actions may seem brutal nowadays, but he was the one man quick enough to react. If he had not, the SAS men would have been the ones to be wiped out.

Tragedy Strikes

The Germans surrendered unconditionally on 8 May 1945 and the fighting war in Europe was finally at an end. It was hard at first for men of the SAS to adjust to relative inaction. Some had been involved in some of the toughest Special Forces operations for up to four long years and now knew little else. There followed a pleasant diversion in Norway for members of 1st SAS as Paddy and his troops were ordered to oversee the capitulation of large numbers of the German occupying forces who had been stationed there since 1940. In the event, there was little trouble from the demoralised German forces and the SAS troops were treated to overwhelming hospitality by the grateful and jubilant Norwegian populace. After the dropping of the atom bombs on Japan which brought about the end of the Second World War on 15 August, the SAS returned home to Britain. Neither they nor David Stirling, having been released from captivity in Colditz, would now be needed for the proposed behind-the-lines missions against the Japanese. All members were devastated to hear that the SAS was to be disbanded on 1 October.

Paddy was like a proverbial fish out of water, suffering from a badly damaged vertebra in his back. The injury, received in the early days of the desert campaign, had been made much worse by the many parachute drops he made into France just prior to and after D-Day. Though in considerable pain at times, he typically hid this fact from his men on missions from France onwards, even though he needed proper medical treatment. It is amazing that he accomplished so much with such a serious disability, but he was to pay the price. In effect, the injury prevented him from following a more active career, and perhaps remaining in the military. He took up an interesting job in the Falklands Dependency Survey, which was offered by the Crown agents, working with a survey team in the South Atlantic, but finally his tortured back gave out completely. Within weeks, he was in hospital in Buenos Aires for a much postponed major operation which entailed the removal of an entire vertebra. He was then shipped home, but despite this drastic surgery, his back never fully recovered.

Shortly after his return home to Newtonwards, Paddy was offered the role of secretary of the Incorporated Law Society of Northern Ireland, a professional body that serves solicitors. He was at last able to use his legal training, gained before the outbreak of war, but though suitable, the post failed to excite or stretch his capabilities in any way. Late-night drinking sessions with friends and former comrades who came to visit him from mainland Britain and elsewhere took up too much of his time over the next ten years. He never married. On one memorable occasion, SAS comrade Bob Bennett, one of the original SAS veterans, arrived at his office in the law courts.

Paddy was delighted and promptly told his secretary he would not be back for two weeks! The pair embarked on a gargantuan bender.

For most of the time, Paddy floundered around without a real purpose in life apart from his family, his job, his friends and his drinking. On 14 December 1955, Paddy was due to go to a teetotal Masonic dinner in his home town, an event he attended as a matter of tradition. His beloved mother Margaret, a major influence throughout his life, watched him roar away from his Mount Pleasant home that evening in his powerful red Riley as he had on countless occasions before. Nothing seemed out of the ordinary.

Paddy went to a poker game and had some drinks in the nearby town of Bangor, calling in the early hours at a friend's house. He had more drinks and left shortly before 4 a.m. Just 5 minutes later, he was only a few hundred yards from home when an unlit, parked lorry suddenly loomed out of the darkness ahead. Paddy's car struck the vehicle a massive, glancing blow and then, shooting across the road out of control, slammed into an electricity line pole with a tremendous crash. Ireland's favourite SAS son, the survivor of scores of desperate hand-to-hand fights with the enemy and victor of all of them, was killed instantly. His body was not found until 7 a.m. the next morning. A post-mortem showed his death was caused by a fracture at the base of the skull.

Paddy Mayne's funeral took place on 16 December 1955. The procession behind the coffin stretched back more than a mile and contained many former SAS comrades, colleagues from the legal profession and the rugby world. He was buried in the family grave at Movilla churchyard, Newtonwards. Maj Roy Farran, one of the most decorated surviving SAS officers from the Second World War, describes Paddy in his appreciation of this book as being like a mighty 'Viking warrior of ancient times' who could mow down his opponents with a sword that no one else would be capable of lifting.

ANDERS LASSEN VC – LIFE ON A KNIFE'S EDGE

Anders Lassen VC, MC and two bars was to the Special Boat Service what Paddy Mayne was to the SAS – the rugged epitome of heroic leadership and ferocious courage in action. There were few finer soldiers in the whole of the British Army, as scores of enemy soldiers found to their cost in hand-to-hand combat. The first encounter with either of these two lethal Special Forces men was usually the last. Both Mayne and Lassen were born killers, ruthless, cold and calculating in action, but with complex characters which were deceptively easy going at times, yet concealing a dark, brooding side that could explode into unpredictable violence once the pressure-cooker atmosphere of action was released. These two famous SAS majors were unquestionably superb commanders, possessing instinctive tactical sense and qualities of leadership that inspired tremendous loyalty and respect among their men.

Anders Frederik Emil Victor Schau Lassen, known as Andy to all his SBS comrades, was born in Denmark and spent all of his younger life there. He was serving on an oil tanker as a merchant seaman when he came to Britain in 1940, desperate to fight the Nazis who had invaded and pillaged his homeland and enslaved the Danish people.

Two of a Kind

Mayne and Lassen shared certain similiarities. Both punched and knocked out their commanding officers when thwarted in minor ways in rest times between missions. Lassen struck his CO, Lord Jellicoe, in a bar in Tel Aviv in a petty difference of opinion. However, Jellicoe, the wise and able commander of the SBS, decided to turn a blind eye to the incident. He knew Lassen was too valuable an officer to be lost on account of such a petulant outburst. Jellicoe's foresight was to be repaid a thousandfold.

Like Mayne, Lassen moved across the raiding battlefields quickly, decisively and with great agility at the first hint of enemy action. Both were deadly marksmen with pistol, rifle, Tommy gun or Bren gun, as well as making liberal use of grenades, and they both used their stiletto-like commando daggers in one-to-one combat whenever it was necessary. It was possible to silence and kill a man in 3 or 4 seconds by severing a main artery in the shoulder or neck, and even more quickly by slitting his throat.

It was with the knife that Lassen, especially, came into his own, relishing killing the enemy in the clinical close-quarter fashion that many soldiers of regular units found repugnant. When Lassen returned from killing his first enemy soldier in this way on one of his early raids he thrust the still bloody knife under the nose of one of his comrades, carried away by the high emotions of the moment, triumphant at his first 'real' kill. In his youth, he was so adept at using a bow and knives of various kinds that he could stalk and kill a stag with a knife – no mean feat.

The Famous Commando Knife

The knife, which Lassen was later to use with such deadly effect in the SBS, was the Fairbairn Sykes Commando knife. Early in November 1940, Fairbairn and Sykes arrived from the Far East at the headquarters of the Wilkinson Sword company in London on a mission that would immortalise their names. They told company executives they wanted to create a mass-production knife that could kill swiftly and silently. The grip had to be heavy so the knife would fit well in the palm, but at the same time the knife had to be manageable and versatile. In fact, Commandos and SAS and SBS men became so accomplished at throwing the knives that they were able to use them as darts, often to the alarm of other units they served with, including the Royal Navy taking them to their targets.

William Fairbairn and his partner Eric Sykes had had a tough baptism in the hardest street fighting of the Far East, where Fairbairn had been assistant commissioner of Shanghai's municipal police and Sykes had commanded a firearms unit. Both were called back to Britain where they were commissioned as Army captains and given a free hand to teach Special Forces recruits the specialities of silent killing, unarmed combat and pistol shooting. It was claimed that the duo had been involved in more than 200 incidents of violent close combat, although their 'harmless', middle-aged appearance belied their experience.

Within a few days of their visit Wilkinson Sword had come up with a prototype knife. A knife from the first batch, including the sheath, cost 13s 6d, and by the end of the Second World War the company had made nearly 250,000 of these. The dagger had a blade almost 7 in long and was popularly known as the Commando knife, but many war veterans called it by the name etched on the squared head of the blade – the Fairbairn Sykes fighting knife. Raiders were trained to creep up on sentries, hook a hand around their victim's chin, yanking the head sideways to expose the shoulder to a powerful, downward thrust. Inflicting damage on the subclavian artery was considered to be the quickest, quietest way to kill a man – 2 seconds later the man would be unconscious, and in 3½ seconds he would be dead, drowned in his own blood. A quick cut to the man's throat would have a similar effect. Many Commando unit badges depict such fighting knives and the SAS badge features a winged dagger, or sword, pointing downwards.

Lassen the Hunter

Many of Lassen's comrades in the SBS later said that he often preferred using the knife to all other weapons, when circumstances allowed. With his homeland ground into submission by the Nazis, Lassen was only too willing to volunteer his services to join the British forces at the first opportunity and put his fighting skills to good use. Lassen landed at Oban in Argyllshire in 1940. He was about

6 ft 1 in tall, slim but powerful and very strong and people who knew him say he was capable of moving across the ground as though he was floating on air. Lassen was the son of the adventurous Capt Emil Lassen of the Danish Life Guards and his great grandfather, Emil Victor Schau, was heroically killed in 1864 in the war against Prussia. His relatives said the Schau strain seemed to pass on a passion for fighting in the Lassen family, a quality that Anders inherited to the full.

After several early adventures in West Africa and elsewhere, Lassen was commissioned second lieutenant in 1942 and joined the Small Scale Raiding Force (SSRF), a special Commando unit, commanded by the gallant officer Gus March-Phillips, who was later killed in a raid on the Normandy coast. The force's cover name was No. 62 Commando, but its true and undisclosed name was the SSRF.

Lassen was a crack shot with any weapon. He could hit a rabbit on the run with his longbow and on one occasion a SSRF colleague saw him hit and ignite a twelve-bore cartridge lodged in the fork of a tree from 25 yd with his bow. The SSRF special raiders were taught how to strip and load sub machine-guns, Allied or enemy, blindfold just like the SAS. They were also taught pistol shooting in the Fairbairn Sykes style. This was a simple but effective way of ensuring accuracy by which even a novice, through pressing the butt hand of his pistol against his navel, could fire like a marksman. They also learned the 'double tap' trick of firing successive shots so that at least one would hit the target. This method is still employed today by the SAS and SBS. The SSRF were taught to aim for the centre of their opponents, as very few people shot in the stomach area recover from their wounds. The SSRF raider's equipment included, typically, items such as a Tommy gun, seven magazines each with twenty rounds, pistol, wire-cutters, grenades, a fighting knife and two half-pound explosive charges.

The Commando raiders hit Sark in the Channel Islands in 1943, with Maj Geoffrey Appleyard DSO, MC and bar and Lassen in the party. Appleyard intended to capture some enemy soldiers, silently without shooting. The prisoners were bound ready for taking back to Britain for interrogation when one suddenly attacked his guard and ran away shouting loudly to raise the alarm. He was caught and, after a scuffle, shot. Two more prisoners broke away and both of them had to be killed too, otherwise the safety of the whole party would have been compromised. It was one of the many unpleasant, but sometimes necessary, things that happen in wartime.

Hitler was informed that the men who had been killed on Sark had been deliberately bound and shot when helpless, and he was beside himself with fury. Subsequently, the raid was used to justify the murder of selected prisoners under the infamous Commando execution order issued by the Führer himself. Only a fortnight after the raid, Hitler authorised the extermination of captured raiders and Commandos, accusing the British of brutal behaviour, of tying up prisoners and killing unarmed captives. Hitler's secret order, which was marked 'in no circumstances to fall into enemy hands', was to have grave repercussions later in the war for many captured SAS, SBS and Commandos. But, reflecting on the Sark mission, Lassen indicated he was no sadist but merely a soldier doing his duty when he wrote in his diary: 'The hardest and most difficult job I have ever done – used my knife for the first time.'

The First and Second Military Crosses

Lassen was awarded a Military Cross in recognition of his early raids, including the controversial attack on Sark. The citation called him 'an inspiring leader and brilliant seaman possessed of sound judgement and quick decision'. The Dane won his second Military Cross after spending nearly three weeks behind enemy lines on the island of Crete in the first independent operation by the Special Boat Squadron, where he led one prong of a devastatingly successful triple raid. Anders Lassen had found his true home – the SBS.

The 'legitimised pirates' of the SBS had been formed under Lord Jellicoe a few months earlier in the spring of 1943 when the 1st SAS was divided into two. Half the unit became the Special Raiding Squadron under Col Mayne and the remainder became the SBS. Jellicoe's share of the manpower included 250 officers and men from the 1st SAS, 55 members of the old Special Boat Section and the remnants of the Small Scale Raiding Force, which included Lassen.

It was in June 1943 that Lassen and six others landed with David Sutherland and his main party on the south coast of Crete. Their destination was the airfield at Maleme, which was on a steep hill and well defended. Lassen killed two Italian sentries with his dagger and by firing his pistol, incredibly without even taking it from his pocket. Unconventional as ever, Lassen thought nothing of cutting corners if it provided a quicker and more effective result. His glowing citation for the second MC reads:

> Great difficulty was experienced in penetrating towards the target, in the process of which a second enemy sentry had to be shot. The enemy then rushed reinforcements from the eastern side of the aerodrome and forming a semi-circle, drove the two attackers into the middle of an anti-aircraft battery where they were fired upon heavily from three sides. Danger was ignored and bombs placed on a caterpillar tractor, which was destroyed.
>
> The increasing numbers of enemy in that area finally forced the party to withdraw. It was entirely due to this officer's [Lassen's] diversion that planes and petrol were successfully destroyed on the eastern side of the airfield, since he drew off all the guards from that area. Throughout this attack and during the very arduous approach march, the keenness, determination and personal disregard of danger of this officer was of the highest order.

A Crack Pistol Shot

Later in 1943, when withdrawn for further training, the SBS had their pistol-shooting skills honed by Maj L.H. Grant Taylor – veterans recall he could flick a coin into the air, draw from his shoulder holster and hit it squarely before it fell, just like in the cowboy films. Lassen was not slow with a pistol either – he could hit a playing card at 25 yd five times out of six with his right hand and at least three times out of six with his left.

The Third Military Cross

Lassen won his third Military Cross in brilliant style on the island of Simi. His citation reads: 'The heavy repulse of the Germans on 7th October, 1943 was due in no small measure to his inspiration and leadership . . . At that time, the Italians were wavering and their recovery is attributed to the personal example and initiative of this officer . . . In the afternoon, he led the Italian counter-attack which finally drove the Germans back to their caiques with the loss of 16 killed, 35 wounded and seven prisoners, as against our loss of one killed and one wounded.' During this action, Lassen personally stalked and killed three Germans at close quarters, some with the knife.

It seemed as though he would end the war as one of the SBS's most decorated soldiers, returning in triumph to his beloved Denmark. However, with the end of the war within sight, Lassen was asked to lead one final mission at Lake Comacchio, near the Po delta in northern Italy. It was to be the scene of his greatest triumph and bitterest tragedy.

An Historic Victoria Cross

Comacchio town and the adjoining harbour of Porto Garibaldi were held by about 1,200 of the enemy, a combination of German troops and their allies, who were stubbornly holding up the Allied advance. Despite courageous attacks by Commandos, the enemy line was only yielding slowly and the general staff were getting impatient. Germany was almost beaten and it seemed only a matter of days before their entire empire collapsed like a pack of cards.

Lassen's job was to stage a diversionary attack to draw the Germans towards the Adriatic side of Comacchio so the Allies could mount a left hook to force a bridgehead on the west side of the lake, where No. 2 Commando Brigade had fought for days to find a gap in atrocious muddy conditions. Lassen split his force into three, with the rear patrol carrying fused bombs and explosives to create a spectacular display intended to create the impression of a much larger attack. Lassen had seventeen men with him, all seasoned veterans who had already survived long years of war. Soon half of them were to be dead or wounded in this near-suicidal mission.

Crucially, there had been no opportunity to reconnoitre the southern defences. Lassen, as commanding officer, could easily have stayed safely behind and ordered another officer in charge of the mission, but typically decided to lead from the front. The men silently paddled their inflatable dinghies across the still waters of the lake with Lassen in the lead, his patrol landing nearly 2 miles from the town. The raiders swiftly disembarked. One soldier, Freddie Crouch, slipped into the mud at the side of the long spit of land which stretched south from the town for 3 miles or more and carried the causeway on which the SBS had to pass. He drowned before the eyes of his comrades as he floundered in the morass, bravely not calling out for help because he knew that would have given away their position and led to the whole patrol's annihilation.

Suddenly, Lassen and his men were challenged in Italian from an enemy machine-gun post directly ahead. Lassen quickly urged one of his men to answer in Italian saying that they were fishermen. But after a tense pause, firing broke out. The game was well and truly up. The patrol dived for cover under the edge of an embankment half a metre above the floodwaters. The area was covered by a series of pillboxes in ascending order of height so they could direct the maximum volume of machine-gun fire. Without hesitation, Lassen worked his way into the lee of the dyke to the roadside opposite the first strong point, threw in a couple of grenades and then killed the four machine-gunners there.

There were at least two more heavily armed defence posts situated higher up the road and machine-gunners were also firing at the raiders from a position on the left. The group sustained some further casualties and Lassen, by now in a cold fury, ran on alone to successfully silence the rest of the pillboxes with grenades and pistol fire. Single-handedly, he wiped out the crew of the second strong point and ran onwards. As he neared the third one, however, there was a shout of 'Kamerad!' as he approached, the occupants indicating that they wanted to give themselves up. He uncharacteristically stood up from behind cover and approached alone to accept the surrender only to receive a treacherous blast of close-range machine-gun fire at near point-blank range.

Lassen fell mortally wounded, but somehow found the strength to shout out to his comrades who could hear, but could not see, the drama happening yards in front of them in the pitch darkness. His men rushed forward to help but Lassen ordered them to get the rest of his surviving men out. Angrily, they made short work of the treacherous defenders in the pillbox, before desperately trying to stem their commander's wounds and carry him back to safety. Sadly, Lassen died within minutes and they had to leave his body as they were being showered with fire from other strong points.

Two more SBS raiders were killed before the group reached their inflatable boats and paddled disconsolately back to the Allied lines. Everyone was stunned – it did not seem possible that the invincible Dane was dead after all he had gone through. Exactly why Lassen took the risk to expose himself and approach that last pillbox is something of a mystery. Perhaps he took the defenders at their word and believed they were going to surrender honourably, or perhaps he had run out of ammunition and was trying to bluff them into submission. It could even have been just a tragic misunderstanding and the surrendering men, suddenly seeing Lassen looming at them out of the darkness, instinctively shot him, suspecting a trick. No one will ever know for sure exactly what occurred.

The only certainty is that Lassen, uniquely within the SAS or SBS during the Second World War, won the ultimate honour for bravery, a posthumous VC. In the face of overwhelming odds he had single-handedly wiped out two strong points, destroyed six machine-guns, killed eight enemy soldiers and wounded others. His body was later found by a partisan patrol on the road where he had breathed his last. He was aged just twenty-four and was buried with full military honours in the Allied war cemetery at Argenta Gap, in Italy.

Lord Jellicoe has paid the Danish hero the greatest tribute, solemnly emphasising in Mike Langley's *Anders Lassen VC, MC of the SAS* that 'Nothing is more important to me than my memory of Andy Lassen.'

ROY FARRAN – BRAVEST OF THE BRAVE

Maj Roy Farran DSO, MC and two bars was showered with a host of medals from grateful foreign nations and became one of the most decorated SAS soldiers of the Second World War. He saw a great deal of hard-fought action in very diverse fields of operations from the bitter bloodbath of Crete, to the slogging battles of the Western Desert and behind-the-lines operations in France and Italy, commanding some of the most legendary missions in SAS history. A colourful character of Irish descent, Farran had an instinctive ability that enabled him to assess dangerous situations rapidly and to deliver an immediate and optimum response, so essential in SAS operations deep behind enemy lines. His steady leadership also inspired deep loyalty and commitment in his men, and in the mixed partisan bands with whom they often fought alongside.

Farran was in many ways the model professional Sandhurst-trained officer – versatile, highly disciplined and ultra reliable. However, like David Stirling and the legendary but volatile Paddy Mayne, he also sometimes rebelled impetuously against the rigid red-tape bureaucracy that at times threatened to destroy everything the SAS was trying so hard to achieve. The most famous example of this wayward obstinacy undoubtedly came when Farran was ordered not to parachute into Italy on a particularly vital mission with his troops towards the end of the war. Furious at this seemingly senseless restriction from those in high command (for which there was undoubtedly a very sound reason) and being convinced he could make the operation work far more effectively in command on the ground, he went along for the ride on the parachute drop over the target and contrived to 'accidentally' fall out of the aeroplane and parachute down to complete the key mission with the rest of his men. Roy knew full well that he risked a court martial for deliberately disobeying orders, but decided that he just had to go with his gut instincts and loyalties. In the event, the mission was a great success and the matter was conveniently forgotten afterwards. But it could easily have had disastrous consequences and signalled the end of Farran's illustrious career.

The very qualities that made the men of the SAS such exceptionally fine soldiers – self-reliance, initiative and resourcefulness – meant that they were far more likely to buck authority on occasion than the ordinary soldiers of the line. In practice, many often followed their instincts and survived to fight another day. But not all were as fortunate, or as irreplaceable, as Roy Farran.

The Bloodbath that was Crete

Farran saw some furious action earlier in the war when serving in the tanks of 3rd King's Own Hussars in Crete in

1941. The defenders of this strategic island were pitted
against forces that included massed battalions of crack
German paratroopers. Ironically, British and New Zealand
resistance was so fierce that the Germans came within an
ace of abandoning their whole invasion during the period
when it seemed the Allies' counter-attack on the vital
Maleme airfield would succeed. But, heartened by the last-
gasp withdrawal of British forces, the Germans pressed
home their attacks and won possession of the key island.
'Such is often the hair's breadth between victory and
defeat' said Farran, who was captured in the Crete debacle
but later made a daring escape from a Greek POW camp to
rejoin British troops in the desert in 1942, before the
disastrous retreat to El Alamein and his decision to join the
newly formed 2nd SAS, under Lt Col Bill Stirling.

Shock Death of a VC Hero

Just before this momentous move, however, fate dealt
Farran one of the cruellest of blows imaginable. He found
himself playing an innocent but instrumental part in the
death of one of the British Army's greatest heroes – the
one man at the time who could have halted Rommel's
seemingly unstoppable advance towards Egypt, gaining
victory at last in the wildly fluctuating desert war – the
charismatic Gen Jock Campbell VC.

After his escape from the POW camp, Farran received
treatment for wounds in his thigh and heel. He was then
appointed to the 7th Armoured Division as an intelligence
officer and shortly afterwards as ADC to Gen Jock Campbell,
who had recently taken over command of the division. The
force was refitting in the Delta with new General Grant
tanks, having secured Cyrenaica at the Battle of Sidi Rezegh
for the second time in a year. However, the ground they had
won was lost by fresh troops from Britain in similar fashion
to the previous spring. 'Jock Campbell was not the sort of
man to rest idle for long in the Delta and within ten days of
receiving command, he resolved upon a tour of the desert to

inspect the new defences at Gazala,' Farran said. 'I picked him up in his famous cut-away Humber staff car from the aerodrome at Sidi Barrani, where he had narrowly avoided being shot down by long-range ME 109s.'

Farran recalls that it was a pleasant trip up through the old battlefields to Tobruk. Gen Jock was, in any event, the hero of every officer and man in the Middle East and loved the Western Desert as no other man could love it.

All the way up from Alexandria, he recounted stories of the fighting in the past two years . . . The General loved to drive his car at fantastic speeds, but was kind enough to hand over the wheel to me when he felt that he was tiring. We visited all the various headquarters and spent the night with General Gott. The most remarkable thing was the new technique of digging trenches for vehicles with bulldozers. Another feature which was quite new to desert warfare was the enormous minefield stretching from Gazala to Bir Hacheim. I felt that the General disapproved of the idea of locking brigades up in defensive positions called 'boxes', which were nothing more than the same type of perimeter camps the Italians had been so ridiculed for using. Mobility is the essence of desert war and, for that matter, all war. It seemed to us that the newly constituted Eighth Army had gone a long way towards losing it.

After we had traversed the length and breadth of the minefield, we drove back towards Cairo. At first the General had contemplated flying from Gambut, but I persuaded him that the presence of long-range enemy intruders made it unnecessarily risky. I think he was more influenced by a cable he had received from his wife, congratulating him on his VC, but asking him to take great care of himself.

We set out to make the long distance to Alexandria before dark, which was an impossible task from Tobruk in any case.

Near Bardia they ran into a thick dustbowl. This slowed them down to about 10mph and gave them the chance to survey the huge stretch of desert between the wire and Tobruk, which had been converted into a gigantic rubbish heap of war by the passage of three armies and countless battles.

Near Halfaya Pass, the storm lifted and after stopping for lunch, Gen Jock asked Farran to take the wheel and to drive fast, still hoping to make Alexandria before dark.

Although I am not excusing myself, it must be recorded that the steering of the car had been loosened by the hard wear it received over bad desert going. Near Bug-Bug the metalled surface of the road had never been completed and instead was paved with soft, blue clay from the salt marsh. Until this clay has been rolled and dried in the sun, its surface can be very slippery.

The car must have been going at about 45mph when I hit a fresh patch of clay, recently laid. Somehow, I lost control of the wheel and the car skidded from side to side of the road over about 200 yards. I just had time to hear the General say 'Keep the bloody thing straight,' when I felt myself falling through the air. I never lost consciousness in spite of the force of my landing on my back.

I picked myself up to notice with horror that the car had overturned, the four wheels still spinning helplessly in the air. I ran round to the other side to find the General lying on his back with blood coming from his mouth. He had been killed instantly. His servant and his driver were both lying unconscious beside him. I did not know what to do.

The country all round was deserted and I contemplated suicide. How could I face the world with the news I had killed the greatest man in the desert in his hour of triumph? I began to run down the lonely road towards 30 Corps headquarters. After I had run about 3 miles, I came across a South African padre, who took me back to the scene of the accident in his truck. The two other men had both recovered consciousness, little the worse for their fall, but there was nothing to be done about General Jock. I sat there with my head in my hands unable to bear the accusing glances of his servant. From then onwards, I lapsed into a sort of coma from which I barely roused myself for a fortnight. I went through the courts of inquiry as if in a trance, dreaming that it had all happened. For it was a grievous loss to Britain. If Jock had been alive, we might not have suffered the terrible defeats we did in the withdrawal to Alamein.

He had been the driving force of the division, whoever was commanding, and without him we were like a man without a soul.

Backs to the Wall at Alamein

My late father, Cpl Jack Morgan, then a driver in the Royal Army Service Corps, was also caught up in the momentous retreat, refusing to surrender at the debacle at Tobruk to bring his truck back hundreds of miles through the desert to the new British front lines at El Alamein without compass, map or navigational aid. Due to this brave initiative, he was selected to join 2nd SAS Intelligence under Maj Eric Barkworth, arguably the best-known SAS intelligence officer of the war, later coincidentally working on the intelligence of Roy Farran's famous missions in Italy.

Because of this connection, I have maintained a regular correspondence with Roy Farran over a number of years and he has kindly given me authorisation to quote extensively from his own classic book on his wartime service, *Winged Dagger*, which illustrates the unique experiences and dangerous risks taken by a Second World War SAS officer in the field.

Farran's Glorious SAS Career Begins

After being wounded again, this time during a German
bombing raid and sent away for convalescence to South
Africa and Britain, Farran volunteered for the SAS after
meeting an old Eighth Army friend Sandy Scratchley, who
had been with David Stirling for some time and had now
transferred to the 2nd SAS in Algiers. Farran was most
impressed with the aggressive, workmanlike set up of the SAS
and the Stirling brothers in particular. 'We had already been
transported to a world which knew no obstacles – a world in
which we felt that we were doing something concrete towards
winning the war,' he said. *'The Stirlings did not leap over red
tape; they broke right through it. I have never met anyone who
equalled their drive and although they made many enemies by
slipping round smaller fry, they always got there in the end.'*
But first Farran had to understand the SAS way of
working at the 2nd SAS training camp at Philippeville:

It was a pleasant tented camp pitched alongside a
wonderful beach. Behind were the towering hills of the
Jebel, covered with thick green cork forest. All day, one
could hear the rattle of small arms or the thud of
explosives from training cadres on the beach. There
seemed to be a complete disregard for the normal army
safety precautions, but nobody appeared to get hurt.

The physical training was very rigorous. Before a
recruit was accepted, he had to run to the top of a
600 ft mountain and back again in 60 minutes.
Failures in this final test were returned to the infantry
depot on the other side of the hill.

There were long route marches with 60 pound
packs, practice in night infiltration and various
schemes to encourage self-reliance in the men. It was
emphasised that the method of approach to the
operational area was of secondary importance. That
which really mattered was what you did when you got
there. We were trained to land by sea in a fast surf

using West African dories, to infiltrate overland by foot or in jeeps and in the normal parachute drill in an old fuselage. We experimented with all kinds of sabotage devices and close-quarter shooting was taught in a style which would have shocked instructors in the Small Arms School at Hythe.

Jumping Fearlessly into the Void

On his introduction to parachuting, Farran recalled the clammy anticipation of the first leap into the void.

The nervous fingers which fumble as they fasten the harness . . . the constant glances at the static line to make sure that it is not entangled . . . the safety pin which will never go first time into its socket . . . that terrible feeling in the pit of the stomach as one stands to the door and of the leap of your heart as the plane bounces in an air pocket.

It is enough to say that the first parachute descent is always the best, because there is usually no difficulty in keying yourself up to get out of the plane. Only when you have experienced those few awful seconds before the parachute opens do you really know what parachuting means. When at last you have completed the gentle thrill of your feathery descent and felt the final bounce as you hit the ground, you are filled with supreme confidence. If you could then go straight up again, you would jump without a single qualm. But given time to think, your thoughts gradually go back to those few terrible seconds in the slipstream. For the only difficult part of a parachute jump is getting out of the hole. All sensible instincts revolt against it. It is stupid. It is against human nature. But you go on doing it just to prove to yourself that you can . . . .

Nevertheless, there was tremendous pride the morning after the recruits' last night jump when they received their new

wings. Farran said: 'Parachutists! We were daredevils – men
playing a man's game. Now we would have something to
show the pretty girls at home!'

Deadly Jeep Raids in Italy

During jeep operations in Italy in 1943, Farran was to see
the results of devastating machine-gun attacks on trucks
full of unsuspecting enemy soldiers.

I led the column in line ahead for about eight miles
beyond Pogiano until we came to an Italian policeman
on a crossroads. He told me that German vehicles were
passing all the time and usually turned left towards a
village called Ginosa.

I waved the jeeps into ambush positions and the last
vehicle was still backing into the trees when I saw the
head of a large column approaching from the west. I
threw myself into the ditch, pointing my Tommy gun
up the road.

I half suspected that they were Italians and the first
vehicle was nearly on top of us before I noticed the
German cockade on the front of the driver's cap. The
squeezing of my Tommy gun trigger was the signal for
the whole weight of our firepower to cut into the
trucks at practically 'nil' range. Having once started
such a colossal barrage of fire, it was very difficult to
stop it in spite of the fact that Germans were waving
pathetic white flags from their bonnets.

I remember screaming at a Frenchman called
Durban to cease fire and making no impression on his
tense, excited face until the whole of his Browning belt
was finished. At last the racket stopped and I walked
down the road towards a tiny knot of Germans waving
white flags from behind the last vehicle. All those in
the front trucks were dead.

Still panting from the excitement of the ambush, we
screamed at them to come forward with their hands

up. A totally demoralised group of Germans was led up the column by an officer, bleeding profusely from a wound in his arm and still shouting for mercy.

It was plain that there would be no question of further resistance from any of them. In all, we took about 40 prisoners and four trucks. Eight other vehicles were destroyed and about ten Germans were killed.

My greatest fear was that the Germans would retaliate from Ginosa or at least investigate the cause of the shooting. We had not sufficient strength for a pitched battle so that, after sending back the prizes with the prisoners, we sabotaged the remaining vehicles and withdrew a short way down the road.

The Germans sent down a number of infantry and armoured troop carriers within an hour of our attack. They halted at the crossroads and began to salvage the remnants of the vehicles and to bury their dead. I sent two men hidden in the back of an Italian hay cart to get a better view of their activities and they returned later to say that the enemy had withdrawn to Ginosa.

Later on the advance to Castellerano, an even more furious battle ensued as the SAS jeeps pressed deeply into enemy territory.

The Germans would certainly be in a state of readiness on the roads, so I decided to take the squadron across untracked country for the first time in Italy. If we were lucky enough to find a good track later on, there was a chance that we might be able to approach Castellerano unobserved from the north.

We moved in desert formation with large intervals between the jeeps . . . the ground was hard enough to reduce the dust, but I feel certain now that we were watched the whole way across . . .

We had motored for miles across the fields, breaking through the fences with our wire cutters, when we came to more hilly ground, thickly covered with young hazel trees. The jeeps laboured up a stony track through a flock of sheep until we came to a steep precipice. Below I could see enemy trucks moving like Dinky toys on the road.

Peter Jackson, who was leading, beckoned me forward to a crest on the left. We were perhaps 300 yards from a village perched on the top of a round knoll. Through my glasses I could see Germans running out of what appeared to be the school and we heard one or two rifle shots. It was clear the alarm had been given.

I had just given the order for the jeeps to turn round when Roach, Peter's Irish driver, spotted a German steel helmet in the bushes about 50 yards away. Almost immediately a tremendous hail of machine gun fire was directed towards us. At least four Spandaus were firing simultaneously. My own jeep had not yet turned round. Leaping into the driver's seat, I set her nose at the wood of young saplings, charging them at top speed.

We crashed down one tree after another in a desperate attempt to get under cover. One other jeep followed me but there was no sign of the others. All around us the bullets splattered into the trees.

My last view of Peter was of his crew still fighting the guns from a blazing jeep. It was a gallant attempt to cover our withdrawal and typical of the grandson of a double VC winner.

Our two jeeps crashed down the slender tree trunks until we were halted by a ditch. Behind us we thought we could hear the sounds of pursuit. The men worked with the desperation of terror to fill in the trench with brushwood and sods. We were across and the trees began to thin when we heard the sound of engines to the left.

Fearing a chase by tanks, we switched off our motors until we laughed at each other with relief when two other jeeps came into the glade. We all returned to brigade together, our hearts heavy at the almost certain death of Peter, Roach and Durban.

After I had reported to the Brigadier, we leaguered for the night in one of those red carabinieri stations which one comes across at intervals all over Italy.

I was just folding my maps for the next day's run when Peter walked in through the door! For some moments I could not speak. Then all I could say was 'I thought you were dead.' He explained how they had avoided being hit by a miracle. Durban had fought his guns until the flames reached the petrol tank. Then they had run under the cover of the black smoke into the woods, pursued by several Germans.

They ran non-stop for over three miles until they came to a farm where they borrowed a pony trap to complete their journey. I poured out two glasses of brandy and we sat back, German cigars in our mouths, exchanging versions of the battle.

The Hell that was Termoli

Like many of the SAS and Commandos who fought so gallantly at Termoli against overwhelming odds, Farran found the battle against elite German troops and tanks one of the hardest of his career. A powerful German advance seized the key cemetery area of the town, forcing the SAS back on the last ridge before the railway goods yard. Farran takes up the story:

Although we only had a strength of 20 men, our firepower was abnormally strong. In all there were six Brens and a two-inch mortar. I covered our 1,000 yard front between the 1st SAS and the sea by putting ten men with three Brens on each side of the railway line. Our main trouble was that we had no tools with which to dig weapon pits.

In spite of the fact that heavy fire was directed on us from the cemetery and that constant attempts were made to advance down the line of the railway, we held our positions for three days.

Mortar bombs swished down at all times but most of them crashed harmlessly in the engine sheds behind. Only one man was wounded, although I am sure we inflicted heavy casualties on the enemy. The range was so short that we could not fail to hit a man advancing in an upright position.

Crossing the railway from one side of the position to the other was a most perilous venture. A sniper cracked bullets dangerously close to our heads as we raced across the open track.

We had been in our position for nearly a day before we discovered that the railway engine and truck in the middle of our front was loaded with high explosive, ready to be detonated. I was terrified during the entire battle that it would be hit by a mortar bomb.

We were short of rations and the nights were bitterly cold. It was the only pure infantry battle I fought in the war and I never want to fight another.

Our spirits were low until we were encouraged by a County of London Yeomanry Sherman tank which came up on our left. It scored a beautiful direct hit on the dome in the cemetery and the green marble disintegrated like the atom at Bikini. Everyone cheered loudly for it had contained an annoying sniper.

On the third day, the Irish Brigade landed in the harbour. The London Irish moved up to our position for a counter-attack and I pointed out the enemy guns to the company commander who was to pass through my sector. He asked me to fire everything we had down the railway line while he advanced from the left.

It was a perfect shoot. Only when the fools stood up and began to run back down the beach did I realise their great strength.

Several hundred figures in blue overcoats began to double back, tacking this way and that to avoid our bullets. The 1st SAS on the left were having the same kind of harvest. I think the enemy must have been surprised at our firepower for we had conserved ammunition carefully until this last moment.

It was a reward which made our miserable three days in the cold worthwhile. The London Irish company commander came back on a stretcher, but he was cheerful enough for he had been wounded in the hour of victory.

Heroes of the Forests of France

During Operation Wallace in France (19 August– 19 September), Farran had one of the closest shaves of his wartime career in a furious fight with the Germans near the Fôret St Jean, losing more than half his squadron of jeeps.

Within 10 miles of the forest, Ramon again ran into trouble. An unreliable civilian told him that a village called Villaines was clear of the enemy. He ran into a number of [former] Afrika Korps troops in the streets and both his jeeps were destroyed.

Ramon, as always, fought bravely and succeeded in escaping on foot to the hills, but three of our best men were left behind. Worse still, there was no way of warning me.

I was breaking all the rules by motoring along quite happily at about 30mph at the head of my column, confident that Ramon would give me notice of any opposition ahead. Only the very slowest speed is wise in enemy country since it is essential that you see the enemy before he sees you.

As it was, we turned a corner to come face-to-face with a 75mm gun blocking the entire road. Even as I told Corporal Clarke my driver to swing into the ditch, two Germans in Afrika Korps hats fired a shell at less than 10 yards range. Perhaps it was because we were so close to the muzzle of the gun that the shell whistled over our heads to burst in the road behind.

And then we were crawling out of the wrecked jeep into the ditch with bullets spattering all round. The little Maquis guide we had picked up at Les Bordes was shot in the knee.

As I huddled under the bank, I could see the spare wheel from the front of the jeep rolling down the middle of the road. There were lots of Germans practically on top of us, shouting loudly and spraying the jeep with machine gun fire. We had crawled about five yards from the vehicle when I remembered the codes and my marked map. Carpendale, the Signals officer, crawled back to get them. We still had the Bren, so that when we came to a convenient gully I sent the others up to the top of the bank to hold them off. I began to run the gauntlet back to organise the rest of the column.

The Germans were now running forward in line, shooting as they came. A big blond brute with a Schmeisser called upon me to surrender, so I wildly fired at him with my carbine. He disappeared, but I cannot say whether he was shot or just taking cover.

I found Jim Mackie with the good old bewildered look on his face standing by the leading jeep. Thank God he had had the sense not to drive round the corner. He had first thought that I had been blown up on a mine. I led him up a convenient lane to the right, from which his two jeeps poured enfilading fire at short range into the German flank. Corporal Clarke was still holding his own out in front with the Bren. Sergeant Major Mitchell moved off to the left with ten men and four Brens to hold the line of the hedge, while I myself commanded the two jeeps in the centre of the road.

By now the enemy fire had become very heavy, including shells and mortar bombs. The Germans made a foolish charge along both sides of the road, giving us a magnificent shoot at less than 50 yards range. Their casualties were very heavy and Jim

Mackie's troop alone accounted for a whole platoon in a field. Instead of abandoning the attack, the idiots came on until they were so far into our rough semi-circle that we were cutting them down from three sides.

I even shot a German with my own carbine – my only definite personal bag of the war.

Corporal Clarke's Bren was silent by now and I feared he had been captured or worse. (In fact he joined up with Ramon Lee some days later.) After we had been fighting for almost an hour, a mortar and a machine gun opened up behind us. I had been holding on in the hope that David Leigh would come along with the other jeeps, but it was now quite clearly time to break off the action. In any case, his arrival had been so long delayed that I assumed that the sound of the firing had made him veer off on another tack.

The trailer containing our wireless set was on fire in the middle of the road and I nearly got myself killed in a vain attempt to rescue it.

Under the cover of Jim Mackie's guns, we withdrew down a small lane which unfortunately proved to be a dead end, leading into a mill. We succeeded, however, in making our way over a stream and across country through many hedges to strike a country lane near Jeux.

A farm labourer then warned the SAS that a whole Panzer division was strung out in the villages between Semur and Montbard, necessitating a wide detour. Tragically, it later transpired that the popular and dashing officer David Leigh had run into the same tough opposition at Villaines after Farran's withdrawal, only this time the Germans were doubly primed and ready. The gallant Leigh was killed and his party only escaped after suffering heavy casualties.

A depressed Farran found himself with only seven of the original twenty jeeps with which he had set out. Later, during a combined squadron attack on Chatillon to seize the important junction of the Montbard and Dijon roads, there was very fierce fighting with the SAS again giving out worse than they got. During a lull, Farran nonchalantly described what happened next as he led a foot patrol around the east of the area, supported by one jeep. As he cautiously looked around a corner, he was astonished to see a German machine-gun post on each side of the lane, facing outwards.

They were all in great coats and had their back to us. I could not think what to do, so we sat in a garden and waited. Lieutenant Pinci begged a bottle of wine, bread and cheese from a French cottage, so we had lunch.

I tossed up which German we should shoot in the back and it turned out to be the left hand one. Sergeant Young took careful aim through his carbine and when I gave the word, he pulled the trigger.

At the same moment Pinci, as excitable as ever, shot a German on a bicycle to the right. All hell was then let loose. I do not know from where they were coming, but our little lane was soon singing with Schmeisser bullets. It was so high banked and so open on each side as to make it a death trap. With angry bullets buzzing around our heads, we burst into the front door of a French house. Running straight through, we scrambled down a bank to a canal.

After we had run along the tow path to a lock, I led the party across country to the east. We had just reached the cover of a thin hedge on the skyline when two machine guns picked us out.

I had not realised that we could be seen. We wriggled on our bellies along the furrows in a ploughed field with the bullets kicking up great clots of earth all round. I have never felt so tired. I knew that if we remained on that crest we would be killed and yet I could not force myself to move any faster.

Sergeant Robinson behind me was hit in the leg and still he moved faster than I. When we had reached a little dead ground I tried to help him, but I was too exhausted. Never have I been so frightened and so incapable of helping myself.

Fortunately, Jim Mackie appeared in the jeep and they managed to get Robinson aboard and dressed his wounds at a friendly farmhouse and then motored back slowly through the forest glades to their base. Farran added: 'The battle of Chatillon was over. They say we killed 100 Germans, wounded many more and destroyed nine trucks, four cars and a motorcycle.'

Near Granrupt, a force of 600 SS with 4 armoured cars and 6 troop carriers prepared to surround Farran's SAS and wipe them out. Luckily, a nineteen-year-old French youth gave the British troops a last-minute warning and they prepared to slip free from the tightening trap. Farran reported:

The field was completely enclosed by woods and the only exit was a lane which led towards the Germans in Granrupt. I knew it would be useless to try to form a defensive position with the Maquis, who would be much better advised to withdraw into the woods. In any case, I had to think of my jeeps and the rest of my command in the Forest of Darney.

By this time, small arms fire had broken out in the woods on the eastern perimeter of the dropping zone, so well marked by white parachutes still sitting in the upper branches of the trees. The Maquis were running back in disorder into the forest. Escape to the east and the north was impossible and although I drove the jeeps around like a string of ponies, I could not find a route to the south or west.

A deep stream ran through the woods on the north which our jeeps could not hope to negotiate. In something like despair, I placed the jeeps in the hull down position behind a small crest in the middle of the field. Suddenly, when we were about to do the Old Guard act, I noticed a gap in the south-west corner. We cut the wire and crashed through a spinney of young saplings, bursting through them like fear-crazed elephants in a jungle. On the other side of a small field, we found a good track which led us down to the main road. In all, we had covered about four miles across country in a straight line.

Now that we had reached safety, my thoughts were for the boy scout Maquis and their first battle. I sent Lieutenant Gurney with two jeeps to attack the enemy's immediate rear along the Granrupt Road. He machine-gunned some German infantry, especially a group of officers standing on a mound and knocked out what appeared to be their headquarters truck. I placed Sergeant Vickers in ambush on the road near Hennezel, hoping to catch the Boches on their way out. He was fortunate enough to catch two staff cars moving towards the battle and it was later reliably reported that amongst the dead were the Colonel and second-in-command of the attacking force.

From the subsequent German reaction, I do not think they were pleased with our day's work. I decided it was better to lie low for a while, so we remained under the dark shadow of the trees all day.

Farran used the lull to summon two French mechanics to come from the German workshops in Bains-les-Bains to repair a burnt-out clutch on one of the jeeps. The men arrived on a motorcycle roaring with laughter at the thought that they were going to fix a British SAS fighting vehicle with German spare parts. 'Only this sort of comedy made life in Occupied Europe worthwhile,' quipped Farran.

At the end of operations in France, Farran's men were suffering from the intense nervous tension brought about by having spent a month behind enemy lines in the most testing of circumstances. However, they had killed and wounded a large number of enemy troops, disrupted communications, tied up a huge number of enemy forces who were engaged in looking for them and destroyed ninety-five trucks, the burnt out carcasses of which littered the roads of France. They returned to Britain well satisfied with their efforts.

Operation Tombola – the Last Dramatic Throw of the Dice

In the spring of 1945, the next major mission was in the Tombola valley, Italy, which Farran was determined to lead, against the wishes of his superiors. He judged his men would need him in command and, in the event, Farran's decision was vindicated, although he fully appreciated the risk he was taking in deliberately disobeying orders.

I put the scheme up to Colonel Riepe, who agreed in principle provided that we did not begin to operate until ordered by Fifteenth Army Group. He categorically refused my application to be allowed to command the party. I pretended to accept with good grace, knowing well that it would not be long before a slender thread would hang between me and a court martial . . .

Officially, an advance party of Captain Jock Eyston and four men would jump on March 4th, having been dispatched from the plane by me. In fact, I intended to lead the stick in front of Eyston and my kit would be pushed out on a separate parachute by an RASC packer. The aircrew was briefed to tell a sad tale of mishap on their return. They did this so successfully that I was reported as a casualty until my first wireless message came through.

I had been shivering in the door for about ten minutes when the aircraft began to lose height. My heart thumped like a bilge pump when I glimpsed a circle of red and yellow parachutes laid out on the snow beneath. There were little black dots moving round it like water spiders on a pond. We circled round slowly for the run-in to the drop.

It was a long, narrow valley and the dropping zone seemed to be in a basin at the southern end. I recognised the largest and whitest mountain as Cusna . . . The red light went on, which meant that we had ten seconds to go. The dispatcher put his hand over the box, but I told him to take it away, preferring to watch for the light myself. I turned round to look at the rest of the stick. They were pale and nervous, but had enough confidence to raise a smile. Kershaw cocked his thumb up with a grin and shouted something, which was blown away in the slipstream. It was his first parachute jump. Orthodoxy had never been our strong point.

The ground seemed very low and we could see white, upturned faces [the partisan reception committee] against the snow. I was just contemplating the advisability of another run-in, when the green light came on. This was no time to argue, having keyed myself up to the pitch of getting out. Then I was in mid-air. My chute opened with a crack, tugging at my shoulders. I heard somebody shout 'Woa Mahomed' [the Para's famous battle cry] as I recovered my breath. Kershaw I suppose.

Fortunately the dropping zone, which was only as big as a suburban back garden, was on a steep slope and the wind was strong enough to make us drift down the valley. I had barely paid out my leg bag, when I hit the snow with tremendous force.

Operation Tombola had begun!

In Praise of Women Partisans

Various squads were raised among the partisans including fighters, runners and, perhaps the most colourful section of all, the intelligence squad organised by an Italian called Keess. This consisted of fifteen strong-legged partisan girls. 'Their functions were numerous', according to Farran. 'Apart from cooking and sewing and mending, they were excellent for reconnoitring German held villages.' He continues:

It was a trick I had learned in France. Where a man could never venture without false identity papers, an attractive girl could pedal a bicycle through a German-held village with impunity. They could also carry messages with greater safety than a man. Keess sent them on numerous long expeditions to the plains for information and they never failed.

Oh, how a woman can loosen a soldier's tongue! These girls could march better than any man in the company and their morale was always high, in spite of the fact that they lived in the same filthy conditions as the men. Later on they cared for the wounded, loaded machine guns, carried dispatches and were always a good influence on morale. When the Germans attacked at Gatta, one of our blondes was the only Italian to stay behind with the British.

One girl in particular will always remain in my memory. Her name was Noris and she was a tall, raven-haired girl with Irish blue eyes. She was as brave and dangerous as a tigress and was completely devoted to the British company.

When she was not dressed in her finery for a reconnaissance she wore a red beret, a battledress blouse and a thick grey skirt made from an Army blanket. The pistol in her waistband was a sign that she was more than capable of taking care of herself. John Stott, the liaison officer from Modena valley, used to say that she had all the devils of the world in those eyes.

Noris was worth ten male partisans!

Many daring actions were fought, but one of the most memorable was at the German Corps headquarters at the Villa Calvi and the Villa Rossi near Casa del Lupo in spring 1945. According to Farran, the partisan band and the SAS contingent made a 'motley crowd of ruffians', comprising thirty Russians, forty Italians and just twenty-four British.

There was plenty of colour in the crowd, however. Here and there, amongst the dirty khaki were red berets, bits of parachute silk, green and yellow plumes, a few red stars and the summer frocks of the girls. Everyone seemed to be armed to the teeth with knives, pistols, sub machine guns and bullets.

I explained the plan for the attack over the air photographs we had received from Florence. Each sentence was translated first into Italian and then into Russian. We would infiltrate through the enemy positions as soon as it became dark, charging quietly in three tightly-packed columns led by me with two local guides and two British scouts.

On the left Lieutenant Harvey, the Rhodesian, would lead a column of ten British and twenty Garibaldini. In the centre, Lieutenant Riccomini would lead ten British, the Goufa Nera [partisans] with Lees bringing up the rear with the girls. Modena and the Russians would form the right-hand column. We would march all night until we reached our lying up position in the farm called Casa del Lupo, ten miles from the objective . . . We would remain under cover during the day until it again became dark, when we would advance in the same three columns towards the German headquarters . . .

The headquarters consisted of two main buildings, separated from the foothills by a large number of small houses in which the troops were billeted. Of the two main buildings, one was the chief of staff's villa and the operations room and other was the residence of the corps commander. Between these villas ran the main road and each was guarded by four sentries. In addition, there were six machine gun positions sited tactically round the camp.

I had decided to concentrate on the two important villas and to place the Russians in a semi-circle to the south to isolate these targets from assistance from the remainder of the headquarters. Ten British would force an entry into each villa, after killing the sentries. They would be immediately reinforced by twenty Italians at each building.

The plan seemed straightforward enough and, in any case, it was too late to worry about any last-minute hitches now. Farran describes in vivid detail the stark heroism of the daring attack:

The firing started first at the Villa Calvi. A tremendous burst, which must have been a whole Bren magazine, was fired by someone. Tracer bullets began to fly in all directions. Although we had reason to congratulate ourselves on getting a hundred men to the target unobserved, the Germans were by no means asleep.

Spandaus were soon spraying the whole area from the south. I thought at first that the Russians were firing in the wrong direction, but it was not long before I realised that at least seven German machine guns were awake. I told Kirkpatrick to strike up Highland Laddie (on his bagpipes) just to let the Germans know that they had the British to contend with.

He had only played a few bars, when the phut-phut of a Spandau picked us out. I pushed him into a slit trench and he continued to play from his cramped position.

At Villa Calvi, Ken Harvey killed two sentries on the lawn before they realised that they were being attacked. The front door was locked, but was soon burst with a bazooka bomb. Four Germans were killed on the ground floor, but others fought back valiantly down the spiral staircase. In one room, Harvey was confronted by a German with a Schmeisser. He ducked, but neglected to extinguish his torch. Fortunately, Sergeant Godwin was quick with his Tommy gun and shot over Harvey's shoulder.

Several attempts were made to get up the stairs, but the Germans kept up a concentrated fire from the first floor, which made it impossible. Corporal Laybourn was wounded by a grenade rolled down from above. Another British parachutist called Mulvey was hit in the knee by a bullet.

From the lawn outside, an equally furious battle raged against the top windows. Several Germans were killed by bazooka and Tommy gun fire. Harvey realised that it was impossible to take the house in the twenty minutes allowed. He therefore decided to start a fire on the ground floor. Working frantically against time, the British heaped up maps, chairs, files and curtains in a great pyre in the middle of the operations room. With the aid of a few pounds of explosive and a bottle of petrol, a trail was laid and ignited. The wounded were carried out to safety, while the Germans were kept inside by Tommy gun fire until the whole house was ablaze.

At Villa Rossi, things had not gone so well. I had not allowed Riccomini sufficient time to cross the road and Ken Harvey had opened fire on Calvi too soon. A siren gave the alarm from the roof of Villa Rossi and all the lights were turned on. Ricky killed four sentries through the iron railing with his Tommy gun and then rushed the door. It was open, but a hail of fire greeted him at the foot of the stairs. Somebody, I think Taylor, shot out the lights. Four Germans were killed and two surrendered on the ground floor . . . Two attempts were made to carry the stairs by assault, but were repulsed with heavy losses. Sergeant Guscott was shot in the head and Mike Lees was seriously wounded as he tried to rally the attackers on the first landing. Ricky was killed in one of the rooms on the ground floor. The Germans made an attempt to come down, but withdrew when three were killed on the landing. It is believed that one of these was a General . . . Kershaw, Green and some others then started a fire in the kitchen, while Ramos and Sergeant Hughes carried the wounded outside.

Bullets were flying everywhere and, over it all, the defiant skirl of the pipes. The Russians were brusquely returning the German fire, but I knew that our ammunition must be nearly finished. Star shells were being fired from Bologna, Modena and Reggio and the

Germans had even opened fire on Villa Calvi with the anti-aircraft guns from Pianello. Rossi was beginning to burn and Villa Calvi was like an inferno. I pointed my pistol at the sky and fired a red Verey light – the signal to withdraw.

The group's losses were, in the circumstances, incredibly light – three British killed and six Russians captured. Included amongst the dead was Ricky, 'One of the bravest chaps to ever have lived,' Farran recorded. The exploits of his brave, motley band in this and other outstanding episodes during the final weeks of the war were to go down in regimental history.

Farran's Battaglione Alleato (SAS), otherwise known as the Battaglione McGinty (the SAS major's codename on this operation was the typically tongue-in-cheek Paddy McGinty), had forged a special comradeship only found among those who have risked their lives together in a vital, common cause. The group was fiercely proud to have as its motto '*Chi osera ci vincera*', which translates not surprisingly as 'Who Dares Wins'.

With victory won at last after so much effort and sacrifice Farran, like so many other comrades in the SAS, felt a deep sense of anti-climax and underwent a period of intense soul searching. He simply could not comprehend why he had survived when so many close friends had not. He had fully expected to be killed on active service and, given the amount of action he had seen over so many years, it was indeed a miracle he had survived unscathed. He turned to his religious roots to find the answer to his deeply troubled feelings of loss and confusion, and prayed to God for reassurance.

Farran's final words in *Winged Dagger* reinforce the double-edged hope with which he resolutely faced an uncertain future: 'Show me the way to use well my freedom and tell me that it has not all been in vain . . .'.

Demons of the Desert

Jock Lewes, Fitzroy Maclean,
Bob Lilley, John Sillito, Johnny Cooper

JOCK LEWES – EXPLOSIVE HERO

Jock Lewes was one of Stirling's key officers and closest allies in the formation of the Special Air Service in the Western Desert. The brilliant, logical, scientific mind of Lt John 'Jock' Steel Lewes perfectly counterbalanced the vivid imagination and impulsive panache of his commanding officer. Stirling greatly admired Lewes' skills as a resourceful commander in the field during the early desert operations. However, he gauged that Jock was the perfect officer to take charge of a major training programme which would provide sufficient numbers of highly trained recruits for his clandestine raiding unit to expand and eventually become a permanent part of the British Army. This was Stirling's burning, long-term ambition.

Bravery, fighting ability and fitness alone would not be sufficient qualities in the men the SAS was seeking. Self-sufficiency, stealth, navigational and survival skills and above all cunning would be needed in plenty – and Jock was the inspirational leader to instil these attributes in the deadly raiders, as Stirling readily acknowledged. Sadly, Lewes' star burned brightly but all too briefly, as he was tragically killed in a devastating fighter attack while returning from a desert airfield raid just as the SAS was proving itself a Rommel-beating force. But Stirling never forgot his loyal lieutenant, who invented the famous 'sticky bomb' that was so deadly to vulnerable aircraft on the ground, saying that he regarded Lewes as one of the key founders of the Regiment and one which it could least afford to lose.

Jock was put in charge of training L Detachment SAS at Kabrit in 1941 when the war was going very badly for Britain and the Allies. Lewes, an Australian and Oxford rowing blue who had joined the Welsh Guards, had an honours degree in science and the right qualifications and organised mind to solve the new technical problems in combat faced by the SAS. Stirling had recruited Lewes from No. 8 Commando by going into Tobruk, which was then beseiged by the Germans. Stirling had a very good reason for wanting to attract Lewes to join his fledgling outfit.

Lewes had managed to acquire some parachutes which had been unloaded at Alexandria in error and he and a small group of Guardsmen were authorised by Brig, later Maj Gen, Robert Laycock, to experiment with them. Laycock commanded Layforce, a Commando-based force, which was raised to seize the strategic island of Rhodes. However, German successes in Cyrenaica and the Balkans sabotaged that plan. As a consequence, the highly trained Commandos of Layforce were being unsuccessfully and wastefully used in large-scale raids on enemy centres along the North African coast.

The only form of air transport available to Lewes was an ancient Vickers Valencia aircraft which was unsuitable for dropping paratroops, but beggars couldn't be choosers. Stirling and a party consisting of two officers and six Guardsmen made the first drop. Stirling became a casualty when his parachute caught on the tail section of the aircraft as he baled out. A jagged hole was torn in the canopy and he fell too fast, injuring his back on landing. He was a very lucky man indeed to get away this lightly, but the mishap did not deter him in the slightest in his plans to raise a special parachuting, sabotage force. While recovering in hospital, Stirling finalised his ideas, which were eventually accepted. Backed enthusiastically by Lewes and a nucleus of tough officers, he set about raising a force of about sixty volunteers which would go into action just before the next big offensive. Splitting into small groups, they would attack enemy aircraft on the ground and then fade away into the desert to strike again another day.

Jock Lewes outlined in great detail the training programme he had in store for the new recruits. During his briefing he told the men they would have to learn to parachute and as there were no airborne training facilities in the Middle East the SAS would have to form their own. They would need to build training towers, scaffolding, swings and gymnastic equipment, which was all vital for the required specialist instruction. Jock instilled into the troops that the purpose of their training was to make them independent in every way, operating in very small groups, or alone if necessary. They would have to develop a natural self-confidence in their ability to navigate across featureless terrain, using maps that gave little or no detail. It would be important to learn to survive on minimum rations and to eke out their limited food and, especially, water during the hot periods of the day. Above all, there would be no back-up or safety net in the event of things going wrong. The raiders would use the cover of darkness for offensive activity wherever possible. Therefore, Jock insisted that night work was to be the most essential part of training, coupled with skill in handling weapons of all types.

The men spent a week constructing 20-ft and 40-ft jumping towers out of scaffolding. Swings and all the other equipment used in parachute training at the time were also assembled from scratch. However, it was not possible to build a simulator for the men to practice their parachute rolls, a manoeuvre essential to avoid injury on landing. So one of Lewes's bright, but inherently dangerous ideas, was to have the soldiers jump from the tail board of a Bedford 15cwt truck speeding across the desert at 30mph. Trainee SAS men had to crouch facing the front of the vehicle and then jump off backwards, hitting the ground with considerable force.

Unfortunately, the parachute rolls they executed were not always sufficient to prevent accidents and a large number of injuries were sustained as a result. Contrary to the expectations of some of the new recruits, such bad luck was met with little sympathy. Anyone permanently injured would be curtly and unceremoniously returned to their parent unit and out of the SAS. The tough unit had tough rules – there was no room for the soft option.

If they survived their basic SAS course unscathed, the recruits were introduced to 216 Squadron of RAF Transport Command which was equipped with old fashioned Bombay aircraft. The aircraft were powered by two Pegasus engines and had a very slow air speed of about 90mph, with crews under orders to turn back if head winds exceeded 50mph. The soldiers attached their static parachute lines to rails bolted on to the floor of the aircraft. There were no reserve chutes and although the process seemed extremely dangerous to some of the men, they nevertheless doggedly perservered with their training.

Unfortunately, a tragic accident occurred early on in the training schedule when two SAS men, Duffy and Warburton, were first to jump out of the plane. The clips that attached their static lines to the rails inside the aircraft broke and the two men plunged to their deaths, to the shock of Stirling and the rest of the stick waiting to jump. Luckily, the RAF dispatcher aboard dived in to stop the others from jumping, otherwise more men could have died. Back at base, Stirling assembled everyone and said immediate modifications to the clips would be made and that parachute training would recommence the following morning and that he would be the first to jump. Stirling reasoned that the situation was similar to a bad fall from a horse and that the best way to preserve confidence was to get straight back in the saddle. He jumped first the very next day and everything thereafter went smoothly to plan, but it was a nerve-racking time for the whole unit, especially for Lewes, who always put his trainees' safety first and foremost.

The first active mission that Lewes and the SAS were involved with was to jump from five 216 Squadron Bombays about 20 miles from the German airfields at Tmimi and

Gazala, west of Tobruk and then attack them in small parties using Lewes' newly invented bombs. These bombs were placed on the wing of an aircraft to blow a hole through and ignite the fuel inside the tanks. Experienced Army engineers had experimented with various devices but concluded that it was impossible to design a bomb to fulfil both explosive and incendiary requirements.

Not to be deterred, Jock began an exhaustive round of experiments himself and eventually developed a bomb that consisted of a pound of plastic explosive, rolled in a mixture of thermite from an incendiary bomb, mixed up with his secret ingredient, old engine oil. One of the SAS originals, Johnny Cooper, remembered him demonstrating his bomb in front of a crowd of sceptical sappers and RAF officers on an old aircraft wing with the tanks half filled with fuel and supported on oil drums. A bomb was placed on top and when detonated, fire triumphantly gushed from the wing. The unlikely mixture worked like a dream. Johnny recalled in his book, *One of the Originals*, 'To set the bombs off, we used a time pencil and number 27 detonator which we carried separately and were only activated just before approaching a target. The time pencil consisted of different strengths of acid which would eat their way through a wire connected to the plunger of a detonator, giving delays of between 10 minutes and two hours, or even longer if required.' The timing depended on the thickness of the wire to be eaten through.

On the fateful first mission, the raiders in the five aircraft were commanded by Stirling, Mayne, Lewes, McGonigal and Bonnington. The group received increasingly alarming reports of rising wind speeds and thunderstorms approaching the central Mediterranean and, in fact, the storm was one of the worst for decades. However, Stirling felt the credibility of the unit could be damaged, perhaps irreparably, if he cancelled at this late stage.

Before jumping Lewes warned his men: 'Now remember this, lads, set the back bearing on your compasses and you will have the best chance of locating the man who has jumped before you.' The jump turned into a disaster, however, with men scattered far and wide, some fatally injured and some too badly harmed to continue. Many were simply lost in the desert and never seen again. It was impossible to attack the chosen targets because the containers with the necessary bombs and equipment had been lost in the chaos. Lewes was one of the sixty-four officers and men taking part in this first, disastrous parachute raid. The drop was made in the teeth of a gale and only Stirling, Mayne, Lewes, Bill Fraser and eighteen men reached the rendezvous. The vital inaugural mission had to be written off as a total disaster. Lewes told his men that with conditions as they were, their only hope was to try to locate their rendezvous with the LRDG and get back to safety. It was later learned that this was the worst hurricane and rainstorm that had been registered in the area for thirty years.

The failure of the operation was a major set-back to the fledgling SAS. In fact, for a time, it looked as though it might even destroy Stirling's dream entirely. After a massive rethink and discussion with Lewes, Mayne and the other officers, Stirling decided to abandon parachuting and use the LRDG from now on as a means to get to and from targets. Consequently, on 8 December 1941 he and Paddy Mayne set off to attack Sirte and Tamet aerodromes. Jock Lewes and Bill Fraser were to leave a few days later for other targets from Jalo oasis.

At last the SAS were successful, with Paddy Mayne raiding Tamet and inflicting great damage with the superbly efficient Lewes bombs. The bag on the Tamet raid was twenty-seven aircraft, three lorries, two trailers carrying spare aircraft parts and several petrol dumps. Fraser's haul soon afterwards was even higher, with a huge total of thirty-seven aircraft confirmed destroyed in a daring night raid at Agedabia. The SAS then repeated a series of raids on Sirte, Tamet, Agedabia and El Agheila, with Lewes taking part in this wide-ranging operation. His patrol at the outset consisted of himself, Sgts Almonds and Lilley and Ptes

Storey, Warburton (not to be confused with Tpr Warburton mentioned on p. 97) and White.

After a raid on Nofilia aerodrome, while returning with the Kiwi LRDG patrol, the party was attacked by an enemy fighter. Lewes was hit by a 20-mm cannon shell and died shortly afterwards. The surprise attack by the Axis planes was devastating with five trucks destroyed out of six. Morris of the LRDG continued to the rendezvous codenamed Marble Arch, but when he arrived he could find no trace of Fraser's patrol. After this fateful last mission for Lewes, the overcrowded LRDG truck was nursed back to the Jalo oasis – all that was left of the convoy.

Jock Lewes' death was a huge blow to David Stirling. Not only was he devoted to him, but he said that he was the officer upon whom he relied the most. Lewes could provide any scheme with a sound, practical basis. Stirling had admired Jock's talents from the first and had hoped that when they returned to base, he would take complete charge of the organisational side of the unit, but it was not to be.

Sgt Lilley, a tall, wiry man, vividly described what happened on that last fateful mission in Virginia Cowles' *The Phantom Major*. Morris had dropped the patrol 30 miles from Nofilia on Christmas Eve. At 2 a.m. on Christmas morning, Lilley, said:

We stopped, sat down and each man took a can of beer from his pack. Jock Lewes produced a tin of cold Christmas pudding and this he shared between the five of us. We all wished each other a merry Christmas, drank the beer, ate the pudding, had a smoke and a yarn and then we were on our way again.

We reached Nofilia before dawn and found a place to hide up where we could watch the aerodrome. There were not many aircraft in the field and the few that were there were very widely dispersed, but we noted the positions of them.

As soon as it was dark, we moved on to the landing

ground and put a bomb on the first plane, then moved off in search of the next plane.

We had just put a bomb on the second plane when the first one went off, we were only using half hour time pencils then. After that, the airfield became alive with troops and we came very near to getting caught as we beat a retreat. It was a big disappointment to all of us that we had only destroyed two planes.

Lilley continued to relate how they had returned to the rendezvous, then started off for Marble Arch. He added that a low-flying Axis plane – a Savoya – spotted them.

He circled over us and came in with all guns firing. We blazed away at him with everything we had, but our fire didn't seem to affect him.

We abandoned the trucks and tried to find some cover. The pilot came gunning for us. He attacked twice and Jock Lewes was hit. We bandaged him with field dressings, but he died about five minutes later and we buried him in a grave about two feet deep.

It was as bare as a billiard table, we had not been able to find any cover. Two more aircraft appeared on the horizon. There was nothing to do but walk away from the trucks and lie down in the sand.

In a few minutes, the fighters had destroyed all the trucks and then they went for the men. When they finally ran out of ammunition, more planes came to take their place. The merciless attack continued for several hours.

Jim Almonds and I thought we were the only two left alive and we began making plans for the march back. The next minute, there were voices calling from all around and on checking up we found that after eight hours strafing and bombing the enemy had only succeeded in destroying the transport. By swapping pieces on the burnt-out vehicles, we managed to get

one going. We all clambered aboard and held each
other on the truck.

Then we carried on to the rendezvous to let Bill
Fraser know that we hadn't forgotten him and tell
him that we would send other trucks out for him.
There was no sign of him or any of the party, so we
decided to make for Jalo as fast as we could.

A second patrol was sent to look for Bill Fraser, but this
was also unable to locate him. Later, it was discovered there
had been some confusion about the meeting place. Fraser
and his four men – Sgts DuVivier and Tait and Pts Byrne
and Phillips – had found the aerodrome near Marble Arch
deserted and had returned to the rendezvous marked on
maps the following day. They waited there for six days
before giving up hope and by this time had nearly run
out of water. They only had half a pint per man left. They
were slightly better off for food, but still only had food
supplies for another 48 hours. There were two options
open to them, either to surrender to the enemy only a few
hours walk away – surrender was not a word found in the
SAS vocabulary – or to try to get back to their own lines.
But this would mean many days in the desert finding water
and food wherever they could to keep alive. After an epic
eight-day march covering 200 miles, they were finally
sighted by a British armoured car patrol within 40 miles of
their own lines and picked up looking like a band of
savages with matted hair and beards, faces caked in dirt
and ragged clothes.

Cooper said of the crushing loss of Lewes: 'Jock had been
our training officer right from the beginning and had
always striven hard to give us the best possible background
to equip us for our tasks. He was a man we all greatly
respected.' Paddy Mayne reluctantly had to take Lewes'
place at the training base and Stirling, who had been
promoted to major, also keenly felt Lewes' loss. Paddy was a
born fighting soldier and did not take kindly to being left
behind to manage the unit's preparation.

However, by this time it was proven beyond doubt that Lewes and Stirling had trained their men magnificently in the principles of small-scale raiding operations with the emphasis on the use of the three-, four-, or five-man patrols and the future of the SAS was assured.

At the opening of the Stirling Lines barracks, at Hereford, in June 1984, Col David Stirling gave the following heartfelt tribute to his old comrade Jock Lewes, a man who had the brightest future in the SAS had he lived to see it through to fruition: 'I have always felt uneasy to be known as the founder of the Regiment. To ease my conscience I would like it to be recognised that I have five co-founders: Jock Lewes and Paddy Blair Mayne of the original L Detachment, Georges Berge whose unit of Free French joined the SAS in January 1942; Brian Franks who re-established 21 SAS Regiment after the SAS had been disbanded at the end of the Second World War and John Woodhouse, who created the modern 22 SAS Regiment during the Malaya campaign by restoring the regiment to its original philosophy.' Significantly, Lewes' name was the first that came to the mind of the man who created the SAS.

FITZROY MACLEAN – SAS SUPER SOLDIER . . . SUPERSPY?

Sir Fitzroy Maclean crammed so much into his action-packed life that his exploits with the SAS in the Western Desert are but one part of the many adventures he enjoyed.

The bold aristocrat was so keen to fight for his country in the Second World War that he used the cunning ruse of becoming an MP so he could escape his job at the Foreign Office and take an active part in the war. Fitzroy became one of Churchill's right-hand men when he daringly parachuted into Yugoslavia later in the war as the premier's special envoy to Tito. After many close shaves, his key guidance enabled the partisans to mount a spectacularly successful guerrilla campaign which tied up many thousands of German troops who were so badly needed on the Russian front.

Maclean's greatest claim to wartime heroism undoubtedly includes his outrageously cheeky dressing down of Italian troops at roadblocks while in full British uniform behind the lines with David Stirling, during one of the SAS's raids on the North African coast. Fitzroy's main weapons against Rommel's heavily armed allies were his faultless command of Italian, a liberal dose of bluff – and an incredibly strong nerve – he pulled off his amazing escape act not once, but numerous times. There is also a very strong claim that the dashing war hero, diplomat, traveller and senior public servant was the model for James Bond 007 himself.

When Maclean reported to Cairo for active service in 1942, he had a chance meeting with David Stirling, formerly a subaltern in the Scots Guards, whose brother Peter, then Secretary at the Cairo embassy, was an old friend of Maclean's. Fitzroy recalled:

David was a tall, dark, strongly built young man with a manner that was unusually vague, but sometimes extremely alert. He asked me what my plans were. I told him.

'Why not join the Special Air Service Brigade?' he said. I asked what it was. He explained that it was not really a brigade, it was more like a platoon. It was only called a brigade to confuse the enemy. But it was a good thing to be in.

He had raised it himself a month or two before with some friends of his after the Commando with which they had come out to the Middle East had been disbanded. Now, there were about half-a-dozen officers and 20 or 30 other ranks.

Maclean jumped at the chance and did not have long to wait for exciting action, when he was asked to take part in a raid on Benghazi in the company of Stirling and Randolph Churchill, son of the British Prime Minister.

The Benghazi mission was risky, but it was the spring of 1942, when the war was going badly for the Allies, and there was a great deal of pressure to make some gains.

Fitzroy said: 'GHQ were toying with the idea of a raid on the docks installations in Benghazi itself. David had said I could go on the first operation after my training was completed. This was it . . . For an operation of this kind, it was necessary to wait for a moonless period. The next one was in the second half of May. This gave us plenty of time to make our preparations.' The raiders decided to use the LRDG to drop them off and pick them up from the target. They would drive into the port with their explosives and weapons hidden in Stirling's converted 'battle-wagon' vehicle, using inflatable small boats to attack enemy shipping supposedly safely berthed in the key harbour area.

The battle-wagon, which was to become a famous part of Stirling's kit, was a cut down Ford station wagon, with room for about six soldiers and equipment. It had a powerful engine and was fitted with two machine-guns in front and two behind. These could be removed and placed out of sight, giving an innocent appearance, if necessary. Stirling had it painted dark grey to resemble a German staff car, with all current enemy air-recognition marks prominently displayed.

On the trip were David Stirling, Gordon Alston, Fitzroy Maclean and Cpls Rose, Cooper and Seekings. Churchill, who had left a staff job in Cairo to join the SAS, insisted on coming along. He had not completed his training, but acted as an observer. The party travelled to Benghazi via Siwa and the Jebel Akhdar, feeling the cold in the open car as the journey was made in the dark. On the approach to the town, the battle-wagon developed a nerve shattering, high-pitched screech. The rough going had damaged one of the track rods and the noise was bound to attract unwelcome attention. Suddenly they turned a corner and a hundred

yards away, straight ahead, a red light was gleaming right
in the middle of the road.

Fitzroy described what happened next in his classic book
Eastern Approaches.

David jammed on the brakes and we slithered to a
standstill. There was a heavy bar of wood across the
road with a red lantern hanging from the middle of it.
On my side of the road stood a sentry who had me
covered with his Tommy gun. He was an Italian.

I bent down and picked up a heavy spanner from
the floor of the car. Then I beckoned to the sentry to
come nearer, waving some papers at him with my free
hand as if I wanted to show them to him. If only he
would come near enough I could knock him on the
head and we could drive on.

He did not move, but kept me covered with his
Tommy gun. Then I saw beyond him in the shadows
were two or three more Italians with Tommy guns and
what looked like a guardroom or machine gun post.
Unless we could bluff our way through, there would
be nothing for it but to shoot it out, which was the last
thing we wanted at this stage of the expedition.

There was a pause and then the sentry asked who we
were. 'Staff officers,' I told him and added peremptorily,
'In a hurry.' I had not spoken a word of Italian for three
years and hoped devoutly that my accent sounded
convincing. Also, that he would not notice in the dark
that we were all wearing British uniforms.

He did not reply immediately. It looked as though his
suspicions were aroused. In the car behind me I heard
a click, as the safety catch of a Tommy gun slid back.
Someone had decided not to take any chances.

Then, just as I had made my mind up that there was
going to be trouble, the sentry pointed at our headlights.
'You ought to get those dimmed,' he said and, saluting
sloppily, opened the gate and stood aside to let us pass.
Screeching loudly, we drove on towards Benghazi.

The raiders decided to abandon the battle-wagon with its noisy wheel and planted a bomb to go off in 30 minutes to destroy it. Suddenly, the party came face to face with an Italian Carabiniere soldier. There was no avoiding him and as, fortuitously, sirens began sounding off, Maclean immediately asked him in Italian what all the noise was about. 'Oh, just another of those damned English air raids,' he said gloomily. 'Might it be', Maclean inquired anxiously, 'that enemy ground forces are raiding the town and that they are the cause of the alert?' The soldier laughed loudly and said there was no need to be nervous because the British were all back on the Egyptian frontier. Maclean thanked him for his reassuring remarks and wished him good night. Although they were stood almost under a street light, the soldier did not seem to have noticed that Maclean was in British uniform. The group hurried back to their vehicle, changing their minds about destroying it and removing the detonator just moments before it went off so they could use the battle-wagon again.

Maclean bluffed another sentry as they looked for suitable targets among the jetties to plant their explosives. Some ships no more than a stone's throw away looked to be ideal. Then suddenly they were challenged from one of the ships by another sentry. '*Chi va la?*' ('Who goes there?') he snapped. '*Militari,*' Maclean shouted back. The suspicious sentry asked what they were up to. 'Nothing to do with you,' Maclean answered, brazenly. The soldier was sent away, his tail firmly between his legs. However, the group found that the inflatable boats they had taken to reach the shipping were punctured and useless. Yet another sentry approached, this time with bayonet fixed. Maclean pretended to be an angry Italian officer and shouted and gesticulated at the man who turned, embarrassed, and walked slowly away. The party packed up their explosives and left, but were ominously trailed by two more sentries with rifles and fixed bayonets.

Assuming as pompous a manner as my ten day's beard
and shabby appearance permitted, I headed for the
main gate of the docks, followed by David [Stirling]
and Corporal Cooper and the two Italian sentries. At
the gate, a sentry was on duty outside the guard tent.
Walking straight up to him, I told him I wished to
speak to the guard commander. To my relief he
disappeared obediently into the tent and came out a
minute or two later followed by a sleepy-looking
Sergeant, hastily pulling on his trousers.

For the second time that night, I introduced myself
as an officer of the General Staff, thereby eliciting a
slovenly salute. Next, I reminded him that he was
responsible for the security of this part of the harbour.
This he admitted sheepishly. How was it I asked him,
that I and my party had been able to wander freely
about the whole area for the best part of the night
without once being properly challenged or asked to
produce identity cards? He had, I added, warming to
my task, been guilty of gross dereliction of duty.

Why, for all he knew, we might have been British
saboteurs carrying loads of high-explosive.

At this, the man laughed incredulously. Maclean said he
would let him off this time but he had better not let him
catch him napping again. And what was more, he added,
he had better do something about smartening up his men's
appearance! Following this the party set off at a brisk pace
through the gate where the sentry presented arms, almost
falling over backwards in the process of trying to impress
the angry officer.

By the time the group got back to the battle-wagon, it
was nearly light and the sabotage raid had to be
abandoned, however they had learned much intelligence for
a repeat attack in future. The raiders got back in their car
and drove off, the wheel screeching disconsolately. One final
sentry at another roadblock was brusquely told that the
group were staff officers and he too let them go unmolested

and within minutes, the raiders were speeding along the road back towards the Jebel to a welcome rendezvous with the LRDG. Maclean's almost comic hoodwinking of the enemy in one of their most strongly defended ports had enabled Stirling, the head of the SAS, and the Prime Minister's son, to live to fight another day! Little did the Italians know they had such massive prizes within their grasp. The capture of Churchill, especially, would have had world-shattering repercussions in propaganda and hostage-bargaining terms.

Returning to the intriguing James Bond claim, certainly, Fitzroy Maclean had all the ingredients exhibited by the superspy. He was exceedingly cool, brave, debonair, handsome and circulated in the highest circles of power and intrigue. He also had that outrageous tongue-in-cheek sense of humour that the author Ian Fleming gave to James Bond as his unmistakable hallmark.

SAS connections are at the heart of this widespread belief, which is accepted by many of the late Sir Fitzroy's close family members and friends. As well as serving at prominent level at the Paris and Moscow embassies in the years preceding the Second World War, Fitzroy was a very close friend of Ian Fleming. Also, Ian's brother Peter worked alongside Mike Calvert, a gallant officer who served with distinction with the Chindits in Burma, later rising to the rank of brigadier and commanding the SAS Brigade in Germany in 1945. Earlier, in 1940, Calvert wrote a paper entitled prophetically 'The Operations of Small Forces Behind The Enemy Lines' and worked with Fleming helping to organise the guerrilla defence of Britain in the event of a Nazi invasion. There were many other SAS connections, for example, David Stirling became godfather to Fitzroy's son Charles, who later explained the enduring Bond connection in detail:

> Over the years, the Bond/Maclean connection has gradually blurred into myth. I first became aware of its public acceptance in 1984 when my father was the

subject of a *This Is Your Life* programme. Driven on to
the ITV sound stage in a London taxi, he emerged under
the glare of lights, genuinely astonished to be greeted by
Douglas Fairbanks Junior and Eamonn Andrews.

I watched from the wings with David Stirling and a
mixed gang of family, SAS originals and old partisans
and couldn't help smiling, mostly with pride, when the
orchestra twanged out the original theme from James
Bond!

Ian Fleming always remained cagey about 007's
identity. But he put a lot of himself into his books,
indulging as most writers do in wish-fulfilment, but he
saw, too, the need to preserve an air of mystery. After
all, his man was a spy.

My father, perhaps for similar reasons, made a point
of neither denying nor confirming rumours that he
was Bond.

In the early stages of the Second World War the career
paths of Fleming and Fitzroy crossed more than once. After
the fall of France, they found themselves at a London
luncheon at which Cdr Wilfred Dunderdale was a guest. It
is said the gathering had all the ingredients for the making
of James Bond sitting around that one table. Dunderdale
was a spy and had been a Secret Intelligence Service (SIS)
operative at the Paris embassy while Maclean was working
there. He had enjoyed a lavish lifestyle, introducing the
young Fitzroy Maclean to a glamorous world of White
Russian nightclubs, intrigue and beautiful women.
Champagne flowed from dusk till dawn and, as a third
secretary, Fitzroy really saw life as Bond lived it.

Maclean travelled without permits through central Asia
in the 1930s, and the Soviets naturally assumed he was a
spy largely because of his lifelong interest in Russia. These
assumptions and allegations persisted throughout his life.
Later, in the 1950s, he made overland journeys to exotic
places like Persia, Montenegro and Afghanistan. Before
leaving on one of these trips, Maclean was asked by

Stewart Menzies, head of SIS – the equivalent of 'M' in the James Bond stories – to carry out a cloak and dagger mission of which Bond would have been proud. Fitzroy was tasked to find out information about a possible Soviet invasion of Turkey from the Caucasus. It was a strictly unofficial request and fortunately no such situation developed, for the man who briefed Maclean was none other than the superspy and super British intelligence traitor, Kim Philby. On another occasion at the height of the Cold War, a group of Albanians confessed in a show trial that they had been recruited to assassinate Albania's Communist dictator Enver Hoxha by the 'Titoist war criminal' Fitzroy Maclean. It was a ridiculously trumped up charge, but intrigue stuck like glue to Maclean for most of his life.

There were incidents among Maclean's wartime exploits that could have been straight out of a James Bond novel. One was his successful kidnapping at gunpoint of the Persian tribal leader and collaborator with the Nazis, Gen Zahidi. With the authority of Gen Maitland Wilson, commander with responsibility for Persia and Iraq, Maclean set about raising a force of 150 volunteers to be trained in SAS operational methods. While engaged in this, he was instructed to report to Wilson's headquarters in Tehran towards the end of 1942. A dangerous situation was developing in southern Persia where German agents were operating among the local tribes. This might have resulted in vital supply routes to the Persian Gulf being threatened, as well as the Persian army in the south of the country becoming involved, joining forces with rebellious tribesmen and forming a potent force. McLean recalled:

A sinister part was being played in all this by a certain General Zahidi, who was in command of the Persian forces in the Isfahan area. Zahidi was known to be one of the worst grain-hoarders in the country. But there was also good reason to believe he was acting in co-operation with the tribal leaders and was in touch with the German agents who were living in the hills, and through them with the German High Command in the Caucasus.

Indeed, reports from secret sources showed he was planning a general rising against the Allied occupation force, in which his troops and those of the Persian general in the Soviet-occupied northern zone would take part and which would coincide with a German airborne attack on the 10th Army, followed by a general German offensive on the Caucasus front.

In short, General Zahidi appeared to be behind most of the trouble in southern Persia.

It was decided by the British high command that the general had to be kidnapped and that Maclean was the best man for the job. He would get into Zahidi's residence in Isfahan under the pretext of accompanying a visiting British brigadier. Maclean would have with him some armed, hand-picked men and the sentry would be distracted by an undercover Persian-speaking RAF intelligence man.

Amazingly, the daring plan worked without a hitch. Maclean continued:

When General Zahidi, a dapper figure in a tight-fitting grey uniform and highly polished boots, entered the room, he found himself looking down the barrel of my Colt automatic.

There was no advantage in prolonging a scene which might easily become embarrassing. Without further ado, I invited the general to put his hands up and informed him that I had instructions to arrest him and that if he made a noise or any attempt at resistance he would be shot. Then I took away his pistol and hustled him through the window into the car, which was waiting outside with the engine running.

To my relief, there was no sign of the much-advertised bodyguard. As we passed the guardroom, the sentry once again interrupted his conversation to present arms, and the general, sitting bolt upright, with my pistol pressed against his ribs and Guardsman Duncan breathing menacingly down his neck, duly returned the salute.

They rushed Zahidi off to the pre-arranged rendezvous and he was unceremoniously flown out of Persia for safe keeping in Palestine. The daring Maclean had triumphed yet again.

With German armies smashed at the war-winning battles of El Alamein and Stalingrad, the threat to Persia evaporated and Maclean continued to train his detachment of troops in the SAS methods, joining up with George Jellicoe's SBS. But plans to raid Crete fell through and another scheme to parachute into Greece also failed to materialise before Maclean went on his historic mission to aid Tito's Yugoslavian partisans.

Another Bond-like wartime episode had sinister and tragic associations. In 1943, Maclean was due to leave Cairo in a Liberator plane bound for London. At the last minute, he received instructions to delay his departure. The Liberator mysteriously crashed into the sea off Gibraltar, killing all passengers on board. Among them was Gen Sikorski, leader of the Polish government in exile. Several theories were later put forward to explain the incident, but Maclean suspected that the traitor Philby, who was in the Spanish section of MI6 at the time, was strongly implicated. Tantalisingly, he never discovered why he was taken off the plane, as Stalin at that time would have wanted him out of the way just as much as he would Sikorski. It was a mystery worthy of Fleming himself.

BOB LILLEY – MORTAL COMBAT IN THE LION'S DEN

Former Commando, Sgt Bob Lilley was one of the toughest original members of L Detachment. He possessed an instinctive mastery of the deadly skills of unarmed combat –

and was well prepared to use them. He had lightning speed of thought and reactions and the determination and ability to fight harder than any opponent he was likely to meet. As a fully trained Commando, Lilley was intensively schooled in a variety of lethal martial arts, silent killing with the knife and a host of 'dirty tricks' moves designed to get a hard-pressed SAS raider out of a tight corner. He and his superbly trained fellow SAS original NCOs from the Commandos, including Bennett, Cooper, Rose and Seekings, were among the first volunteers when Stirling formed L Detachment of the SAS. All subsequently won decorations and became experienced veterans who helped train and guide the new recruits in later vital areas of SAS operations.

During a spectacularly successful series of raids along the Axis-dominated coast of North Africa under Jock Lewes and later David Stirling and Paddy Mayne, Lilley helped set the desert ablaze with consistent deeds of bravery, particularly evident during raids at El Agheila, Nofilia, Berka, Tripoli, Fuka and the big Benghazi raid, which was held in conjunction with the major, disastrous raid on Tobruk. The tough and unyielding Commando training that had been so much a part of Lilley's early Army life was to come to his aid and save his life on one memorably brutal one-to-one occasion, when courage alone was not enough and instinctive fighting skills were all that stood between his return to safety and oblivion.

In June 1942, Stirling was summoned to headquarters in Cairo and ordered to step up his SAS raids and destroy as many enemy warplanes as possible, as the pressure on the key Mediterranean island of Malta was mounting to such an extent that convoy supplies were reaching a critically low level. A further series of co-ordinated raids were planned and unleashed on the Benghazi area, Derna and Barce. A mainly French SAS party was nearly wiped out by a full German company after being betrayed, despite putting up a fierce resistance, but Stirling's group wreaked havoc at Benghazi, blowing up numerous aircraft and spare engines in hangars and workshops. Other SAS groups of raiders destroyed more aircraft and stores and inflicted casualties in savage firefights, but were soon hotly pursued by large enemy forces intent on tracking down the British phantoms and annihilating them. A brief passage in Philip Warner's superb history *The Special Air Service* makes it abundantly clear that the raiders could not always use their weapons to fight their way out to freedom and that sometimes more sinister, silent methods had to be employed. These unconventional methods were often frowned upon in regular Army circles where a code of chivalry still existed, even in the heat of battle. But behind-the-lines raiders were often forced to live, or die, by different rules. The iron-hard Lilley was one of the prime exponents of this deadly art of self-defence:

> In making their exit, the SAS ran into different problems, but one of the most interesting escapes was that of Sergeant Lilley.
>
> Looking for a way back, he wandered inside the perimeter of a large German camp. After a short time, he realised that it would be impossible for him to slip unnoticed through the German lines, so he stood up and walked for two miles.
>
> He was dirty and dusty and no one noticed he was not a German until he met an Italian outside the perimeter; the latter unwisely tried to arrest him but had his neck broken for his trouble.
>
> Lilley kept on walking. A dozen miles later, he ran into other members of the expedition and soon after linked up with the LRDG at the appointed rendezvous.

It does not take much imagination to conjure up the primeval, life-or-death struggle that must have taken place in the midst of the enemy encampment, as both men grappled violently for supremacy, the enemy soldier desperately trying to bring his weapons to bear, or shout to his comrades to come quickly to his aid and kill the intruder. Lilley had been surprised literally in the midst of the enemy lion's den, surrounded by numerous foes. Any alarm raised by the guard would almost certainly have spelt his sudden death, preceded probably by some very unpleasant treatment at the hands of his captors. However, his quick reflexes and deadly Commando training gave him a swift, decisive victory.

As Lilley made his way back to the main SAS group, the re-united raiders should have, at this point, returned to base. However, Stirling and Mayne could not resist going to have a look at the extent of the damage done by their men's deadly bombing attacks. A truck was borrowed from the LRDG's Capt Robin Gurdon, as their own transport had been destroyed, and off they sped for a recce. However, the raiders were quickly thwarted in their scheme to view the destruction at close hand as they approached Bernina airfield, near Benghazi, which they had earlier devastated. They were halted abruptly by enemy troops at a road block within a few hundred yards of their goal. They were all in British uniform and the heavily armed guards were turned out, headed by a German NCO brandishing a grenade menacingly in one hand and a pistol in the other. He appeared to become suspicious, even though one of the SAS, a German-speaker, was shouting in German that it was OK to let them through. An impatient Paddy Mayne menacingly cocked his pistol as the guard approached to look into the truck. Immediately, the rest of the SAS in the back readied Tommy guns and grenades for what seemed like a desperate shoot-out. But the startled German NCO abruptly changed his mind and quickly withdrew, deciding correctly that, as he was nearest, he would be the first to die and that his life would be preserved longer if he waved the truck on its way.

The SAS men shot up and bombed a few opportunist targets before they headed back into the desert pursued by what appeared to be a German patrol of trucks or armoured cars. To Mayne, always a fast and at times reckless driver, it was like a red rag to a bull and he floored the accelerator as the LRDG truck attained a speed over

The brilliant David Stirling in SAS officer's cap, in the domain he made his own, the Western Desert. (*IWM E21340*)

David Stirling discussing tactics with his key fellow SAS founder Jock Lewes (right) in the Western Desert, shortly before Lewes was tragically killed in a low-level aircraft attack, 1941.
(*Drawing by Penny Morgan*)

Desert SAS parachute trainees in their antiquated looking original jump gear, rubber helmets and knee protection, worn in training before the advent of berets and parachute smocks.
(*Denis Bell/Mike Morgan*)

A top-level inspection by the Duke of Gloucester of SAS stripping Spandau machine-guns and Schmeissers in the Western Desert in the early days of the unit's formation. (*IWM E12971*)

Cpl John Sillito MM, one of an SAS unit despatched to blow up the railway line near Alamein. After being separated from his colleagues in a fierce firefight, Sillito trudged back well over 100 miles through the burning desert to British lines with no water or food. (*IWM E19781*)

This side view of a desert SAS jeep, heavily armed with Browning and Vickers K machine-guns, gives a good idea of the number of jerry cans that had to be carried for petrol and water, spare tyres, ammunition, provisions and other gear essential on deep-ranging raids behind the lines. A stray bullet could cause havoc. (*IWM NA676*)

The world-renowned photograph of Stirling and his desert raiders taken shortly before his disastrous capture in 1943. Note the officer's dagger, foreground right. (*IWM E21338*)

Cpl John Henderson Melville, L Detachment SAS, formerly of the Scots Greys and from Fife, with heavy Browning jeep machine-gun in the Western Desert, 1943. This tenacious soldier saw much action and was later a hero in the forests of France fighting ferociously alongside equally tough and determined SAS comrades. (*IWM E21343*)

Fitzroy Maclean, the roguish epitome of SAS courage and panache – and a perfect model for James Bond. This illustration, inspired by a pre-war diplomatic tour of duty by Maclean in Russia, perfectly captures the irrepressible spirit of a truly extraordinary man. (*Drawing by Penny Morgan*)

Maj Sandy Scratchley and Roy Farran (front row, left to right) of 2nd SAS after the bitter battle for Termoli, Italy, 1943. Note the use of captured enemy Schmeisser sub machine-guns among the other Allied weaponry. (*IWM E26182*)

Lt Col Paddy Mayne, wearing the famous beige SAS beret prior to D-Day, 1944. (*IWM AP6069*)

One of the true heroes of the
Second World War,
Maj Roy Farran.
(*Courtesy of Roy Farran*)

Maj Anders Lassen, just before
the fateful Battle of Comacchio,
where he was killed leading a
daring solo attack on a series of
strong points, winning a
posthumous VC.
(*IWM HU71361*)

Maj the Earl Jellicoe (left), the brave and gifted SBS commander,
with Capt Chevilier and a Greek officer on board the Special Boat
Squadron headquarters boat Tewfik,
c. 1944. (*IWM HU71413*)

Portrait of the brilliant SAS avenger and Intelligence chief Maj Eric 'Bill' Barkworth. (*Barkworth family*)

The author's late father Cpl Jack Morgan, one of Maj Barkworth's key right-hand men in the elite 2nd SAS Intelligence unit, Italy, 1944. This photograph was taken just before he returned to the UK for intensive secret planning work to help co-ordinate the SAS Brigade's massive behind-the-lines drops in France in support of D-Day. He is wearing on his left breast the Eighth Army campaign medal ribbon awarded for victory in the North African desert. (*Morgan collection*)

The resourceful Sgt George Daniels MM, Algiers, 1943. (*Daniels collection*)

Tough as they come – Sgt Pete Tomasso, George Daniels' close comrade, Algiers, 1943. (*Daniels collection*)

Battle-hardened ex-11th Scottish Commando and L Detachment, 1st SAS and SRS veteran L/Cpl Denis Bell (rear left) and comrades 'somewhere behind the lines' with armed jeep in the forests of France, after D-Day, 1944. A rare and candid shot – note the armoured heavy calibre Browning machine-gun at the front of the vehicle. (*Denis Bell/Mike Morgan*)

SAS L/Cpl Denis Bell's wedding to wartime bride Alice on a short spell of leave just prior to dropping behind the lines after D-Day, 1944. (*Denis Bell/Mike Morgan*)

The brave, but doomed, SAS Maj Ian Fenwick behind the wheel of an armed jeep, just before he was killed in a do-or-die attempt to break through a formidable German road block, France, 1944. (*Drawing by Penny Morgan*)

One of the bravest and finest, SAS Lt David Leigh, Algiers, 1943. He was tragically killed in action in France in 1944 while fighting his way out of an enemy ambush, which shortly beforehand almost claimed the lives of Maj Roy Farran and comrades. (*Daniels collection*)

An extremely rare previously unpublished photograph of SAS raiders, including Sgt Robert Young (centre), actually in the process of blowing up an enemy road block behind the lines in France, 1944. Sgt George Daniels recalls that by this late stage in the war some of the raiders sometimes did not wear their famous winged dagger beret badges on active service, but instead wore unit badges to try and conceal their true SAS identities and avoid brutal torture and execution if caught. (*Daniels collection*)

Capt Darryl Morris (left) and men on a covert behind-the-lines mission in France, 1944. Sadly this brave and experienced officer was later cut down by enemy fire and killed just yards from comrades in a surprise attack. (*Daniels collection*)

SAS brigands in a cut-down Citroën car, France, 1944. The group includes Capt Anthony Greville-Bell DSO and Sgt George Daniels, the decorated stars of the highly acclaimed Operation Speedwell which took place in Italy. (*Daniels collection*)

The SAS bringing in Gestapo thugs by jeep to Celle, Germany, to face their just retribution for war crimes towards the end of the war in Europe. (*IWM BU3495*)

An SAS 3-in mortar crew in action, backing partisans at Alba in the Cuneo province of northern Italy as the fight for liberation reached its peak. (*IWM NA25411*)

Three tough-looking SAS troopers carrying a Vickers heavy machine-gun dismantled in pieces over mountains in Italy, April 1945. They had been parachuted into the Castino area with heavy weapons to carry out raids behind the lines. (*IWM NA25407*)

During fierce fighting near Essen, Germany, towards the end of the war in Europe, battle-experienced Sgt Joe Schofield and Tpr Jeavons embark on a dangerous mission to kill snipers – all in a day's work for the wartime SAS. Their jeep is armed with twin and single Vickers machine-guns. The absence of most of the radiator grill shows their jeep was almost certainly a veteran of the desert campaign, when it would have been fitted with a condenser for use in the hot climate. (*IWM B11921*)

Sgt George Daniels and a 2nd SAS comrade in a captured enemy VW military vehicle, Germany 1945. (*Daniels collection*)

Armoured jeeps and SAS move through Germany, with final victory in sight, 1945. To the right of the twin Vickers K machine-guns is a sheet of armour plate topped with a semi circle of bullet-proof glass, which protected the driver. (*Daniels collection*)

The spoils of victory as the Allies advance deep into Europe. SAS raiders with a huge captured Nazi flag and jubilant, liberated civilians. (*Daniels collection*)

A rare and historic photograph of Paddy Mayne (centre, front) and 1st SAS veterans at the end of the war, Norway, 1945. (*Denis Bell/Mike Morgan*)

A superb, laconic portrait of 2nd SAS stalwart Frederick 'Chick' Howard. *(Weekes family)*

The Villa Degler in the Black Forest, Germany, post-war HQ of Major Barkworth's War Crimes Investigation Team who were hunting German war criminals and SS murderers of their SAS comrades. Chick Howard is centre with Fred 'Dusty' Rhodes far right and Arthur Relf second right with other team members. Chick was a support member for the intelligence unit, many of whom were wartime comrades of the author's late father Cpl Jack Morgan, 2nd SAS Intelligence. *(Weekes family)*

Some of the hand-picked SAS War Crimes Team at the Villa Degler gather around a German car. *(Weekes family)*

Paddy Mayne's brave and resourceful driver Billy Hull with French Resistance and SAS. Left to right: Capt Anderson SAS, Billy Hull, Camille Raymond, French Resistance and Andre Lemee, French SAS. This photo was taken in the Coulonges-sur-Sarthe area of Normandy, in 1944. *(Hull collection)*

Billy Hull, a tough SAS fighter and skilful boxer (far left) with 1st SAS comrades relaxing nonchalantly outside their billet behind the lines in France in 1944. *(Hull collection)*

A V2 missile with sinister message for England checked out by 1st SAS behind the lines in enemy occupied Europe, 1944. *(Hull collection)*

By the KING'S Order the name of
Trooper W. Hull,
Army Air Corps,
was published in the London Gazette on
22 March, 1945,
as mentioned in a Despatch for distinguished service.
I am charged to record
His Majesty's high appreciation.

Secretary of State for War

Billy Hull's mention in despatches for exceptional SAS service.
(Courtesy of Gary Hull)

A superb portrait of
Ulsterman Billy Hull –
one of the SAS's
finest. *(Hull collection)*

The famous wartime battle honours issued at the end of the war to members of the 1st SAS. *(Courtesy of Gary Hull)*

SPECIAL
AIR SERVICE REGIMENT

EGYPT · ITALY
LIBYA · FRANCE
TRIPOLI · BELGIUM
TUNISIA · HOLLAND
CRETE · GERMANY
SICILY · NORWAY

WHO DARES WINS

1941 · 1945

SAS jeep being unloaded under fire at Rhine Crossing, 1945.
(Sydney Rhodes collection)

SAS unloading jeeps from amphibious Buffalo armoured vehicle under fire at the crossing of the Rhine, Germany, 1945. Syd Rhodes 2nd SAS is pictured foreground right.
(Sydney Rhodes collection)

Sydney Rhodes marries wartime bride Gladys. Note his proudly worn SAS wings and medal ribbons. *(Courtesy Mark Rhodes)*

The famous Norway scroll, signed by King Olav – an honour proudly given by the monarch to the SAS fighters who liberated Norway, 1945.
(Courtesy Gary Hull)

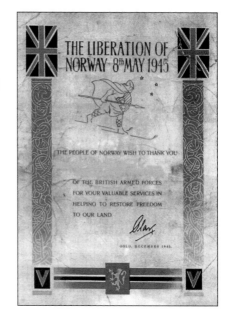

2nd SAS stalwarts Capt Greville-Bell DSO, foreground and George Daniels MM (rear) and Tpr Rushworth in cut down French saloon commandeered by the SAS in France.
(Daniels collection)

Capt Greville-Bell DSO, third from left, and SAS confer with American troops in France. *(Daniels collection)*

A superb group study of the 1st Squadron 2nd SAS in autumn 1945, containing many famous SAS veterans. Legendary behind-enemy-lines escaper Tanky Challenor MM is pictured second row, far right, along with several other Military Medal winners in the front row. *(Daniels collection)*

Veteran tough guys Jimmy Laybourn, left, and Dave Morrison, 2nd SAS, pose with captured Swastika on their jeep, Germany 1945. *(Courtesy Steve James)*

The SAS War Crimes Investigation Team on the prowl in post-war Germany catching Gestapo torturers and war criminals for the hangman's noose. The late Arthur Relf is pictured at the rear of the jeep. *(Morgan collection)*

One of the first 200 of the SAS and one of its toughest fighting veterans, Denis 'Taffy' James, 1st SAS. *(James collection)*

A brilliant shot of Curtiss Commando aircraft being loaded with 1st SAS jeeps bound for Norway, 1945.
(Courtesy of 1st SAS veteran Tom Robinson)

1st SAS stalwart Tom Robinson and A Squadron members relaxing in Norway in 1945, but still armed and dangerous! Tom is pictured far right. *(Robinson collection)*

An early shot of SAS veteran Taffy James, second left at rear, and comrades in forage caps in the Western Desert. *(James collection)*

A rare action shot taken during the historic Battle of El Alamein as Taffy James's SAS jeep inadvertently gate crashes the action whilst returning from a patrol. *(James collection)*

Troops going forward into action at Alamein under fire observed briefly by roving 1st SAS patrol. *(James collection)*

Photo of German soldiers found on the body of a dead enemy soldier in the Western Desert by SAS trooper Taffy James. The deceased former owner is believed to be one of those pictured. *(James collection)*

An extremely rare shot of SAS jeeps massed ready to go on operations behind the Mareth Line as the Allied Western Desert campaign reaches its victorious climax. *(James collection)*

A rare and evocative study of Paddy Mayne in 11th Scottish Commando uniform before joining the SAS and becoming its greatest legend. *(Courtesy of the Blair Mayne Society of Northern Ireland)*

2nd SAS veteran Arthur Huntbach (right) and SAS comrades, left to right, Parachutist Frank Herringsweet and Signalman Rickman celebrate a hard won victory at Ostend, May 1945, with captured Nazi flag. *(Courtesy Arthur Huntbach)*

SAS troops wait for the historic crossing of the Rhine with jeeps, Vickers Ks and amphibious vehicles awaiting the order to 'go' clearly visible. *(Daniels collection)*

SAS raiders far behind the lines somewhere in France or Germany – a study taken late in the war. George Daniels MM is far left. Note the familiar Fairbairn Sykes dagger on the belt of the SAS trooper pictured right. *(Daniels collection)*

Some legendary SAS soldiers gather around armed jeeps in the victorious drive through France, 1944. They include (left to right) Frank Craig, Tom Moody, Syd 'Dusty' Rhodes, the incomparable Tanky Challenor, one of the greatest of all the survivors of the tough behind-the-lines war, SSM Mitchell MM, unidentified trooper and signals veteran Freddie Oakes. *(Oakes collection)*

Confident, war-winning SAS troopers surround their trusty jeep near Paris, September 1944. These include (left to right front) SSM Mitchell MM kneeling, Bob Fyffe and Tpr Tate. Back: Tanky Challenor, unidentified trooper and Syd "Dusty" Rhodes – one of three Yorkshire brothers who saw distinguished service in the SAS during the Second World War. *(Oakes collection)*

rough ground that it had never reached before. At a break-neck rate of knots, the SAS band lost their pursuers and luckily found the wadi they were aiming for, or they could have been helplessly stranded, away from their intended route. Then suddenly Lilley shouted a desperate warning for everyone to jump out of the truck.

Lilley had detected the distinctive smell and heard the click as acid started to eat through one of their time pencils – not a recommended occurrence as they were still carrying upwards of 40 lb of high explosive. All the raiders jumped out and ran frantically to reach a safe distance away from the truck when, just seconds later, the bomb went up, setting off a tremendous explosion and blowing the borrowed LRDG truck to smithereens. The rest of the journey back to base had to be covered on foot until they met some Senussi Arabs who sent a message to the LRDG, who motored out to collect the dishevelled SAS party, minus, unfortunately, their shiny LRDG truck.

The SAS men returned via the Siwa oasis, with Stirling planning to make amends for the loss of the precious LRDG transport by ordering a gigantic round of drinks for his fellow desert raiders in the bar at the famous Shepheards Hotel in Cairo! The joy at the success of their raids, however, was tempered by the catastrophic news that Tobruk had fallen and that Rommel was at the very gates of Egypt, with a final, backs-to-the-wall stand being organised by the British Army and their Commonwealth allies at El Alamein. There was a long way to go yet and many more raids and campaigns to be fought and won before either Lilley, or any of his hard-bitten desert SAS veterans, could celebrate victory.

SILLITO'S NIGHTMARE MARCH THROUGH THE MERCILESS DESERT

Most soldiers win awards for gallantry by performing a miraculous feat of arms on the field of combat, or by saving a comrade's life under fire. Tpr, later Acting Sgt John Sillito, of the 1st SAS, won a well-deserved Military Medal near Tobruk in 1942 for defeating not just the enemy, but also an equally deadly foe – the burning wastes of the waterless desert.

After his mission to blow up a railway line in the run-up to the Battle of El Alamein had to be aborted after a surprise attack by enemy guards, Sillito walked, without food and with hardly any water, nearly 200 miles back to a desert rendezvous. As a feat of navigation in featureless terrain it was incredible. As a demonstration of iron determination, courage and an overwhelming will to survive at all costs, it was magnificent. It is an indelible part of SAS folklore still talked about to this day in regimental circles with pride and admiration. However, to put Sillito's historic feat into context, it is necessary to look at what had occurred in the wider field of operations in the Western Desert for Stirling's men as the unit grew in strength following its successful earlier raids on airfields and enemy installations.

Against all advice from Stirling, the planners at headquarters now disastrously decided to raid Tobruk and Benghazi simultaneously in a massive combined forces' raid, employing a very large party of SAS troops. This was going against all the principles on which the SAS was formed and threw away all its usual advantages of stealth and surprise in employing small-scale hit-and-run attacks. SAS forces would strike from the land, while naval and Commando units would attack from the sea with the aim of maximum destruction in an overwhelming raid. Stirling had a large, highly obtrusive force of 200 men, 40 jeeps and 40 supply trucks to somehow get to the target and back undetected.

The Tobruk raid was an utter catastrophe with numerous ships lost and many soldiers and sailors killed, including the irreplaceable commander, Col John Haselden, who had carried out such daring spying missions in the desert, on one memorable occasion driving sheep across an enemy airfield dressed as an Arab. It was widely believed that the Germans had prior warning of the operation and that the enemy was ready and waiting, and subsequent findings bear this out.

On the way to Benghazi, the SAS were also hit hard in an ambush on a heavily mined road. They fought off their attackers, but the element of surprise was totally lost and Stirling reluctantly gave the order to return to base. On their way back, the SAS raiders were strafed heavily from the air and lost eighteen jeeps and twenty-five trucks and had to borrow enough petrol from the Sudan Defence Force to get back to Kufra. From the SAS point of view, the raid had not been just a dismal failure but a disastrous waste of highly trained men and precious materiel.

Ironically, it was after the failure of the Benghazi/Tobruk raid that Gen, later FM, Alexander decided that the SAS should be given regimental status and its future was assured. Meanwhile, Stirling tried to persuade Gen Montgomery to allow him to take badly needed recruits from the trained men in the Eighth Army. But Montgomery flatly refused. He insisted he required all his men for the forthcoming major offensive at El Alamein and that Stirling would have to pick his new recruits from raw, freshly arrived troops. Consequently, Stirling now had personally to take charge of a training programme lasting three and a half months, effectively curtailing a major SAS offensive in the interim. However, he kept the SAS in action by sending a squadron of experienced men commanded by Paddy Mayne to the Kufra oasis, with orders to hit coastal communications hard before the decisive Alamein battle got underway.

Mayne's A Squadron destroyed many trains and sections of track before setting out on 7 October 1942 with eighty men, just under two weeks before the battle that was to change the course of the war. As the raiders spilt up into smaller groups for various missions, this was an operation that was to be forever associated with the tough and resolute Tpr Sillito, who together with a lieutenant, was detailed to blow up yet another rail track to stop vital supplies getting through to the Axis forces. This was a battle Britain and her Commonwealth allies had to win, or risk losing the whole war.

Sillito and the officer were stealthily attempting to lay a charge to demolish the track and, hopefully a train passing over it, when they were spotted and attacked by guards. The officer was killed when his Tommy gun jammed. Sillito also came under fire but managed to evade his pursuers, but soon found himself on his own and lost in the wilderness. He had three courses open to him: he could surrender to the nearby enemy, he could try to hide with some friendly Arabs and wait until British forces came or he could try to walk back to base, more than 180 miles across the desert. There was only one choice in Sillito's mind – he must try to return to his comrades, at whatever cost, despite the fact that he had no food and only enough water to last a day, and just a compass and a revolver. Sillito said in his own account recorded soon afterwards:

The first night I just kept slogging on, with nothing to eat and nothing to drink. Occasionally I came across piles of empty petrol tins upon which was collected dew and was able to wet my tongue on them. There was not much of it.

Then, in a wrecked tank, I found a tin of bully beef but when I opened it and tried to eat the meat I found that I couldn't as my tongue had become like dry putty and mastication was out of the question. I threw the meat away but kept the tin.

It came in handy for holding my urine, which I then started to drink. It stopped me from desiccating and drying out altogether. Of course it was acrid and unpleasant, but it was better than dying of thirst.

I kept this up for seven days – marching on the bearing in daylight and using the stars at night.

During the hottest part of the day I used to lie on my back and used my greatcoat as a tent until that became too heavy to carry.

Eventually, I hit a wadi called Hatiet Etla, which was the one we had rested in prior to setting off on the final stage to the railway and I knew that the LRDG had a store of emergency rations of biscuits, bully beef and water hidden in a broken down three tonner (lorry) they had left there.

I hit the northern extremity of this wadi – it was about a mile long by about 100 yards across. At first I thought I was at the wrong place and followed some jeep tracks for several miles until I found a haversack. It contained nothing of use to me, so dragging my blistered feet I returned to the wadi. Just as I got there it began to rain. Oh what a joy! What a relief.

According to another contemporary account of his epic journey by Malcolm James Pleydell:

It started to rain and he was soaked to the skin. Starting to walk at 2 o'clock, he had covered 25 miles by dawn the next day. He tried to sleep but couldn't and so walked all that day covering another 30 miles. During the next night, he covered a further 20 miles, still without food or water. A puddle saved him for a time. The remaining distance . . . was a horrible nightmare and falling unconscious many times, lying helpless for long periods too weak to stand, giving up once and preparing to die and, being saved by rain and much more that is not clear due to delirium. Shortly afterwards, eight days after beginning this nightmare, Sillito was found unconscious and barely alive by SAS comrades.

Pleydell, an Army medical officer with the SAS who shared many of their exploits in 1942 and 1943, gave yet more fascinating details of Sillito's courage in his book *Born Of The Desert, With the SAS in North Africa*. Pleydell says that at the time of Sillito's raid, SAS patrols had only two or three days in which to approach their targets undetected, as their advance headquarters were at Kufra oasis at the heart of the Sand Sea. This was no easy task with enemy planes constantly on the lookout for them. Lt Jim Chambers had only recently returned from a raid, suffering from bad desert sores that had become infected. He gave Pleydell a first-hand account of Sillito's disappearance and said he was depressed about the raid because he had not been able to confirm the results.

Chambers described how the raiders had first successfully buried charges beneath the track and then waited nearby to watch the next train blow up. However, when the train did come puffing along, nothing happened and it carried on into the distance! A hurried council of war decided that due to the dampness of the soil, the charge or detonator could have been affected, so two men, Sillito, the party's navigator, and an officer, went forward to lay another charge using a different technique. This was the point at which they were apprehended by a well-armed enemy patrol and attacked, and when Sillito dramatically became detached from the rest.

Pleydell relates below Sillito's amazing tale after the brave SAS man had miraculously made it to the rendezvous:

> When, quite suddenly, he had found himself completely alone in the vicinity of Tobruk, he squatted down for a minute to reckon out what his next move should be. He had neither food nor water – only a compass and a revolver.
>
> He considered what he should do. He could march northwards and give himself up to the enemy; start heading east towards Alamein keeping well within the coastal belt where the Arabs might help him . . . where derelict trucks and lorries might well contain something in the way of necessities; or finally he could walk due south, away from the life of the coastal belt, through the arid desert where there was next to no chance of meeting any form of life or water, and where a mistake in direction meant a certain and unpleasant death.
>
> It was the final alternative that he chose – a lonely march of nearly 200 miles towards that little hollow in the middle of the Sand Sea which we had chosen for our rendezvous.

Off he set, trudging steadily southwards and apparently not worrying much about the distance at first. On account of the recent rains, he was able to drink from puddles . . . but as he progressed, the ground became dry and more stony and it was imperative for him to make each mouthful of water last. The skies became piteously blue and unchanging; he took to resting during the real heat of the day, continuing with his march only when it had grown cooler and when the glare and shudder of the skyline [desert heat haze] had disappeared.

Imagine the loneliness of this! Day after day with the sun arching up over him; without a soul to whom he could voice his thoughts; with a flat landscape that stretched on and on in front of him; with no indication of his whereabouts nor how far he had travelled. Just the day and night to show him how time was passing and the conviction that he was correct in his compass-course to give him encouragement.

On the second day, the water gave out and from then on he stored his urine in an old bully beef tin that he found lying on the ground but, he said, the urine became more and more concentrated. The contents of the tin he threw away for the bully beef was too hard to swallow.

To lie-down and rest could not have been an easy decision, for it must have seemed that an hour without advancement was an hour wasted; yet it was the only logical way by which he could reach his goal.

A fourth day passed, then the fifth and his progress began to slow down. His feet were sore, cut and blistered; it became a question of determination and staying power – a lone figure trudging for mile after barren mile across the vast emptiness of the desert.

On the sixth day he saw some dots on the skyline. . . . Were they real? He wondered. Was this a trick of the eyes? Was it the heat haze? No, they actually were vehicles. They were coming towards him. On their present bearing they would pass by him a little to the west.

Yes they were jeeps! He could see them quite clearly now; he could make out the machine gun mountings. Almost beside himself with joy, he waved and waved and tried to shout. But they were going on as if they had not seen him! Surely this was not possible! Suddenly an idea occurred to him and, tearing off his shirt, he rummaged in his pockets and found some matches. In a moment he had set fire to his shirt and was waving it slowly backwards and forwards over his head.

It burned with a smouldering flame and the smoke faded readily on the hot air. With something akin to despair, he watched the jeeps drive past. They became distorted shapes in the heat haze, then they were dots, then they had vanished completely.

He was alone once more with the heat, the sweat and his thoughts. He turned and went on.

It was on the eighth day that first he sighted the white pointed slopes of the Sand Sea as it lay sprawled out in front of him, extending about 100 miles to the east and west. Somewhere along this northern border there might be a few jeeps which were preparing to go out on a raid or had just returned from one; he was dependent upon his own navigational judgement and the entrance and exit tracks of the vehicles for finding the exact location and, if the jeeps were not there, he would be forced to cross another 40 miles of soft, sinking sand dunes before he reached the advance rendezvous.

It is doubtful whether he could have achieved this extra march, but luckily it was not necessary as he found tracks and soon afterwards came upon a small patrol.

In this, fortune was with him; for the men would have left on the previous day had not one of their jeeps broken down and their departure been thus delayed.

Soon after, he was sent back to Kufra and thence to base for some leave. His feet were being dressed daily and even when he had been with us for a week, he still found it painful to hobble about.

But that was all he had to show for his experience – that and a hesitancy of manner and an expression in the eyes that told their own story of mental strain and physical hardship.

Reproduced courtesy of Greenhill Books

Amazingly, within a matter of weeks Sillito had been discharged from hospital and was fully recovered to rejoin his unit.

At about this time, on 4 November, as Allied forces smashed through the Axis lines at El Alamein, the tide of war began to turn Britain's way at last with the famous victory beginning the long, slow road to Germany's final, crushing defeat. The courage and resilience shown by Stirling's SAS desert raiders, like the indefatigable Sillito, had played a magnificent and unforgettable part. Amazingly, Sillito, known to his close mates as Jack, whose parent regiment was the Staffordshire Yeomanry, won a bar to his MM for further courageous acts carried out later in the war during the invasion of Sicily while serving with the Special Raiding Squadron.

JOHNNY COOPER – ONE OF THE REGIMENT'S BRAVEST YOUNG TIGERS

Johnny Cooper was aged just eighteen when he volunteered to join David Stirling's original L Detachment of the SAS in the Western Desert in 1941. Before the war was over, he had become one of the unit's most seasoned veterans, playing a key role in many of the Regiment's most successful escapades, especially in the arid wastes of North Africa, later becoming one of the finest officers the SAS has known. At the climax of the Desert War, he courageously evaded the specially trained German anti-SAS unit which caught David Stirling in Tunisia in 1943 and, in the dying stages of Germany's Third Reich, witnessed the appalling horrors of the Holocaust at one of Nazi Germany's most notorious death camps, Belsen.

The keen, fit and resourceful teenager had earlier lied about his age to enlist in the famous Scots Guards, aged just seventeen, following a tradition of patriotism and enthusiasm to serve his country and a path to adventure trodden by countless young men before him. In the autumn of 1940, he was one of the volunteers who joined Bob Laycock's Commando force, which was training hard in Scotland for raiding deployment overseas.

Fifty Scots Guards volunteers, including the young Cooper, were accepted to form Number 3 Troop of 8 Guards Commando and were billeted around the picturesque riverside town of Largs in Ayrshire, near the Isle of Arran where tough Commando training forays soon sorted the men out from the boys. The bleakness of the landscape and the unforgiving climate added an extra dimension to the tough weapons, endurance and survival training, which many veterans remember with chagrin to this day. Veteran Denis Bell, a volunteer in the 11th Scottish Commandos and later a comrade of Cooper's in 1st SAS, remembers being one of the first band of Commandos who trained under live ammunition exercises. He had to crawl underneath heavy machine-gun fire and keep his head well down to stay alive and complete the course in the most realistic, but dangerous, conditions possible.

Cooper's section commander at this time was none other than Lt David Stirling, who had arrived from the 8th Battalion Scots Guards, recruited partly because of his skiing experience. In the years prior to the outbreak of the Second World War, it had been one of Stirling's burning ambitions to be part of the first group to climb Everest, which was then still unconquered. It was a patriotic dream never to be fulfilled as Europe was literally torn apart by Germany's insatiable appetite for conquest. Stirling's thirst for adventure was equally unquenchable, as the Germans would soon find out to their cost.

As fate would have it, a posting to the Middle East with the Commandos was the key piece of the jigsaw that was to lead to Cooper's chance to volunteer for his date with destiny with the SAS.

In his colourful book *One of the Originals, The Story of a Founder Member of the SAS* Johnny Cooper describes his first impressions of the tall, unassuming, well-bred future creator of the SAS: 'Stirling came from an ancient Scottish family with a long association with the Scots Guards, yet he was different from the officers I had come into contact with up to that time. This quietly spoken young lieutenant commanded far more respect and confidence, with his ability to put soldiers at their ease and his willingness to help. He did not bark orders; he asked people to do things. He was immensely tall, six feet five inches which, like many tall men, he attempted to disguise with a slight stoop.' Their meeting was the start of a long association punctuated with high drama, adventure and a lasting mutual respect for the other's abilities.

Before the end of the war, Cooper had won a daring Distinguished Conduct Medal with the SAS, had risen to the rank of captain and was widely regarded as one of the Regiment's most reliable and audacious officers. Yet, amazingly, he was still only in his early twenties. His keen intelligence and natural initiative were distinctive hallmarks of his distinguished service with the Regiment. He was an almost ever–present figure, especially during the famous desert raids led by David Stirling and Paddy Mayne, later fighting his way through France and Germany with 1st SAS in the wake of the dangerous but vital parachute missions that followed the D-Day invasion to liberate Europe. Cooper's vivid memories of the disastrous capture of SAS warlord Stirling just as the desert war reached a victorious conclusion in 1943 are a key record of that desperately unlucky but momentous event.

The Capture of Stirling

David Stirling had lived life in the fast lane during three action-packed years in command of the SAS. On many occasions, Stirling had led from the front and diced with death or capture on his daring missions among hardened enemy forces all along the coastal strip of North Africa. But each time he gave his pursuers the slip to return to his oasis hideaways in triumph. He rode his luck with the consummate skill and daring of the great leader he undoubtedly was. But as the Axis powers staggered to an inevitable total defeat in the desert, the bold raider just could not resist taking one last gamble and completing a final patrol in January 1943, with a prestigious first link up between the converging British and American armies as the prize that would help further secure the future of the SAS Regiment. This decision was to prove to be his unwitting downfall.

Stirling's plan was to move rapidly across uncharted country south of Tripoli with a small, fast-moving jeep patrol, penetrating as far as the Tunisian border some 300 miles south of the coast. The party would then turn north to get behind the heavily defended Mareth line to join up with the American First Army in Tunisia. It sounded deceptively straightforward. To the veterans of the SAS so used to taking high risks in their stride, almost on a daily basis, it seemed a reasonably routine procedure. However, events, including the formation of a special German anti-SAS unit designed to hunt down the raiders at all costs, were to prove that theory totally wrong.

Stirling's group had a Free French patrol with them which had planned to pass through the narrow Gabes Gap. This would pose many problems as the area was swarming with enemy troops and armoured units. However, the SAS commander had a supreme confidence bred from taking on and beating such daunting tasks many times in the past. At the last minute, Stirling decided to abandon his scheme to flank the Mareth line and aim instead to drive the direct route – straight through the gap. It was a typical SAS tactic, relying on audacity and catching the enemy totally by surprise.

The SAS party set out on 22 January heading north towards Lake Djerid, a large area of impassable salt marsh which restricted the possible entry zone near the town of Gabes on the coast. Stirling gambled that his party of five jeeps could simply race down the main road where he hoped they would not be recognised as British troops. Countless times in the past, the ruse had worked like a charm in the confused midst of overwhelming enemy forces, so why not now?

As dawn was breaking, the SAS party booted the accelerators of their trusty jeeps to the floor and raced for the tantalising Gabes Gap. Before long, they cheekily passed right through the middle of a German armoured division which was resting and enjoying breakfast on either side of the road, stretching along for a distance of several miles. Tank crews and many curious German soldiers looked right at the SAS raiders, but like many of their comrades before them, they wrongly assumed that no enemy troops could possibly be operating so far behind the lines. With practised disdain, the SAS boldly stared right back and drove on. More enemy units were encountered on the move, but, apparently causing no alarm, the raiders decided to leave the main road and climb steadily towards some scrub–covered hilly ravines where they judged they could camouflage their jeeps, rest and eat and get their bearings.

Stirling asked for lookouts and Cooper and the ace navigator Mike Sadler volunteered and crept up to the highest point to fix their position using binoculars, compasses and maps. They noted some enemy vehicles that stopped near the track leading to their position, but were not concerned as it looked as though the soldiers had merely paused to relieve themselves. However, all hell was about to break loose. Unknown to Stirling, suspicion had been aroused among some of the German forces the jeeps had driven past earlier that day. The SAS lookouts had not

witnessed a harmless group of German soldiers
approaching but had glimpsed the crack reconnaissance
group from the German paratroop battalion that had been
ordered to search the area and capture them.

Meanwhile, Stirling, Cooper and the rest were still
unaware of the impending danger and, as they were
exhausted, all dozed fitfully. This was not carelessness, as all
their vehicles were carefully camouflaged and they were
following a long-established procedure. Cooper, however, was
one of the first to be rudely alerted to the impending trap. In
One of the Originals he said: 'At about 3 o'clock, I was
awakened by a kick on my feet. I looked up. Standing at the
foot of my 'bed' was a fully equipped German parachutist
with his Schmeisser sub machine-gun slung loosely across
his chest. He motioned me to stay where I was and then
disappeared around the corner, breaking into a run. He was
joined by another German and they continued their fast exit
out of the wadi, obviously to report that they had found us
and to bring up reinforcements.'

Cooper leapt up, woke Stirling and rapidly explained what
had happened. Stirling ordered the signallers to destroy all
logs and codes and then the Germans opened fire and
Stirling shouted 'every man for himself!'. Mike Sadler, French
Sgt Freddie Taxis, Cooper and the signallers ran uphill
towards the end of the wadi. The signallers and the rest of
the SAS group split up, with Stirling racing off in the
opposite direction. This fleeting glimpse was the last that
Cooper saw of the great commander until he was released
from Colditz prison at the end of the war. Stirling's capture
was a massive propaganda victory for the Germans, who
literally could not believe their luck. More significantly, the
SAS was robbed of its finest brain and greatest inspiration for
the duration, even though Paddy Mayne and other senior
officers worked like Trojans to limit the damage and keep the
Regiment on an even keel. The short-term fall out from the
catastrophic capture of Stirling, however, was immense and
posed many difficulties, as he carried much of the planning
for future operations in his head.

Cooper and his colleagues, meanwhile, were literally running for their lives. They found a shallow hollow about 3 ft deep covered at one end by camel scrub and dived headlong into it. Well-armed German paratroopers were by now swarming all over the area, firing indiscriminately to winkle the raiders out. Luckily for Cooper and his comrades, a group of hungry goats wandered over to their hide-out looking for food and very effectively hid them! After an agonising half-hour listening and tensely waiting, the group heard the enemy troops rounding up the rest of the patrol and driving their SAS jeeps away. Any hopes of a quick getaway back to Allied lines were now well and truly scuppered, but at least they had survived. Cooper said: 'The situation was not enviable. All we had was a map and compass but no water or food. There were two courses of action open to us. One was to walk back towards the Eighth Army, but to do that we would again have to contend with the Gabes Gap which was swarming with the enemy soldiery. The other possibility was to move north and west and hope to meet up with the French Foreign Legion who had taken the oasis town of Tozeur on the north bank of Lake Djerid.'

The group waited for night to fall and chose the latter course, relying on the uncannily accurate navigating skills of Mike Sadler to lead the way. They banked on slipping through any large enemy troop concentrations they encountered using their wits and stealth bred by hard experience. When dawn broke, the SAS raiders hid on a flat escarpment near to a small Arab camp. The French soldier Freddy Taxis spoke Arabic and suggested they should approach the encampment to see if they could obtain some food and water. Luckily for the SAS men, the Arabs there turned out to be friendly and gave the party dates, bread and water and the group trudged on until they were so exhausted by the fierce sun that they had to lie up in whatever shade they could find. The group fell into a deep sleep and later that afternoon Cooper was again rudely awoken, this time finding himself looking into a shotgun held by an angry looking Berber tribesman – the man wanted Cooper's clothes! Some children then appeared on the scene and threw stones, one of which hit Cooper and cut his forehead badly.

The group ran off, still determined to make contact with the Foreign Legion and marched all that night without stopping. Next morning, they found themselves in a dead flat, arid wasteland of white sand and salt. The sun was searingly hot, but through the shimmering heat haze they spied in the distance what appeared to be palm trees. They could hardly believe their eyes. They had made it to the edge of Lake Djerid and as they walked deeper into the oasis, they came to a watercourse and feverishly scooped up some of the water to drink. An elderly Arab appeared giving them some dates and then a French Senegalese soldier approached. In broken French, the SAS raiders told him they were British and in a poor state. The soldier disappeared and came back soon after with a sergeant accompanied by more soldiers.

The group then walked slowly along a track that led to one of the finest Beau Geste forts Cooper had ever seen. It was brilliant white, surrounded by palm trees with strangely garbed soldiers all around. The garrison commandant welcomed the SAS men, giving them medical help and a fine meal of potatoes and goat meat, washed down liberally with white rum, which Cooper described as a 'magnificent feast'. Signals were sent off to the nearest American headquarters about 124 miles to the north. The French sent a quaintly worded signal that said words to the effect of 'We commemorate the meeting of the glorious British Eighth Army with our forces here in Tunisia.'

A patrol was actually sent out by the Americans to *arrest* the group, as they had no knowledge of any SAS operations so deep in the territory. Fortunately, they informed Gen Alexander at his headquarters who was well aware of the situation. Cooper said: 'We must have looked a motley crew, my head was swathed in bandages and all our feet had been similarly treated as we were covered in blisters from our march across the desert. Without any nourishment whatsoever we were driven through the mountains to Tebessa . . . on arrival the Americans had red faces, for confirmation had arrived from Generals Alexander and Mark Clark that we were indeed members of David Stirling's SAS patrol and our American captors began to fête us with canned substances of all types. To our chagrin though, there was only Coca-Cola to drink and no beer!'

Belsen – a Memory Seared on the Soul

As one of the first Allied troops into Belsen concentration camp, Cooper experienced unforgettable horrors, which were imprinted on the minds of the young soldier and all the SAS comrades who were chosen to go first into the camp because of the mobility of their jeep units.

This situation resulted from the historic crossing of the Rhine in March 1945, as 1st SAS advanced deep into Germany, alongside the main British Army, in support of the 8th Parachute Battalion and other units. They ploughed on without serious loss northwards to Munster and Osnabrück, but soon came across a terrible atrocity centred on the railway station in the town of Celle. German guards had opened fire on defenceless concentration-camp prisoners, mowing down hundreds of men, women and children after being panicked by an Allied bombing raid. It was a shock to the system, even to the battle-hardened veterans of the SAS and an ominous warning of worse nightmares to come. The SAS were then ordered to drive to the nearby town of Bergen Belsen, the location of the notorious concentration camp to which the victims of the Celle railway massacre were being moved when they were gunned down.

After five years of war, Nazi Germany was almost at its last gasp, with the Russians ploughing on inexorably towards Berlin from the East and the Allies advancing steadily in the opposite direction in the West. The writing was on the wall at last for the sadistic Belsen guards and those in charge who had orchestrated unimaginable horrors at the camp of death. One of the most notorious of all the concentration camps, Belsen was massively overcrowded with upwards of 60,000 inmates crammed into its stinking, barbed wire-encased and heavily guarded perimeter. Even at this late stage, thousands more prisoners were daily transported to the camp as the Germans remorselessly retreated. Right to the very end the Germans were doing their utmost to stop the starving hordes of prisoners from falling into Allied or Russian hands and freedom.

The SAS were sent to Belsen to investigate the situation before the camp was evacuated by the Germans and taken over by the advancing main British Army. No one at that stage had any firm idea about the horrors that lay within. Cooper and his comrades were met by a notorious SS officer called Kramer, who claimed to be merely an administrative officer and cynically denied he was responsible for the appalling scenes of cruelty and depravity in the camp. He was later one of those tried by a British war crimes court, found guilty and hanged.

Cooper, shocked to the core by the indescribable horrors that met the gaze of the SAS men wherever they looked, said:

Once inside we realised the vast size of the camp and I'll never forget my first sight of the inmates. Ostensibly they were living human beings, but to me the men, women and even children were just walking skeletons. When they realised that we had come to liberate them, some managed to find enough energy to swarm towards the barbed wire which contained them. In fact, in their joy, some impaled themselves on the barbs without any apparent registration of pain. Moving on, we then discovered a whole series of communal graves, consisting of trenches about a hundred yards long and 20 feet deep, which were being steadily filled with naked skeletal bodies. Lime was casually thrown over them, presumably to try to contain the danger of infection.

Walking stunned and disgusted into the barrack huts, they found many more dead bodies which had been left to rot as the other inmates were too weak to drag them outside for burial.

Soup was rapidly prepared for the ravenous inmates, but most were so weak they could only stomach tiny amounts. Any substantial nourishment would have killed them. Some of the British soldiers flew into a terrible rage when they saw the SS guards, still arrogant and defiant, beating and threatening the prisoners. A woman prisoner who thrust her hand under the wire to grab a rotten turnip was shot dead by one of the Hungarian auxiliaries who were assisting the SS to guard the camp.

Many years after the war, SAS NCO Reg Seekings admitted that a number of the guards were shot out of hand in retaliation by some SAS comrades. Feelings were running very high after the mind-numbing scenes they had witnessed and many of the SAS already knew full well that the SS had brutally tortured and shot many of their own friends since the D-Day invasion, in France, Italy and elsewhere. It was done in the heat of the moment, quickly and cleanly and, in all honesty, not regretted for a moment.

The SAS men were very glad to receive orders soon after to move on, with yet more fighting missions to complete. Later, when they reached Luneburg, the SAS troops were amazed on explaining to German civilians what they had seen in the death camp to be told in reply that it was 'just British propaganda.' Most flatly refused to believe that concentration camps even existed, a fact that was soon remedied when the Allies took hundreds of local people to see for themselves the lasting shame that would forever be Hitler's poisoned legacy to the world. Cooper commented, poignantly, 'As long as I live I will never forget the Germans who perpetrated such acts. Although I was only 21 at the time, I had been in action for three years and was no stranger to violent death. What I saw in that camp, however, defies adequate description and those scenes will stay with me for ever.'

After the war, it was not long before Cooper received the

call, along with many other wartime veterans, to rejoin the SAS, serving with distinction in Malaya, Oman and North Yemen, rising to the rank of lieutenant colonel and being mentioned in dispatches three times in 1946, 1959 and 1970, when he also received the Sultan of Oman's Award. These campaigns were vastly different from those fought in the Second World War, but the skill and courage of the veterans of the SAS remained as a hugely prized and highly effective commodity.

Blistering Action – France and Germany

Derrick Harrison, Chalky White,
Ian Fenwick, Bill Fraser

DERRICK HARRISON – THE BLOODIEST SHOOT-OUT

Lt, later Capt, Derrick Harrison MC, parent regiment the
Cheshires, joined 1st SAS in the Western Desert, taking part
in raids in Sicily and Italy, including the bloody action at
Termoli, before being dropped with C Squadron into the
Orleans area of occupied France immediately after D-Day in
June 1944 as part of Operation Kipling. It was to be a
cataclysmic baptism of fire without equal on the long-awaited
Second Front. Harrison and four other SAS comrades were to
become involved in one of the most spectacularly one-sided
hand-to-hand battles of the war against the infamous SS in
France, with no quarter asked or given.

The fact that the SAS emerged victorious, though
bloodied, from this savage encounter, with Harrison for a
time single-handedly taking on more than 200 heavily
armed storm troopers and living to tell the tale, is little
short of miraculous. By all normal odds, he should have
been killed several times over, but the cornered SAS officer
unleashed a fury born of desperation to leave the battle
scene littered with the bodies of his black-hearted foes.
Harrison's amazing story is a tribute to the devastating
firepower of the machine-guns of the SAS jeeps and to the
deep bond of loyalty among the Winged Dagger men,
which meant that a comrade in trouble was never
abandoned, no matter how hopeless the situation seemed.

Prior to being parachuted into France, Harrison and his men were kept cooped up in isolation in barbed wire cages in the depths of the countryside miles from prying eyes at Fairford in Gloucestershire, until the order to 'go' came at last. Few had any real inkling of the barbarities they would shortly face from their German opponents, especially the SS, with so many comrades brutally tortured and shot after capture or beaten to death with rifle butts in front of assembled civilians as a 'warning' to stay in line and do their Nazi masters' bidding. The SAS knew full well that Hitler had issued an order that they were dangerous men who should be handed over to the Gestapo to be 'ruthlessly exterminated' when caught. But not one of the raiders preparing to parachute into the unknown in France backed out.

Harrison, who broke a finger as he dropped into his designated operational area, was assigned to lead a risky reconnaissance, driving at the head of a couple of jeep crews deep into enemy territory, as he remembered in his classic book *These Men Are Dangerous*. At top speed, they raced away along the bumpy, dusty road towards an ominously growing column of smoke. Breasting the top of the hill outside Les Ormes, Harrison signalled the jeep behind to stop and they both screamed to a halt as they approached a fork in the road. From the left came the sound of firing and a number of buildings were well ablaze. The crossroads was just over a hundred yards from the village, but as the SAS squad strained their ears to detect the source of the trouble, it was obvious that all the noise seemed to be coming from the far end. While Harrison debated what to do next, an old woman on a bicycle came pedalling furiously down the left-hand fork towards the Englishmen. Tears were streaming down her shocked face and she managed to blurt out a warning to the SAS men that the 'Boche', the Germans, were in the village killing hostages and burning the buildings. She was determined to fetch help from the Maquis resistance fighters. Incensed, Harrison asked how many Germans there were. The woman shrugged her shoulders. '200 . . . 300,' she guessed, 'Who knows? A lot. Yes, a lot. Too many for you Monsieur. Now I must go.' Harrison's mind was crystal clear. He told the woman the SAS men would go instead. With their jeeps it would be much quicker. 'Leave it to us,' he said. Astonishment showed in the woman's face and she thanked the troopers enthusiastically before climbing back on her bike and cycling slowly back into the burning village.

The patrol gathered round and Harrison held a hurried council of war. He asked the men outright what they thought they should do. Should they go for the Maquis or attack the village themselves? It was a tough decision. His mind was already made up, but he did not think it fair to risk all their lives without a general agreement. There were just five SAS in all against several hundred crack German troops. Fauchois, who had been sent to the unit from the French SAS, was the first to speak, urging an all-out attack. The audacious Frenchman carried false papers showing him to be a Canadian to ensure that, should he be captured, his family would not suffer, as they inevitably would otherwise from recriminations. Like many of his countrymen who had seen at first hand what atrocities the German occupying forces were capable of, Fanchois was fired up, dependable and always anxious to kill the 'Sales Boches' ('dirty Germans').

Harrison turned to his stalwart driver, Curly Hall, who argued that by the time they had driven to Aillant to alert the Maquis, a golden opportunity to ambush the Nazis would have been thrown away. Stewart was in command of the other jeep with Brearton as his driver. Both were hard nuts, ex-tank men. 'Let's have a crack at them,' was Brearton's terse reply. Stewart too said there simply was not time to get the Maquis. Harrison snapped out his orders. He assured his men that he wanted to strike, but cautioned that they could not make an open attack. He suggested that they took the right-hand fork into the part of the village that was quiet. Once in, they could drive through at high speed with all their guns blazing and they would have the element of surprise and be able to shoot their way out of anything they met. The odds were something like 50:1, he said, but he hoped that would cause such a shock that they just might pull it off.

Union Jacks fluttering in the wind, Vickers K machine-guns loaded, cocked and at the ready the raiders tore down the road, round a bend and straight into the village. Harrison takes up the story:

> Even as we came into the square, I saw him [an officer]. He was dressed in SS uniform walking towards us pistol in hand. He looked up in surprise – and died.
>
> I took in the scene in an instant. The church in the middle of the square . . . a large truck . . . two German staff cars . . . the crowd of SS men in front of the church.
>
> The staff cars and the truck burst into flames as, standing in my seat, I raked the square with fire from my twin machine-guns. The crowds of SS men stampeded for cover. Many of them died in those first few seconds in front of the church, lit by the flickering flames of the burning vehicles.

Even as Harrison fired he shouted to Hall to reverse. The jeep jerked to a halt about 30 yds from the church, but the Germans who had escaped the first fury of the SAS assault were now returning fire. As Harrison turned to see why Hall had not got the jeep speeding backwards he saw his comrade lying slumped over the wheel. Blood gushing out of his wounds told its own story. Curly Hall was dead. Harrison continued:

> Still firing, I pressed the starter with my foot. The engine was still, hit by the burst of fire that had got Hall. Then my guns jammed with no time to try to put them right. I dashed round to use the rear gun. It fired one burst and stopped.
>
> There was now only the single gun by the driver's seat. I got round to it, managed to fire a couple of

short bursts before that, too, jammed. A dud jeep and three jammed guns. Hell, what a mess!

Harrison had forgotten all about the second jeep, but now he could hear its guns hammering away over his shoulder. Suddenly, he spotted it drawn up against the wall of the road leading into the square. There were Germans at the upper windows of the building immediately overlooking the tiny British force hammering fire down. But again and again Harrison heard Stewart's Colt (automatic pistol) crack as he desperately stopped them trying to wipe out the ferocious English raiders. Harrison vividly describes the scene:

All this I took in a flash, My own plight was too desperate, standing as I was in the middle of the crossroads. I reached over and snatched up my carbine. Thank heavens it was semi-automatic. I fired off the fifteen rounds in the magazine . . . changed the magazine. Blast this broken finger! The damned splint got in the way.

I fired whenever I saw movement. A German made a dash for safety. I fired from the hip and he pitched forward onto his face. Now I grabbed Hall, lifting him from the jeep. A sniper stepped from a doorway on my right. I took a quick pot shot and dropped him. Aim was instinctive.

Harrison managed to get Hall to the centre of the crossroads, but the fire from the Germans intensified. He started shooting again and could see tracer streaming towards him.

I weaved backwards and forwards like a boxer as if to dodge the flying bullets and then came a shout behind me. 'Look out. The orchard on your left.'

There was a low stone wall to the left. I ran to it. On the other side was the orchard. Germans were advancing through it at the double. I fired as fast as I could pull the trigger. They disappeared.

Back to the jeep. Fauchois had run forward and was trying to drag Hall back to the second jeep. 'Get back, you fool. Get back,' he yelled. The Germans were concentrating their fire on him now. No sense in having another man killed.

Standing by the disabled jeep I kept up a rapid rate of fire. How many magazines left? I didn't know . . . My right hand jerked and went numb. I looked down. It was smothered in blood. With my fingertips, I fished out another magazine from the pocket of my smock and after much fumbling managed to clip it into the carbine. With both hands partly out of commission now, my aim was getting erratic.

The Germans who had seen me jump when hit, increased their fire. The sound of firing from the second jeep had stopped. I dared not look round. Keep on firing, keep on firing . . . the words went round and round in my head.

A German stepped from behind one of the trees and took careful aim. Harrison raised his carbine, now slippery with blood, and squeezed the trigger. Nothing happened. As he lowered the carbine his hand jerked again involuntarily as the marksman's bullets snicked across his knuckles. Harrison tells the story:

I looked down. Two rounds were jammed in the breach. No time to put it right now. I grabbed for my Colt. The holster was empty. I swore. The damn thing must have jerked loose in the fight. Nothing for it but to get that jammed magazine out. Resting one foot on the jeep I wrestled with it as best I could with my gammy hands. The Germans were still firing, but there was nothing I could do about it until I got that carbine firing again.

The new magazine was in. Miraculously I was still alive. I raised the carbine. From behind came a shout 'Dash for it!'

Almost at the end of his tether, Harrison heard the wild revving of an engine. The second jeep had turned around and Stewart, Brearton and Fauchois were racing to the rescue. They shouted again. Harrison said: 'Firing as I ran, I dashed crabwise towards them. The jeep moved forward even as I leapt for it. Fauchois seized the guns and poured a last, long burst into the square. In a cloud of dust, we disappeared down the road.

Hardly believing their luck at still being alive, yet mourning their dead comrade Curly Hall, the shell-shocked soldiers in the jeep blasted straight into the nearest woods, down a narrow almost non-existent track at breakneck speed. Swinging violently around a bend, a weary Harrison was nearly flung from his seat. To save himself, he grabbed at the guns and a final burst rent the air, narrowly missing the engine.

Back in camp, Harrison broke the news that Hall was dead, which was difficult to bear. The brave and cocky little Hall had been with Harrison ever since he joined the SAS and was a real character — always bright, cheery and philosophical. Harrison also knew for sure that, had he not stood up to fire his first burst on entering the village, he would certainly have been the one to take the shots that killed Hall.

That night, news reached Harrison of the reasons why the SS soldiers had swooped on the village. They were either thought to be the advance guard of a German convoy and were protecting its passage through the area or, far more likely, it was a reprisal raid for the presence of the SAS in the area. In addition to burning down numerous houses, the SS seized twenty men for summary execution. It was this act that the SAS raiders had so unexpectedly interrupted outside the church in their headlong dash forward in their jeeps. The first two of the doomed men had been shot just as the British soldiers arrived, but the other eighteen escaped amid the confusion. Besides the truck and two staff cars destroyed by the SAS fire, the Germans had lost a colossal total of at least sixty men dead and wounded. The rest withdrew as soon as the fight was broken off to lick their wounds without further harm to the village or its inhabitants. In all the illustrious exploits of the Special Air Service, the force never saw a finer, or more courageous, hour.

CHALKY WHITE – FIGHTING FURY

Sgt Frederick 'Chalky' White DCM, MM was one of the bravest of all the wartime SAS soldiers. Veterans say he was one of a select band of comrades about whom even the legendary Paddy Mayne spoke with reverence. A measure of White's formidable fighting ability lies in the fact that to this day his campaign medals are displayed so prominently at the headquarters of the Special Air Service Regimental Association, alongside those of Stirling, Mayne and other veterans.

By the time the 1st and 2nd SAS parachuted into occupied France in 1944, this was no death or glory enterprise for the battle-hardened veterans of the unit, but a lethal game of shoot first or die, kill or be killed, with decisions being made in split seconds so far behind the lines that every SAS team was, in many cases, fighting for its life.

Chalky had an additional burden as he prepared to take on the best that the SS and German Army could throw at the vastly outnumbered SAS invaders. He had acquired an unwanted 'jinxed' reputation by this time. Though regarded as an outstandingly courageous soldier by his comrades, having won the DCM and MM on previous operations with the SAS, officers who accompanied him on his trips unfortunately and unluckily tended not to survive to tell the tale. Chalky's platoon commander had been killed on every single operation, and up to this point in the war, six officers had lost their lives on patrols or skirmishes with

Chalky. It was an unenviable record, especially for the superstitious.

Now, as the momentous D-Day invasion got underway to liberate Europe from Nazi tyranny, White, an original from the first L Detachment force of the SAS and veteran of many desert actions from the early days, including the Tamet and Sirte, Fuka and Benghazi raids, parachuted into France as part of Operation Houndsworth. This time, it was intended to outwit the curse by giving Chalky command of his own section. The following account of White's tenacious courage and never-say-die attitude is based on the report made by Capt Ian Wellsted, who was parachuted into the Morvan area on 6 June and on 7 August took over No. 3 Troop SAS.

While at the Chalaux camp on 20 July, Wellsted learned that No. 3 Troop was moving into the Fôret des Dames area. An advance party, including Sgt Jeff Duvivier, had set off on bicycles on the evening of 17 July. Capt Roy Bradford, with Sgt Chalky White as front gunner, Sgt 'Maggie' McGinn as rear gunner and Tpr Devine as driver, set off in a jeep on the evening of 19 July to join them. Bradford took as his interpreter Jacques Morvillier from the Maquis Jean Resistance group.

The next Wellsted heard of what had happened to the troop was on 21 July. It was almost dusk when the message came from the Maquis to say that a British soldier had been brought in and was desperate to make a report. Capt Wellsted said: 'A jeep was sent down to fetch him and when he was brought to us he looked a sorry sight. His shirt was torn, his face was white and drawn and as he spoke he quivered with nervous tension and the strain of what he had been through. It was Maggie McGinn and the tale he had to tell was a sad one.'

It transpired that, after setting out from Chalaux in the late evening, the SAS raiders' jeep had travelled all night, moving cautiously in a north-easterly direction by side roads, taking all usual precautions to remain undetected. By 8 a.m. the next day, they found themselves in the little village of

Lucy-sur-Yonne, where they literally blundered into a face-to-face showdown with a German officer and his sergeant. At first the officer did not appear to realise the vehicle was British and waved them down as though greeting one of his own vehicles. But this was when the hair-trigger reactions of the vastly experienced Chalky White came into play. Without hesitation, White let loose a devastating burst from his twin Vickers machine-guns and Germans tumbled left and right as they dived for cover – and their lives. Many were killed in this first withering burst.

The wildly accelerating jeep ploughed on, but almost immediately came upon a German lorry parked at the roadside, packed full of heavily armed German troops and behind it the SAS crew could see another and yet another. Enemy troops on both sides of the road had been caught completely by surprise lazing in the fields and, in a matter of split seconds, the jeep crew knew they had found a large German troop convoy preparing breakfast. It was already far too late to turn back. They had to fight their way out or face certain death. Capt Wellsted said:

> Already the Germans were sprinting for their guns. There was only one thing for the SAS lads to do and they did it.
>
> On Roy Bradford's orders, Sergeant McGinn put the accelerator to the boards and, as the jeep passed the trucks, Chalky White riddled them with his twin Vickers.
>
> There were seven lorries, each containing at least 20 men. In the jeep, apart from ammunition for the Vickers, there were explosives which could blow at any minute. However, a burst of machine-gun fire from a Spandau hit the jeep from behind. Devine slumped, fatally hit and Bradford was hit in the arm.

The indomitable Chalky, despite having one of his hands shattered by a burst of the machine-gun fire, kept firing his Vickers Ks, dropping more and more of the enemy soldiers. It was the crew's only hope of survival. Three times he stopped to change magazines as he fired about 800 rounds into the Germans at point-blank range, wreaking havoc. Jacques and Roy Bradford passed magazines to Chalky who hammered away without pause at the vastly superior enemy force.

The jeep had almost got through the deadly mêlée when, as the SAS men passed the last truck, a long burst from a Spandau almost cut Bradford in two and severely damaged the elbow of the Frenchman. Chalky White himself also sustained further wounds. He had fired the Vickers and changed magazines even though his left hand was shattered. He now had bullet wounds to the leg and his shoulder was torn. Capt Wellsted continues the story:

> The engine of the jeep was in a bad state and it was only just possible for it to coast out of sight, before it finally came to a standstill . . . Maggie McGinn leapt out and after ensuring that Devine and Bradford were dead, he quickly helped White and the Frenchman from the jeep.
>
> He dragged them both across the roadway and pushed them through a hedge. Behind he could hear Germans running down the road in hot pursuit. From the cover of a nearby wood, they watched the Germans search the jeep and the bodies of the dead men. When night fell, McGinn insisted that the wounded should move in case the Germans began to search the area at dawn.
>
> When the wounded were eventually too weak to travel, he built them a shelter from corn sheaves. At daylight, the three moved on. At one point, McGinn swam the River Yonne and brought back a lock keeper's boat.
>
> He ferried Chalky and the Maquisard across the river and the party remained in an orchard throughout the day. McGinn persuaded the injured Jacques to contact civilians which he did and the Maquis came for them that evening.

It is surprising that the German soldiers did not pursue the SAS fugitives with more vigour as they broke off the engagement, but their reticence could be explained by the shock nature of the attack and the very high numbers of casualties sustained in such a short space of time. An interesting side note is that when the Germans searched the body of Roy Bradford after the action, they removed a photo of Chalky which was later made into a wanted poster and plastered on walls all over the area offering a large reward!

Chalky described the incident in similar terms to the authors of *Rogue Warrior of the SAS*, Martin Dillon and Roy Bradford (unrelated to the SAS fatality), when they compiled their book about Lt Col Paddy Blair Mayne. With a glint in his eye, Chalky said: 'When that officer appeared, I tripped the Vickers. I could feel the jeep running over the bodies of the Germans in the street. I had a field day, but the problem was the tail end Charlie. When the Germans laagered up, they always left a tail end man with a Spandau and he was the one that got us.'

When asked for his assessment of the heroes of the SAS, Chalky said David Stirling was the thinker of the outfit and a gentleman, whereas Paddy Mayne was the 'action-man'. 'Paddy was the best professional killer I have ever seen,' Chalky said. 'In our job you needed a killer. You knew not to mess with Paddy. It was not that he was menacing, but people knew there was a line never to cross. After Stirling was captured, Paddy began to take life more seriously. He knew his settling-in period was over. Our job really was about killing, resting – killing and resting. The war did something to you. You lost all sense of feeling. Became almost a sadist. But Paddy was to me a man without faults.'

In the battle at Lucy-sur-Yonne, Chalky sustained such severe wounds to his left hand that three fingers had to be amputated. However, not for a moment did this prevent him from fighting on – in fact, White redoubled his efforts, fighting like a cornered tiger, dropping the opposition like human skittles. Many observers have noted that there was a ruggedness, determination, and bravery about the wartime SAS and SBS. However, there was also a distinct quality of the loner about men like Chalky.

Chalky White stands out as one of the men from the original days of the Regiment who was most similar to and, in many ways can be compared with, the ferocious Paddy Mayne. Close comrade L/Cpl Denis Bell, of B Squadron 1st SAS, told me: 'Chalky was absolutely fearless in action, he had no fear at all. But he wasn't reckless. He was cast in the same mould as Paddy.' There is no finer tribute.

IAN FENWICK AND THE SAS 'CHARGE OF THE LIGHT BRIGADE'

Maj Ian Fenwick of D Squadron 1st SAS emulated a glorious tragedy in the history of British armed forces when he received a message that his comrades, who were parachuted into occupied France after D-Day, were cut off by overwhelming German forces and facing annihilation. Leaping into his jeep, with a handful of troopers to man the machine-guns, he headed straight towards a heavily armed SS ambush that lay between him and his men. Fenwick was actually warned of the deadly Nazi trap by a local woman a matter of yards before he blasted full speed at it, all guns blazing in an amazingly brave death or glory charge. But he calmly replied to her desperate warning: 'Thank you madame, but I intend to attack them!' The die was irrevocably cast.

Just as a century before the 'glorious 600' cavalrymen in the Crimea rushed into the wrong valley to their near-certain deaths due to faulty information, so Fenwick and his men charged the ambush in similar brave but futile fashion. The information received by Fenwick from the Resistance was also unsound. Although it was true that his men had been surrounded by hundreds of heavily armed Germans, after a desperate battle, they had managed to fight their way out of the trap and had got away safely to new hiding places.

It had all begun so differently just days before when Fenwick and his squadron began a destructive campaign of hit-and-run sabotage when they dropped into the Pithiviers area of France on the night of 16 June, just ten days after D-Day, on Operation Gain. Their raids caused a huge amount of damage to enemy trains, vehicles and supplies. Working on foot in the first dozen or so days, Fenwick attacked and blew up the three main railway lines running through the area, successfully derailing a goods train on the Malesherbes–Puisseau line.

Cunningly keeping one step ahead of his Nazi pursuers, Fenwick moved his camp to the Fôret d'Orleans where, safe temporarily from prying eyes, he again attacked the railways in the locality, derailing another train, on this occasion on the Bellegarde–Beaune line. So successful were the operations, that the stealthy SAS parties could drive their jeeps up to their chosen targets on key railway lines, walk down the track to a suitable spot, lay their charges and get away unmolested, as they caught the Germans on the hop in the first fortnight of their operations. It was a situation that the Nazis, especially the SS and Gestapo who were charged with hunting down the SAS at all costs, were to rectify before long with violent and savage reprisals. To the Germans' fury, as fast as the severed railway lines were repaired, up popped the SAS on another stretch to blow them up again. With forces pushing ever deeper into France after the massive D-Day invasion, it was a situation that could not and would not be tolerated for very long.

But in the meantime, while the going was good, the SAS took full advantage and struck at widely dispersed targets, using the full advantage of surprise and speed. Fenwick noted that German vehicles in the area drove around with headlights blazing. So he ordered his men to remove the covers from the jeep lights, driving around boldly in a blaze of light, gambling that the Germans would not expect

British 'terrorists' to travel around so brazenly and that they would be taken for their own men. However, the raiders very nearly met their Waterloo through a rare case of treachery during an audacious raid at a railway yard where the primary objective was the locomotive shed.

All went well initially as the squad successfully evaded the sentries and quickly worked to plant their bombs, setting the detonators with a short fuse. But before they could slip away, a shot rang out. They had been rumbled. To their horror, they realised that they had been betrayed by one of their French contacts who had directed them to the target and had tried to warn the Germans. Thinking quickly, Fenwick ordered his team to engage the encircling enemy until the first of the bombs had gone off, otherwise all their efforts would have been wasted. A force of more than 200 Germans closed in on the little party which put up such a fierce fight in the cover of darkness that the enemy force was held off until the charges blasted apart an engine and badly damaged the locomotive shed. This caused such confusion that the raiders got clean away.

The firepower of Fenwick's party was significantly increased when at the end of July they were told by radio to expect a vital drop of armed jeeps, which had twin Vickers K machine-guns front and rear. These deadly weapons fired a mixture of tracer, incendiary and armour-piercing rounds at an incredibly fast rate of about 1,200 rounds a minute and meant that raids need not be confined to explosive demolition. Random, or opportunist, targets could now be hit on the move, with the outnumbered SAS men invariably giving better than they got in lightning strikes.

Sorties using these vehicles were initially marked with resounding success. At Ascouy, a large German transport was destroyed and on the Orleans–Pithiviers road, German trucks were set on fire after being raked with machine-gun fire. A petrol lorry was ambushed, lighting up the surrounding countryside for miles. Fatefully, Fenwick now decided to disperse his parties to help to avoid detection as the German response was being marshalled with devastating force. It was a sensible decision in the circumstances, but it was one that was to cost the young, impetuous Fenwick his life.

More raids swiftly followed, however. Railway trains were attacked and many wagonloads of supplies destroyed by the doggedly determined SAS group. The situation was going so well that Lt Col Paddy Mayne, commanding officer of the 1st SAS, planned to parachute into the area as soon as a suitable dropping zone could be arranged. The confirmation message was never sent to London, however, for the Germans unleashed a massive attack on Fenwick's troopers' main camp.

As many as 600 German troops surrounded a trio of hopelessly outnumbered SAS squads who fought tenaciously for 7 hours in a bitter battle to break out of the trap. It was every man for himself and the SAS made every bullet count. Final orders were issued to rendezvous with Lt Watson if anyone succeeded in breaking out of the ring of German steel. However, miraculously, the SAS men *did* manage to cut their way through the cordon and escape.

The following day, 8 August, news of the attack reached Ian Fenwick through Resistance channels. Tragically, the details he received were completely muddled and gave a totally false impression, a very common occurrence when dealing with the Resistance. There were obviously language difficulties. Fenwick was told that many of his men had been killed and all the jeeps lost. However, the truth was that every man had managed to elude what had seemed a certain death trap.

Without hesitation, Fenwick roared off in his jeep towards the scene of the attack to see for himself what had happened and if he could rescue anything from what appeared to be a catastrophic debacle. In the jeep with him were Sgt Dunkley, Cpl Duffy, L/Cpl Menginou of the 4th French SAS and a sergeant of the FFI (part of the Maquis Resistance Forces Français de l'Interieur). Fenwick was seething with rage and some believe his anger clouded his judgement and that this led to him putting his mens' lives unnecessarily at risk. However, his decision was crucial and bravely taken in the heat of the moment without the benefit of hindsight. They had not travelled far when a German spotter aircraft saw their jeep. The pilot immediately radioed the information back to the Germans at Chambon and an ambush was rapidly organised. Fenwick, at this stage unaware that he had been rumbled, drove his avenging jeep at full speed towards its fate with destiny. At the very last minute, a final card was played that could have yet prevented the sad outcome of the saga. A woman stepped out into the road, waving wildly for the jeep to stop. She had recognised the British uniforms at once and courageously gave the SAS men a desperate warning of what lay ahead, just out of sight. She told Fenwick the Germans were waiting in ambush just up the road and begged him to turn back. But Fenwick did not waver for an instant and told her firmly that he intended to blast his way through. Without delay, the jeep shot off towards the Germans, all guns hammering out a deadly message of defiance.

Fenwick almost fought his way through the first group of enemy soldiers, who were stunned by the ferocity of the onslaught, but the odds were suicidally against the SAS quintet. Another group of SS troopers were blazing away at the jeep from positions further back in the village and a 20-mm cannon shell hit Fenwick in the head, killing him instantly. Careering out of control, the jeep skidded wildly towards the woods and crashed. Menginou and the FFI sergeant were killed outright. Cpl Duffy survived the tragedy, however, and miraculously managed to escape back to the Allied lines.

Having been knocked out in the jeep crash, when he came to, Duffy saw Sgt Dunkley being led away by the Germans, handcuffed and with blood on his face. Duffy passed out again and when he regained his senses, he was lying in a German truck on his way to Orleans hospital.

From there, he was later moved to another hospital just north of Fontainebleau.

This hospital had been requisitioned from the French by the German Army medical corps and Duffy found himself sharing a ward with German wounded. He was fortunate to be moved to another ward which was cleaned by some French girls employed by the Germans. One of the girl patriots bravely said she could help him escape. The penalty for such assistance was death, but many of the French by now hated their German oppressors so much that they were willing to risk everything to help the Allies. Naturally, Duffy jumped at the chance. The girl later told him the alarming news that the hospital was going to be evacuated by the Germans, as the advancing American troops had reached nearby Chartres. Duffy had to make his move quickly. The fateful day for the attempt was to be 22 August. The French girl obtained for him a German medical officers' uniform and brought it into the ward in a bucket that she put down at the side of his bed. Duffy quickly hid the contents under his bedclothes while a group of other cleaners distracted the Germans in the ward. He later received a pair of shoes in the same way.

Duffy waited for everyone to fall asleep, dressed quickly and walked out of the hospital posing as a German medical officer, boldly saluting a guard on the way out. After many adventures, he was finally picked up by a party of Resistance men who took him to a doctor. His feet were horrifically blistered as the shoes were too small and he had walked for many miles in stockinged feet towards the Allied lines. He was later treated by the American forces and awarded the order of the Purple Heart. Amazingly, it later transpired that Sgt Dunkley also survived the ambush. He was released from capture and probable death at the hands of Gestapo interrogators when the advancing American forces took the German hospital in which he was being held.

Back at Thimory, two parties of SAS under Lts Bateman and Parsons were devastated to hear of the news of the

death of Maj Fenwick. They contacted Agrippa, a local
Maquis leader, and moved into his camp, which was
guarded by about 600 Maquisards. Capt C.L. Riding took
over Maj Fenwick's command deep in the Fôret d'Orleans.
Two days later, Lt Col Mayne parachuted into the area and
while the units temporarily lay low, dynamically issued
fresh plans and strategies for the men as he thoroughly
reassessed the situation.

The campaign was not yet won and many more fresh
challenges, hardships and dramatic developments faced the
men of the SAS as they fought their way through to victory
and the long-awaited liberation of Europe. But the
chivalrous Fenwick and his fearless comrades are
remembered to this day by the French with great pride.

BILL FRASER – THE GOLDEN CHANCE TO KILL ROMMEL AT HIS SECRET HQ

Lt, later Maj, Bill Fraser MC led an SAS raiding party that
destroyed an incredible total of thirty-seven enemy planes
with Lewes bombs during one night in the Western Desert.
This was more 'kills' than many fighter pilots could achieve
in months of hard dog-fighting. Fraser was one of the
outstanding officers with L Detachment SAS from the
outset. However, it was not until the Regiment parachuted
into France to support the Operation Overlord invasion of
Europe that he stumbled across information that led
directly to Rommel's headquarters and a chance to
eliminate the one man who might possibly turn the tide
and force the Allies back into the sea – the great Field
Marshal himself.

Fraser, who had obtained the priceless details from
French contacts at the base he was establishing behind the
lines in central France, urgently radioed SAS headquarters
back in Britain for permission to attack and kill, or kidnap,
the legendary German commander. More will be revealed
later about this dramatic and little-known story, as this

doggedly determined officer had already carved his name in the annals of regimental history with one of the most devastating single night attacks on an enemy airfield in the history of modern warfare.

Fraser's early success in the North African desert came at Agedabia, soon after the formation of L Detachment, where his tiny group of just four SAS raiders had to sneak up to the closely guarded airfield, dodge the patrolling enemy guards, lie silent for a nerve-racking hour in the midst of the heavily armed enemy, plant their Lewes bombs and then slip away undetected as the explosions ripped the planes apart one after the other. They blew apart all but a couple of the forty or so enemy aircraft that were scattered around the airfield that night. It was an almost unbelievable accomplishment, which helped underline the destructive credibility of Stirling's raiding force.

As recorded in John Strawson's *A History of the SAS Regiment*, Brig Reid noted Fraser's impressive record score in his diary:

At first light there was a certain amount of excitement amongst the forward troops and recognition signals by Very light were fired. I drove forward to see what was the matter and met Fraser of Stirling's L Detachment whom I eagerly asked how he got on. He said [laconically]: 'Very sorry, sir, I had to leave two aircraft on the ground as I ran out of explosives, but we destroyed 37!'

This indeed was a wonderful achievement by one officer and three men. Incidentally, we heard later that Rommel had been in Agedabia that night. He must have had a bit of a headache . . .

Like Stirling, Fraser was a tough, uncompromising Scot, a battle-hardened lieutenant who had come to the SAS via the Gordon Highlanders and 11th Scottish Commandos, a unit ironically disbanded, as already noted, after the courageous but abortive raid to kill or capture Rommel in his desert headquarters near Benghazi in 1941. Fraser's former commanding officer, Lt Col Geoffrey Keyes, was tragically killed in the raid, but his bravery was marked with a posthumous VC. It was to be three long years before the ex-Commandos in the SAS were to have the 'Desert Fox' in their sights again. And, ironically, it was to be Fraser – one of Keyes' best former officers – who was to play a leading role in the new assassination drama.

In the interim, as one of the most dependable officers of the original SAS, Fraser took part in many desert missions and was also heavily involved, after being promoted captain, in the seaborne missions in support of the invasion of Sicily and Italy. Later, he parachuted into France after D-Day as part of the extensive SAS operations in support of the Overlord invasion as a major operating from the important Houndsworth base in central France. It was here, by chance, that Fraser made his stunning discovery, which could have changed the course of the war. He had achieved what countless others had tried but failed to do – he had tracked down and located the hiding place of the 'Desert Fox'.

On 14 July 1944, Fraser confirmed that, without doubt, Rommel's secret headquarters were at the Château de Roche-Guyon, near Mantes. This red-hot information had come from an extremely reliable French source and was totally accurate, but Maj Fraser was at that time 200 miles away from the château and the opportunity to mount any possible raid on Rommel. In addition, his prime responsibility was to establish a guerrilla base ready for the arrival of a large SAS force tasked to harass the German routes used to supply men and materiel to the Normandy beachhead.

David Irving in *Rommel: The Trail Of The Fox* notes that Fraser sent a dramatic radio signal to London that read: 'Rommel arrives left Bank Seine, crosses by motor launch. Walks and shoots in Fôret de Moisson. Send maps from this area to area (of) Mantes, also three sniper's rifles. Would prefer you not to send another party for this job as

(I) consider it is my pigeon.' After carefully considering all the available information at SAS headquarters, near London, it was decided that Fraser was too far away to reach the château safely with an accompanying assassination, or kidnap, team and his commander Brig R. McLeod radioed back: 'Regret must forbid your personal attack on Rommel . . . your task (is) to remain in command present area. This "pigeon" will be attacked by a special party . . .'.

Frustrated at the knock-back, but determined not to give in without a fight, Fraser signalled back: 'Have here Monsieur Defors who owns the estates all around the Rommel headquarters. All the keepers etc. have been in his family service for years. His relations live all around and he has contacts all the way en route.' However, there were too many risks to take into account and too little time available to allow Fraser his golden chance to repay the debt of honour on behalf of his former commanding officer, the heroic Keyes, by personally eliminating the brilliant Rommel.

Brig McLeod rigidly stuck to his guns and insisted that his original decision must stand. He reasoned that a highly trained specialist assault force should parachute into the area near the headquarters to have a much greater chance of remaining undetected and completing what would, in any event, be a very hazardous mission. Rommel was still as cunning a fox as ever and would be heavily protected and guarded. He had already evaded everything the Allies could throw at him and bounced back to further triumphs. There would, clearly, be only one bite at this priceless cherry. However, the stakes were unimaginably high. Rommel was at this time not only Germany's finest field commander, he was commander-in-chief of all Nazi forces opposing the massive invasion in Normandy. If he could be permanently taken out of the picture at this crucial stage of the invasion of France, the effect would be devastating.

Immediately, SAS HQ went into overdrive. McLeod ordered air photographs of the château, which showed the whole area was surrounded by barbed wire and heavily guarded. A special SAS squad was quickly assembled and parachuted into France near the city of Chartres with orders to kill or kidnap Rommel at any cost. In practice, this was virtually a death sentence for the Field Marshal, as it would have been almost impossible to abduct him and get him safely back to Britain. But there was no time for sentiment with Germany still far from defeat and capable of a shock turn of the tables against the invading Allies.

Capt Raymond Lee, of the SAS, a crack shot well experienced for such a professional assassination, was chosen to lead the special five-man team. But, ironically, as Lee parachuted into the darkness over France on 25 July he and his comrades were unaware that their high-profile victim lay gravely injured and had come within an ace of being eliminated by another unexpected source.

The reason for this dramatic turn of events was that on 17 July Spitfires flying on a daring low-level sortie over France had, by sheer chance, strafed and shot up Rommel's Horch staff car as he made a tour to inspect his defences, severely wounding the Field Marshal in a blistering machine-gun and cannon attack. Rommel was rushed away for emergency attention and his life was saved, though hospital X-rays showed he had sustained a quadruple skull fracture. His legendary iron constitution came to his aid and he rallied, though his survival astounded the Army surgeons treating him.

Lee, meanwhile, initially unaware of these developments, was to spend the next few weeks searching in vain for his intended victim. Tragically, the great Field Marshal's reprieve was only temporary for yet another cruel twist of fortune intervened just days later. The bungled bomb attack on Hitler's life by would-be assassin Von Stauffenberg on 20 July at the Führer's bunker in East Prussia finally sealed Rommel's fate. Numerous conspirators were arrested and tortured one by one and, as the net of retribution was cast ever wider, Rommel was, rightly or wrongly, fatally implicated as a sympathiser with the 'treacherous' plot to topple Hitler and was forced to commit suicide.

It was ironic in the extreme that after so many years of dodging Commando killer squads and bombs and tank shells in two world wars, the 'indestructible' Rommel was to die, not in action by an SAS bullet – perhaps defending his headquarters against the crack raiding squad heroically to the last – but by being blackmailed into saving the lives of his family and his considerable reputation by taking poison.

Three Great SBS Commanders

George Jellicoe,
David Sutherland, John Lapraik

GEORGE JELLICOE

Lt Col George Jellicoe DSO, MC was one of the most courageous and influential figures in the development of the Special Boat Service during the Second World War. Earl Jellicoe, son of the famous First World War Admiral, had his studies at Cambridge University interrupted by the outbreak of war, joining the Coldstream Guards before volunteering for the Special Air Service in the North African desert. He quickly proved himself to be daring and resourceful, becoming one of Stirling's finest officers.

An energetic, thick-set young man with a shock of curly hair, Jellicoe later went on to command the Special Boat Squadron, employing ingenuity, tact and solid leadership to get the very best out of the men under his command – especially the brave, but often unpredictable Anders Lassen. SBS veterans who served under Jellicoe in the Mediterranean, Aegean, Greece and elsewhere testify to the popularity of his leadership, which was modestly underscored by genuine ability and refreshing common sense. Never one to stand on ceremony, he was known as plain George to his fellow officers.

The SBS as we now know it was born through the major reorganisation of the various SAS squadrons at Azzib, north of Haifa, as part of the Middle East Raiding Forces based in Palestine. The North Africa veterans of A and B Squadrons were amalgamated into the Special Raiding Squadron under Lt Col Paddy Mayne. These 246 officers

and men carried out a daring series of parachute and
seaborne raids on Sicily and Italy before returning to
Britain to prepare for the invasion of France. D Squadron,
commanded by George Jellicoe from March 1943, was
renamed the Special Boat Squadron, comprising a roughly
equal complement of 230 men. Using the fine sandy
beaches of Athlit, in the shadow of the old Crusader castle,
the SBS began training hard for the tough missions that lay
ahead in the Mediterranean, Aegean and Adriatic. Jellicoe's
forward base later in the war was on the schooner *Tewfik*,
which was moored near the island of Kastellorizon off the
Turkish coast. Turkey turned a blind eye to SBS activities
along their coastline throughout the war. SBS operations
were wideranging and highly effective, making a crucial
and telling contribution to the war effort.

One of Jellicoe's most outstanding individual missions
came in June 1942, prior to joining the SBS. Stirling
received an urgent request to help take pressure off a vital
convoy bound for the besieged island of Malta. It was
decided that the most effective way to do this was by
raiding the airfield bases of the bombers which were at that
very moment preparing to mount further devastating air
attacks on the vulnerable merchantmen taking the vital
supplies to the island. These convoys were being decimated
by a ferocious air blockade and the situation was becoming
critical. In response, a series of raids were urgently
arranged to strike not only at key North African bases, but
also at enemy airfields on Crete, including Heraklion. These
attacks were principally aimed at destroying bombers,
although fuel and bomb dumps would also be hit.

Simultaneous SBS raids on the Cretan airfields at Maleme
and Timbaki achieved mixed results, but bomb dumps were
destroyed at Kastelli via an audacious attack by George
Duncan and teams from M Section, SBS. As fate would have
it, the Heraklion mission would strike the jackpot with many
enemy aircraft destroyed, but at a heavy price. Ironically,
Jellicoe would be the sole SAS survivor. He was second in
command of the raid, which was led by Cdr Berge MC, Croix

de Guerre, a veteran of the Free French forces. Jellicoe had not been with the SAS long, but was an obvious choice for the hazardous mission as he spoke fluent French and knew the island of Crete well.

Jellicoe's party covertly approached the island in the Greek submarine *Triton*. As wartime records show, all went well on landing but once ashore progress was slow, as the route through the mountains was rough and the raiders' packs were very heavy, loaded down with many kilos of explosives and ammunition. The SAS party pressed on doggedly and after two nights marching reached their airfield destination, where they found to their satisfaction more than sixty Junkers 88 bombers parked and waiting – a perfect target. However, the airfield was, as expected, surrounded by barbed wire and well guarded.

The raiders hid up until the next night before silently making their way down, laden with delayed action bombs, to make their attack. They carefully used wire cutters to make a hole in the outer fence, but were nearly discovered when a guard patrol passed close by on the inside wire. The game seemed up, but with some inspired ad libbing, one of the Frenchmen cleverly made a loud, drunken snore that fooled the enemy sentry into thinking nothing was wrong. Perhaps it was thought that the shadowy figure, or figures, glimpsed were off-duty comrades who had been indulging in a heavy drinking session. For whatever reason, the trick worked and the raiders were able to proceed further into the airfield's defences.

Some time later, however, another sentry returned to the spot, this time discovering an obvious gap in the wire. But just as it seemed that the SAS party was now trapped inside the enemy airfield to be wiped out, or captured red-handed, fate intervened. A flight of Stukas suddenly plunged out of the sky coming in ready to land, followed immediately by a marauding RAF Blenheim bomber, which dropped a stick of bombs across the runway. In the ensuing pandemonium, all thoughts of gaps in wire were forgotten as guards and defending troops raced for cover or action stations. The SAS, however, were quick to take full advantage of the confusion. Feverishly persisting with their task they managed to plant all their bombs, which later exploded to destroy at least sixteen aeroplanes and other choice targets, including trucks and aero engines under repair.

The first of these charges went off while Jellicoe's team was still inside the perimeter wire. But, with the airfield temporarily thrown into chaos, with typical SAS aplomb, he was able to lead his men out through the main gate by tagging behind a German patrol. The pre-dawn light was still poor and the cheeky ruse worked like a charm. The SAS raiders slipped away undetected and looking back saw, with satisfaction, the inferno erupting behind them. Some of the aircraft attacked, however, did not catch fire as the Germans had cunningly emptied the fuel tanks to lessen the risk.

Returning to near the beach where they had landed, they hid until they could be taken off again when the submarine returned. Jellicoe and the group's Greek guide, Lt Costi, went to a nearby village to contact an agent working on behalf of the Allies, to facilitate a rendezvous with the SBS. However, disaster struck as the hiding place of the main SAS party was accidentally stumbled across by a party of Cretans who betrayed their presence to the Germans. Berge and the others were surrounded and outnumbered by strong German forces and, after their Tommy guns ran out of ammunition, were all killed or captured.

On his return, Jellicoe was dismayed to find no trace of Berge or his party, but was told by friendly local peasants that the French commander and some other prisoners had been forcibly taken to Heraklion. With a heavy heart, Jellicoe had no choice but to embark, as arranged, three days later, powerless to help his comrades. It later transpired that the courageous Berge and his men were shot by the German authorities. Tragically, sixty Greek hostages were also executed by the Germans in reprisal for the raid.

The vital Malta convoy took a tremendous hammering despite the attacks, losing fifteen out of seventeen ships. However, the two ships that did get through carried just enough supplies to keep Malta going until the next convoy arrived. A total of thirty-seven aircraft were destroyed by the SAS in the combined raids on Crete and North Africa. In the final analysis the Crete raid, though costly in human terms, was a resounding success as far as the number of targets destroyed was concerned. But little did Jellicoe imagine before setting out that he would be the only member of the party who would return to fight again, in his case on many other occasions. This modest, but fiercely determined, commander was one of a rare breed – a fighting soldier, who was genuinely gifted in the broader tactical sense.

DAVID SUTHERLAND

Maj (later Lt Col) David Sutherland DSO, MC and bar, who was to take over command of Jellicoe's SBS squadron as a lieutenant colonel later in the war, was involved in some of the most hair-raising early SBS raids. The following account, derived from the former Black Watch officer's original reports, is a fine example of his courage, calm leadership and tenacity against seemingly insurmountable odds, the survivors of his party finally having to make a near suicidal swim out to a waiting submarine after being hunted down by enemy soldiers furious at a devastating attack on their airfield.

In September 1942, S Section SBS prepared for raids on the two main airfields on the island of Rhodes: Maritza and Calato. These attacks were to take place on Saturday 12 September. A Greek officer and two guides landed alongside the British party, which included Sutherland, Capt Ken Allott, Sgt Moss, a corporal and three Marines. They went ashore from the Greek submarine *Papanikolis* about a week before the raids were to be made. Each man carried a heavy pack of rations, explosives and ammunition, travelling over the mountains by night and hiding by day.

Progress towards the target was, in the difficult terrain, understandably slow, but Moss and Allott reached a hill overlooking Maritza airfield three days later. Spread before them in the valley were runways surrounded by wire, well patrolled by German guards. Allott, Sgt Moss and Cpl McKenzie crept through the defences, planted their time bombs and got away undetected to rejoin Sutherland at a pre–arranged rendezvous on 16 September. Sutherland was at this time high up in the mountains overlooking Maritza airfield. He divided his men into two teams: Marine Duggan and himself, with a Greek officer and Marines Barrow and Harris forming the other.

The raiders set out at dusk picking their way down the mountain towards their targets. Sutherland and Duggan reached the first bomber at Calato airfield, only to be thwarted by a sentry sheltering under its wing. The two Britons waited patiently, however, and after a while the guard moved away. Sutherland laid some small charges on the aircraft propellers, as this was the most efficient way of disposing of an isolated aircraft. He also placed bombs on two other aircraft before getting out of the main runway area, having to cross some barbed wire and an anti-tank ditch between buildings. Here a sentry challenged them, but the raiders slipped behind a building. They then found the petrol dump, placed more bombs and made their escape.

Sutherland and Duggan reached the shelter of a riverbed before their charges went up, followed shortly after by those of the Greek officer and the Marines, from their separate attack. Within minutes the airfield was lit up with many individual fires, with searchlights frantically probing the air for imaginary air attackers. However, the Italians soon began searching the mountainside with lights, though Sutherland and Duggan were able to make their way safely to the rendezvous. They heard machine-gun fire and shooting, indicating the other party had been attacked and either killed or captured. In fact, Allott and his party were all taken prisoner.

At first light Sutherland made a recce on the target and observed many burnt-out aircraft, damage to wrecked store dumps and repair gangs working away. Then he and Duggan made their way to a hiding place above the bay where a submarine would come to pick them up on 16 September. Swarms of enemy soldiers arrived to search for them and the raiders had to conceal themselves on a sloping ledge, remaining completely motionless. One party of Italians passed within just a few feet of them, but the SBS men were not detected. That night the two crept down to a cave but another large party of enemy soldiers arrived and started combing the area. It was obvious that someone had been captured and had talked, and later Sutherland learned that one of the guides had been tortured for information.

Sutherland and Duggan had to remain in their cramped hide among the rocks and, as more search parties scoured the cliffs, their thirst became almost unbearable. But at dusk, Sutherland and Duggan went down to the shore and later that night flashed signals from their torch and received a reply from the submarine. There was now no means of getting out to the vessel, so they had to take a considerable chance and swim for it.

Sutherland and Duggan swam with difficulty, as they had not eaten properly for five days or had water for two and both were extremely weak. After an hour, during which they covered well over 2 km, they heard the welcoming noise of the submarine's electric motors and shortly afterwards the submarine loomed out of the darkness. They could not believe their luck – they were saved! However, the price was, as sometimes was the case in special force raiding, tragically high.

JOHN LAPRAIK

Maj John Lapraik, DSO, MC and bar, formerly of the Cameron Highlanders, was commanding officer of M Detachment, SBS. He was a key figure who operated with great skill and verve at the sharp end of SBS raiding. In October 1943, HQ Raiding Forces Middle East was established in Cairo under the command of Lt Col Turnbull. Together he and Lapraik planned the first of what were to become the bloodiest series of raids in SBS history. A mission illustrating the mayhem inflicted on the enemy by the SBS occurred in November 1943, when S Squadron returned to Simi. The garrison stationed there comprised a German major with 18 men and 2 Italian captains commanding 60 Fascist militia, as well as 10 other soldiers and the island's police force.

Lapraik's patrols silently went ashore on 20 November. Bob Bury's unit moved cautiously into Kastello, but near the governor's castle they ran into a machine-gun post. Without hesitation, Bury lobbed a well-aimed grenade, wounding several soldiers, and his sergeant opened up on troops on a nearby pier with a captured Schmeisser sub machine-pistol, hitting seven others. One man who crawled away was killed in a second burst of fire. Bury himself riddled yet another soldier before detonating 10 kg of high explosives, bringing down part of the castle quarters. Withdrawing swiftly after this lightning attack, the SBS quickly set a booby trap bomb in the street, which their pursuers blundered into, causing yet more casualties.

Lapraik, meanwhile, and three others set the boatyard ablaze, attacked the power station and killed another soldier, while comrades manning Bren light machine-guns shielded the other raiders by engaging the harbour guard in a fierce firefight. By the time the SBS finally withdrew, nearly all the enemy garrison had been killed or wounded, establishing a pattern that was to be repeated time and again in future raids, only on a much larger scale. The enemy never knew from which quarter the next raid was to come.

The SBS, like their comrades in the SAS, gained a fearsome reputation, with their destructive lightning strikes causing casualties and damage way out of proportion to the numbers involved. No unit fought harder to achieve its objectives and casualties in all ranks were high. Jellicoe reorganised the squadrons, as L and S Squadrons had lost many of their original members. The regrouped unit absorbed sections trained at Athlit under Maj Ian Patterson, a skilled former Parachute Regiment officer whom Jellicoe recruited on Kos.

Patterson, like many others in the SAS/SBS, was a perfectionist and sent several officers and fifty men back to their units almost as soon as they had arrived because they were not up to the required standard. But the battle-experienced officer was only re-emphasising the tried and trusted ethos of the SBS. It was obvious to all that the traditional key qualities of discipline and determination would be needed more than ever in the dangerous raiding operations in the coming months, in the various theatres of war. By early 1944, the SBS had made a staggering total of 381 raids on about 70 islands in the Mediterranean and Aegean, before going on to complete yet more arduous operations in Yugoslavia, Greece, Italy and elsewhere.

The SBS force carved out for itself a distinctive and worthy place in history, creating an on-going specialist role, which persists to this day, as part of Britain's elite Special Forces.

The Hell that was Italy

George 'Bebe' Daniels, Philip Pinckney,
Reg Seekings

GEORGE DANIELS – SEVENTY-THREE DAYS BEHIND ENEMY
LINES – HEROES OF OPERATION SPEEDWELL

The amazing story of Sgt George 'Bebe' Daniels and his
comrades is one of the lesser known, but most memorable
and inspiring accounts in the annals of the wartime SAS. It
began when three small groups of expert SAS saboteurs,
numbering a total of thirteen men, parachuted into the far
north of Italy at midnight on 7 September 1943, to carry
out a series of daring raids codenamed Operation Speedwell.
The object was to blow up trains – preferably in tunnels – to
disrupt supplies of tanks, troops and materiel that were being
rushed to the distant southern front to counter the main
Allied invasion, which had begun in the toe of Italy just
three days before.

The crucial mission occurred just before Italy capitulated
and broke its Axis pact with Nazi Germany. This threw the
country into a highly dangerous and volatile state with
pro-Allied bands of partisans roaming haphazardly behind
the lines among many thousands of angry and trigger-
happy Germans who were itching to gain revenge over
their 'treacherous' former allies. It was about as dangerous
a situation as could be imagined for the SAS band who had
first to risk their lives in a highly perilous parachute drop
among towering mountains, successfully complete their
attacks and then, somehow, walk the length of Italy to
escape back to their own lines. They had little idea of who
would help them, or who they could trust.

The fact that this was an extremely risky mission was fully appreciated in advance by the small groups of experienced SAS raiders, commanded by Capt Philip Pinckney. The men had been hand-picked by Pinckney, who had spent two months drilling them to a peak of readiness in North Africa. Now they were winging their way in Albermarle aircraft towards their lofty Italian target. Flying unescorted across enemy territory, Daniels remembers they had to take evasive action to avoid flak before dropping by parachute from a very high level, about 7,000 ft, into the mountains between Florence and Bologna to ensure adequate clearance for the aircraft. 'It meant a very long wait before we hit the ground,' George remembers. 'We usually dropped from very low level, just a few hundred feet high to avoid detection, but we couldn't in this case because of the mountains. This was Pinckney's project. One of the officer's commanding the other stick of SAS paratroopers was Capt Dudgeon, another fine officer, who sadly also did not make it back.' Pinckney was an expert in survival foraging and his men were trained to eat anything to extend their endurance behind the lines. 'We could live on nettles, dandelions – or even slugs if we had to,' said Daniels, who was navigator for the arduous trip. This training was invaluable for the raiders on this mission as, at times, most of its members were near starvation. Often they found their way solely by their silk maps and the stars.

As the men parachuted down, a special German security unit pledged to hunt down the SAS was actively operating in the area. Those who evaded the Germans and survived the drop unscathed made the call of the curlew – the group's rallying sound – and searched the drop zone in vain for 2 hours looking for Pinckney, who was nowhere to be found. He had disguised a painful back injury sustained on a previous mission and may have been further injured in a heavy landing and captured. But nothing definite is known of his eventual fate. However, his comrades are convinced it is almost certain he was shot by Italian Blackshirts within hours of landing. Others in the SAS party were also captured and shot after operating successfully for a period.

The depleted survivors, however, doggedly persisted with their missions. There was just Sgt Daniels' small group of four and two other parties, one under Sgt Tim Robinson and another made up of Lt Wedderburn and Sgt Harold 'Tanky' Challenor, whose story of sheer guts and endurance has become famous, as recorded in his book *Tanky Challenor SAS and the Met*. Challenor and Lt Wedderburn blew up trains on the Spezia–Bologna line, blocked tunnels and created mayhem. Challenor made it back to the Allied lines after seven months, during which time he was captured twice, tortured and first escaped disguised as an Italian peasant woman before finally breaking free. Wedderburn was taken prisoner but did not survive. All Challenor could say when he arrived back among British troops at last was 'I've done it, you bastards' over and over again.

In fact, all of Pinckney's surviving and much-weakened SAS raiders successfully blew up and destroyed a number of trains, including troop carriers, and totally blocked the main rail lines running south in the Spezia area, disrupting communications with Bologna, Genoa and Pistoia. The brave and resourceful Sgt Robinson also eventually made it back to safety in southern Italy after surviving some amazing escapades. Incredibly, they were all faced with a march of several hundred miles down the full length of the Italian Appenines, an area seething with thousands of hostile German troops. The SAS men could not carry sufficient food and had to live off the land and beg shelter from any friendly local peasants they could find before making a final break through the front lines to reach the advancing Allies.

Daniels' problems were compounded by the fact that his officer, Lt Anthony Greville-Bell, had badly broken his ribs on landing and was incapacitated and in great pain, with the shattered bones grinding together as he walked in the rough, mountainous territory. The tough desert-veteran sergeant temporarily took command while the officer slowly recovered, the bones gradually mending themselves after heavy strapping. They managed to blow up four trains, including one packed with hundreds of German soldiers heading for the front. As Sgt Daniels recalled:

We had already blown up three trains in tunnels and had just laid the last of our explosives on another railway line with a trip switch set to catch the next train along, when we heard a train approaching. We just hid in cover and watched. It was a troop train taking soldiers down to the front to fight our lads and the Americans. We could actually see the German soldiers inside as it was all lit up, the Germans feeling safe as houses being so far behind the lines.

Then our explosives went up with a deafening roar, lifting the electric locomotive off the tracks. As if in slow motion, it plunged on to its side in a great cloud of dirt and dust, dragging over the derailed carriages after it. It was awesome, I'll never forget it. There must have been hundreds of casualties because the train was so packed with soldiers, but we couldn't afford to hang around and find out. This was the only train we actually saw being blown up as the others were deliberately hit inside tunnels to cause maximum damage and make it hard for the Germans to extricate the trains and repair the tracks.

As well as directing the missions and helping the injured Lt Greville-Bell, Sgt Daniels overcame a severe bout of dysentery as a result of the poor diet he was forced to exist on, and this indirectly gave rise to one of his most amazing escapes. After starting on the long trek home, Daniels was sheltering in a house belonging to friendly locals in the mountains when the woman of the house came in shouting '*Tedeschi* [Germans] are coming!' Two soldiers were rapidly approaching on horseback but Daniels thought very quickly: 'As the house was surrounded by large boulders I just grabbed a blanket off the bed, went outside, sat very still and disguised myself as a rock! I had seen the Arabs doing a similar trick in the desert. The soldiers passed within a few yards of me, but never spotted me.'

On another occasion, the tiny SAS group was climbing a mountain road when a German truck came round the bend. 'We opened fire and two German soldiers gave themselves up,' said George. They were soon relieved of their boots as those of the SAS were worn out. They also survived when an American bomber being chased by a German fighter at low level dropped its bomb load almost on top of the group, frightening them half to death.

Daniels stoically encouraged his comrades to reach the Allied lines safely, and as a result was at once granted the Military Medal. Daniels' award is highly unusual as it was granted with immediate effect and there are only two authorising signatures, those of Lt Col Bill Stirling, the officer commanding the 2nd SAS Regiment, and FM Alexander. Normally, the award of an MM had to be approved by a whole chain of command. However, the high command banned any publicity for this well-won award at the time owing to the fact that other SAS troops were still operating behind the lines in Italy, which also explains why so little has been known before about this outstanding exploit. The citation reads:

This NCO was dropped north of Florence on 7th/8th September 1943 and returned to our lines 73 days later. The commander of his stick, Lieutenant Bell 2nd SAS Regiment, broke two ribs on landing and being in considerable pain for three days he handed over command of his party to Sergeant Daniels while taking morphine to ease his pain.

Sergeant Daniels succeeded in keeping Lieutenant Bell with the party and was conspicuous throughout the operation during which three trains were sabotaged and much other damage caused to other enemy lines of communication. By his leadership, he made the operation a great success when failure seemed likely.

Ironically, Daniels did not see this citation for fifty years until a friend, Brian Stoker, a military enthusiast, tracked it down at the War Records Office where it was stamped 'No publicity to be given to this citation'.

Sgt Daniels has also given permission to the author to include a previously unpublished letter from a German officer who was present at the execution of SAS Capt Dudgeon, the officer in command of the other parachute 'stick' involved. It demonstrates the great courage with which Dudgeon faced his certain death after capture. The letter, dated 22 June 1945, was written to Dudgeon's family, with copies sent to Brig Mike Calvert and Lt Col Paddy Mayne and Dudgeon's comrades on the fatal mission, Capt Greville-Bell DSO and Sgt Daniels MM. It stated that the writer, a German interpreter, had promised Capt Dudgeon on the night before his execution that he would convey the brave manner in which he had died to his family, together with details of his place of burial.

It was revealed in the letter that Parachutist Brunt was shot by firing squad along with Dudgeon after they were captured at a roadblock having ambushed a German vehicle and killed the occupants in order to drive to their operational area. Sgt Foster and Cpl Shorthall simply vanished and their fate is unknown. The letter was signed by Victor Schmit-Zoller, an officer in the German Army, whose testimony not only solved the mystery, but led to an order for the arrest of Gen Von Zeilberg as a war criminal. He was subsequently tracked down by the SAS war crimes team and jailed for ten years for his part in the atrocity. All personal references to Capt Dudgeon's family have been deleted by the author.

By this letter I fulfil my pledged word to the bravest of English officers that I met in all my life . . . Captain Dudgeon, who fell for his country in Italy on October 3rd, 1943. . . . I was at that time, a platoon commander in the 65th Infantry Division of the German Army. My unit lay in the Passo della Cisa about 30 miles west of Parma on the road Parma–La Spezia.

About 10am [on the day of Dudgeon's capture], I was awakened by my men who told me they had captured two English soldiers driving in the direction of Parma, their clothes smeared with blood. In their bags they had about 40lbs of explosives. I went down and found in the guardroom two English soldiers, one of them a captain. When I asked who they were they gave me their military cards. I reported to the company commander and later to the division. The divisional officer on duty told me that half an hour ago, a German sergeant and a private driving towards La Spezia had been shot and their car stolen.

This having [occurred] several hundred miles behind the lines and two soldiers carrying explosives, they had to be treated as Greischarler [terrorists] and would probably be shot.

The battalion commander who had arrived in the meantime, tried to get out of [Dudgeon] anything about his purposes, where he was coming from etc. I being the interpreter.

Schmit-Zoller said that when pressed, Dudgeon asked him to translate 'If you were my prisoner, should you betray your country by talking about your mission?'

Upon this, my captain told him that probably he had to be shot by an existing order of the Führer. Captain Dudgeon took the news answering something like this. 'Alright – I'll die for my country.'

When my captain had withdrawn, I sat beside Dudgeon on the straw and we were speaking together all night long. He told me he knew little of Germany, that he had spent his holidays in Switzerland, etc.

In the morning the divisional commander, General von Zeilberg, informed the battalion that he would come and see the English captain before he was to be shot. I told him [Dudgeon] that the German officers were scandalised that an enemy who had behaved in so brilliant a manner had to be shot, but were mightless against an order of the Führer. To me the behaviour of the young officer of 23 years old had made such an impression that I couldn't help telling him when we were alone. 'Your country may be proud of you. If you were not my enemy, I should ask you to be my friend.' Captain Dudgeon gave me his hand saying 'I thank you for telling me that.'

The interview with the general was quite resultless. At the end of it (all the German officers were present), the general told me to translate . . . the following sentence. '*Sagen sie ihm dass ich vor Seinen Haltung alle Achtung habe. Er wird, mit seinen Kamaraden in einer Stunde erschossen.*' [Roughly translated: 'Tell him that I have taken care of his arrest. He will be shot in one hour with his comrade.']

[Dudgeon, he said, then saluted militarily and left the general.] He asked me to stay with him until it will be over . . . He asked for a Protestant priest. Before he died, he asked to die with his hands free and open eyes. He knelt down for a short while praying with his hands in front of his face. Then he got up and died like a hero.

. . . The enemy was to have no information whatever regarding the efficiency of the parachutists.

It is impossible to ascertain whether this German officer was telling the whole truth about the manner of Dudgeon's interrogation, which appears suspiciously mild by SAS standards, especially after the violent deaths of two of the German unit's comrades, for which the SAS duo were known to be responsible. Nevertheless, there could be no reason whatsoever to dispute the gallant way in which Dudgeon and his compatriot faced death by firing squad on that lonely autumn day in 1943.

Daniels' Route to the SAS

At the age of twenty, George Daniels joined the
Northamptonshire Regiment in 1939 and watched the Battle
of Britain raging in the skies above southern England, before
reaching the rank of sergeant and being shipped out to the
Middle East in 1941. After seeing action in the desert, he
was recruited by Maj Barlow for the 1st SAS and underwent
a gruelling training programme which, as well as parachute
training and tough marches carrying 70-lb packs, included a
half-mile swim. George said: 'I never fancied getting killed for
some obscure cause. With the SAS you knew the odds and
what your target was – it was up to you and your own
initiative and resources. Major Barlow and myself and
Sergeants Dave Leigh and Dave Kershaw, of the original SAS,
were ordered to recruit and train 2nd SAS Regiment recruits,
then being raised at Philippeville in Algeria, North Africa.
I started off at a place called Bone and met many of the
famous names in 1st SAS, including Johnny Cooper and Reg
Seekings.'

The fresh 2nd SAS recruits soon responded to the hard
but knowledgeable training by the battle-hardened NCOs
and soon they were in action themselves in the desert. 'I
went on a couple of airfield raids and then was with
Popski, of Popski's Private Army fame, for about three
months on jeep operations. They were the experts at the
time on desert reconnaissance.' On one jeep patrol, Daniels
and his comrades spotted an armoured car which had
pulled into a defile. The officer ordered George to get closer
and identify its nationality. 'We could just see the top of its
turret and we weren't sure it was German. But when we
were a couple of hundred yards away, it started spraying us
with its cannon. I saw the flashes first before I heard the
noise. We drove off like a bat out of hell, but the shells
were kicking up sand all around and passing over me. We
were lucky to get away unscathed.'

Later, 2nd SAS were engaged in numerous raids across
Italy, before being pulled back to the UK with all other SAS

units for the invasion of France, where 2nd SAS suffered
some heavy casualties under Hitler's infamous Commando
execution order. There were no trials, it was just murder,
George recalled. He, like the rest of his comrades, dropped
into France to fight doggedly through into Germany itself.
He took part in a total of about fifteen operations on the
continent. 'We were keyed up but ready, the training kicks
in,' George said. 'But one incident when I had just landed
in the forest near the Loire sticks in my mind. My chute
had got caught in the trees and I was just swinging there
in the pitch dark, swaying in my harness and wondering
whether to cut myself down and risk breaking a leg. I
decided to get out of my harness and dropped – all of six
inches! I couldn't help but laugh after I got over the shock.'

George remembers SAS patrols returning from the
Ardennes and actually warning the Americans that they
had seen Germans in American uniform and massed
panzers before the Battle of the Bulge, the last big German
offensive of the war, when saboteurs in GI uniform tried to
spread confusion behind the Allied lines. 'They were
planning to drop SAS among the panzers to cause havoc
with explosives at the critical time of the advance, but
thankfully it was called off at the last minute. I think that
would have been my last mission if we had had to do it – a
real suicide job,' said George.

Later, when the Germans were on the run, some strange
liberties were taken, especially in the transport field. He
remembers: 'One of the vehicles we appropriated for service
was a brand new Citroën car with just 500 km on the clock.
We cut the roof completely off so we could use our weapons
freely and drove in style all the way through Germany!' The
climax of the war for George came when he saw
FM Von Rundstedt coming through the lines on his way to
the surrender on Luneburg Heath.

Afterwards, George Daniels was flown with the rest of the
SAS to Norway, where it was thought pockets of Germans
might still put up a fight. On arrival, however, they found the
large German forces had surrendered. 'We supervised the

return of the loot the Nazis had stolen from the Norwegians during five years' occupation,' George said. 'It was my most pleasant task of the entire war!'

PHILIP PINCKNEY – UNSOLVED MYSTERY OF A UNIQUE STAR OF THE SAS

Capt Philip Pinckney was so audaciously brave during numerous daring operations with the Commandos and SAS that his comrades considered him a sure bet to win the ultimate accolade – a VC. Few men could boast they had hatched a plot to steal one of Germany's top fighters from an enemy airfield, or crawled to within 20 yd of enemy strong points during a reconnaissance of enemy positions. However, Pinckney was destined to go down in history not just for his outstanding gallantry, but because of the highly mysterious nature of his demise, which remains a puzzle to this day.

Capt Pinckney, while serving in the Commandos, came within an ace of embarking on an audacious plot to steal a Focke Wulf 190 fighter from a German airfield in occupied France in June 1942, with the aid of his friend, top RAF test pilot, Jeffrey Quill. At that time, the FW 190 was Germany's top secret fighter and was shooting down the latest Spitfires in alarming numbers. After covertly sneaking into France, the pair planned to penetrate an enemy airfield's defences by stealth, then Quill would have flown the fighter back to the UK while Pinckney stood guard as he departed, before escaping to a previously reconnoitred hide-out. Fighter Command would have been briefed not to shoot down the captured plane, which would have flown with its undercarriage lowered as a means of identification.

British boffins needed an undamaged FW 190 to strip down and discover the secrets of its fantastic performance and Pinckney's amazing scheme to hijack one was approved by the top brass. However, just before the pair were due to embark on what appeared to be a near 'suicide' mission, a Nazi pilot got lost in a fierce Channel dogfight with a Polish Spitfire squadron and landed by mistake at RAF Pembrey in Carmarthen in a brand-new FW 190. Quill was mightily relieved when the so-called 'Operation Airthief' was subsequently cancelled, but the redoubtable Pinckney was deeply disappointed, even though their chances of success, or even survival, had been very low.

Bold and brave though Pinckney was, however, even he could not cheat such massive odds indefinitely and he later vanished without trace on Operation Speedwell, a top-secret cloak and dagger SAS raid in Italy in September 1943, just before the Italian capitulation. He had spent months specially training a band of hand-picked SAS for this high-profile mission which, it was planned, he would command from start to finish. It was to have a crucial benefit to the Allied invasion of Italy, which began almost simultaneously, as the raiders disrupted supplies of tanks, troops and materiel to the fighting front. However, as said, Pinckney had badly injured his back during a previous operation and, according to comrades who survived Operation Speedwell, was in pain and had secretly had a freezing treatment to deaden and mask the injury. He stubbornly evaded all attempts to ground him from taking part in the mission.

Although nothing is known for certain of the manner in which he met his death, survivors of the mission believe he had a heavy landing in the rough terrain and was probably captured by a special Italian or German unit trained to hunt down the SAS parachutists, possibly after being knocked unconscious or being further injured during the landing. His existing back injury, if worsened during the drop, would have been a potentially fatal handicap and would have prevented him from defending himself. If he was captured, as is highly likely – and even German records fail to state his fate, he would almost certainly have been shot as a saboteur under Hitler's special Commando Order. Many of the SAS who were taken prisoner faced harrowing torture in an attempt to extract vital information, though most bravely gave nothing away. Exactly what happened in Pinckney's case is still tantalisingly uncertain.

The mission for the tiny SAS group under his command was to parachute into the mountains in the far north of Italy to blow up trains in tunnels to block the supply of German tanks and reinforcements being rushed to counter the Allied invasion in the far south. The survivors of Pinckney's brave band, numbering six men, achieved just that, as has been recorded in Sgt Daniels' stirring eyewitness account. As Pinckney parachuted down with his characteristic 'Whoop!' war cry as he left the plane, his last known words to Sgt Stokes who had followed him drifting down slowly in mid-air, were 'Watch your drift, Stokes.' Stokes was seen to wave to acknowledge the order, but from then on there was only silence.

Pinckney's immaculate War Record deserves a more in-depth look, however. The burly 28-year-old was a 6 ft 3 in powerhouse of pure determination and had already distinguished himself in some incredible exploits. But he had also proved himself to be a calm, dedicated and highly honourable leader of men and certainly not out for 'death or glory', despite the dangerous nature of most of his missions. He also shunned the idea of medals, though had he lived, he would surely have received many.

Pinckney had taken part in the successful Commando raid on the Lofoten Islands off the Norwegian coast earlier in the war and was furious at being ordered to withdraw due to an unopposed enemy air attack. Later, on a training exercise on Salisbury Plain, a blacked-up Pinckney was bayoneted through the arm by an over-enthusiastic sentry. Far from being angry, Pinckney congratulated the man for his alertness and he was rewarded with promotion to corporal! He then took part in raids on the Channel Islands before being selected for the SAS.

Pinckney quickly gained a reputation for ice-cold bravery among the Winged Dagger men and was soon recognised as a born leader. But on survival training, he tested his men's stomachs with some amazing, stomach-churning concoctions including grasshoppers, butterflies and snails! Pinckney's unshakeable conviction was that SAS men should be prepared to eat anything behind the lines to survive, including wild plants. This has since become a routine part of modern SAS survival training.

But it was in Sicily that Pinckney showed cool gallantry way beyond the call of duty. He travelled deep behind the lines on a solo mission for the American 2nd Corps to gain an accurate picture of the enemy positions. At one point, he lay hidden in scrub less than 20 yd from a German machine-gun post, quietly sketching his clandestine observations. Unfortunately, at this point the gunners decided to burn down the surrounding area to get a clearer field of fire and Pinckney was gradually engulfed in flames and searing heat. Maintaining incredible nerve and self-control, he remained still as the fire licked ever nearer his meagre hiding place, grasping stones in each hand to beat out the flames as quietly as possible. He managed this in the nick of time before the German soldiers saw him and opened fire. It was a very close call, but Pinckney returned to the American lines after three days with a complete sketch of the German positions – intelligence of inestimable value to the American allies, which undoubtedly saved countless lives.

Former 2nd SAS Major Roy Farran, one of the Regiment's most decorated and legendary soldiers, has described Pinckney as a 'larger than life' glutton for adventure. He said: 'Philip was the bravest of the brave, a true British type of hero.'

REG SEEKINGS – A FORMIDABLE 'ORIGINAL'

Tough, dependable Reg Seekings was one of the priceless characters of the Special Air Service, who is remembered with great pride and affection by the Regiment to this day. Brave, resilient and highly decorated, he was a great favourite with his commanding officers David Stirling and Paddy Mayne. He could always be relied on to do the right things in a tight corner – and crack a joke to bolster morale among his comrades when necessary.

Sgt Seekings took part in most of the famous desert raids, from the first baptisms of fire for L Detachment at Tmimi and Gazala, to the highly destructive later missions at Sirte, Tamet, Berka, Buerat, Benina, Fuka and Benghazi, which wreaked such havoc on the Axis airforces and helped to change the course of the Desert Campaign. Seekings had an uncanny ability to detect the smell of high-octane aviation fuel at a great distance and so helped to guide desert patrols as they approached their enemy airfield targets. Ironically, in his latter years, he could not abide the smell of petrol, or anything that was similar, or reminded him of it. However, such foibles are common among men who have seen such a large amount of action at close quarters as he did.

The part Seekings played in the desert victories reads like a glorious version of the regimental roll of battle honours, and he later displayed even more deeds of valour in the raids in support of the invasions of Sicily, Italy and continental Europe, fighting his way through to see the final victory in Germany in 1945. Seekings' story is so interwoven with that of the other members of the SAS that many aspects have already been covered elsewhere in this book. To avoid repetition, some tales that have not been told elsewhere, and which help to throw more light on the exploits of a very special and unforgettable 'Original', are detailed here.

At Termoli, one of the hardest battles the Special Raiding Squadron (SRS) ever fought, Seekings had to report to Paddy Mayne and tell him that a serious counter-attack was underway. The Germans had bolstered their superior forces with crack troops of the 1st Parachute Division, brought in especially for the purpose from the Anzio beach-head area. The situation became critical when an impending break through was reported. As Seekings hurried to a monastery, which was being used as SRS headquarters, shells began raining down in support of the attack. As other Termoli veterans have testified, what happened next was pure British, or more accurately Irish, coolness personified.

After Seekings had battled bravely through the welter of shells he found Paddy Mayne, the SRS commander, was playing snooker with some other officers, including the Medical Officer Phil Gunn. He was continuing with the game unconcernedly just as though he was back in his local club at Newtownards on a peacetime afternoon. After receiving Seekings' urgent report, though shells were now landing close outside and rattling the building, Mayne insisted on finishing his next shot then, and only then, ordered all his available forces to get up to the cemetery to meet and beat the German attack, which included tanks. Seekings and the others who witnessed this typical piece of Mayne mystique were suitably impressed by his sang-froid in the face of such colossal danger, and the incident has since become a much-related piece of regimental folklore.

Just after Termoli, which was the last operation carried out by the SRS (1st SAS) in Italy, another raid was proposed. It promised to be a suicide mission which could have spelled the end for Seekings, Paddy Mayne and many of the cream of the veterans of the SAS, who were still exhausted by the fierce struggle to defend Termoli. Perhaps more than any other, this incident underlines Mayne's sheer fearlessness and also his deep, but seldom stated, personal ambition to win the ultimate prize for valour. It also highlights Seekings' bravery and willingness to follow his commander no matter what the odds or chances of survival.

The crack British Guards Division had twice before attempted to cross the strongly defended Sangro River and spearhead a further general advance of the Allied army, but had been repulsed with heavy casualties. The SRS (SAS) were asked to do the job and Seekings bravely volunteered to go in with his own troop. After his loyal sergeant's unhesitating acceptance of what appeared to be a one-way ticket to a glorious, but certain, death, Lt Col Mayne then said he intended to join the party too and asked confidentially if Seekings was a good swimmer. Seekings, recalling the conversation in Bradford and Dillon's *Rogue Warrior of the SAS*, said: 'I told him I was good enough.

We reckoned that if we were lucky enough to get a line across, the rest could follow.' Even if the operation had been attempted under cover of darkness, it appeared to have little realistic chance of success. The raging torrent of machine-gun bullets and mortars had already claimed numerous brave men's lives. However, Paddy calmly replied to Seekings: 'By the way, I've been told there are two VCs for this. I've put my name on one. You put yours on the other.' He was deadly serious.

Luckily for the SRS, Corps headquarters shelved the scheme at the last minute. This 'mission impossible' was realised to be beyond the scope of even the superhuman stalwarts of the SAS, who were by this stage of the war beginning to be appreciated in many quarters for their true worth and as being too valuable a resource to waste. Instead, the SRS men were sent for a well-earned rest to Molfetta, on the east coast of Italy near Bari. But the fact that Seekings was willing, with Mayne, to take on such an impossible task amply shows the calibre of the man – one of a handful of comrades who the legendary Irishman respected as an equal spirit.

Leading from the Front

Brian Franks, Bill Stirling,
Eric Barkworth

THE ICE COLD COURAGE OF BRIAN FRANKS

Lt Col Brian Franks DSO, MC was one of the top-class officers of the British Army who found no difficulty whatsoever in fitting into the unconventional hurly-burly of life behind enemy lines with the SAS. Franks was an old Etonian public schoolboy and, unlike many of his contemporaries who served with distinction in the Guards and other leading regiments, he chose Special Forces, initially the Commandos and later the SAS, becoming one of the Regiment's most famous commanding officers. He re-established 21 SAS Regiment after the shock disbandment of all SAS units after the end of the Second World War, laying the cornerstone of Britain's modern-day, world-leading force.

When the chips were down in the thickest of action during the Second World War, Lt Col Franks led from the front with great bravery, coolness, intelligence and resourcefulness. He was in good company in the SAS and SBS, however, as not all fellow old Etonians followed the traditional route into the established top-drawer regiments. Fellow scholars Lord Jellicoe and David Sutherland of the SBS were among those who volunteered for exciting, but unconventional, warfare and became legends in their own right.

Paddy Mayne, Jock Lewes, Fitzroy Maclean and many others who were such outstanding soldiers in the SAS were also former public schoolboys from privileged backgrounds. In sharp contrast, many of their troops were working class and, in some cases, from exceedingly poor and streetwise communities, where they had learned their trade in rough house fighting the hard way and were well used to using their wits to survive what was, in the Depression-hit 1930s, the harshest of upbringings. Amazingly, both sets of people worked together harmoniously to form the tough but well-disciplined and versatile SAS and SBS, whose members could turn their hands as easily to parachuting into action or surprise seaborne landings by specialised craft, as they could to a conventional attack or defensive role.

It was at the desperate defence of Termoli, involving the Special Raiding Squadron (re-named SAS) and Commando units that Franks' leadership qualities really came to the fore, however. His inspirational command was noted and admired by all present as the raiders faced a welter of shells and savage attacks by superior German forces. The SRS had been ordered to take Termoli, on the Adriatic coast, due east of Rome, which was then occupied by a substantial German force. The mission seemed on the face of it a difficult but reasonable task, but the high command had not counted on the ferocity of the Germans' reaction, or the top quality of their defending troops.

By this time, at the beginning of October 1943, the Americans had captured Naples, but just north of the city the Germans were dug in and well protected in heavily defended positions. The SRS was going into action with two similarly tough and well-prepared British units, No. 3 Commando and No. 40 Commando. The assault group left Manfredonia on the Adriatic south of Termoli in an American LCI landing craft with two key bridges as its main objective. The SRS swiftly advanced inland from the beach-head and over the railway, then through No. 3 Commando's bridgehead and up the road from Termoli towards Vasto, a coastal town about 10 miles further north.

However, the Germans, highly alarmed at the possibility of a tactical threat to the north of Rome, rallied rapidly and counter-attacked violently the very next day. They used seasoned troops of the 1st Parachute Division, some of

Germany's finest fighting troops, which had come across from Anzio, the graveyard of countless Allied service-men in the costly battle for Italy. The Germans also switched to the east coast the 16th Panzer Division, which was being held in reserve near Naples. Their orders, which later fell into British hands, were to re-capture Termoli 'at all costs' and to drive the British back into the sea. But for the tenacity and fighting skills of the SRS and their Commando comrades, they would have succeeded, but the cost was high.

Heavy shelling fell upon the SRS positions and there were serious casualties. Virtually a whole section was wiped out when what was thought to be an unlucky mortar shell hit a truck load of SRS on its way to repulse a German attack near the cemetery, which included tanks. The men were carrying special detonators and grenades in their packs and never stood a chance as these ignited in an instant, and there were several civilian casualties too. The only survivors were the section commander Capt Johnny Wiseman and desert veteran Reg Seekings, who was just kicking the tailgate of the truck down as the section scrambled aboard. Wiseman had joined the SAS as a young 2nd Lieutenant in the Western Desert from the North Somerset Yeomanry.

Seekings said: 'It blew us to hell. Mine was the only pack not to explode. I was covered in blood and bits of flesh and stank for days after it.' Wiseman, stunned to the core at losing so many of his men in one tragic moment, also could not believe that he had survived unwounded. He had actually been sitting beside the driver inside the truck when the shell hit. The driver and the rest of the men were killed or mortally wounded. Wiseman said 'there was not a living soul' around him. But he walked out of the vehicle untouched to fight on through the rest of the war. A total of twenty-nine SRS men were killed.

Almost all the German troops facing the comparatively light British forces defending the town were elite paratroops, with ample reserves and heavy weapons support. However, although many all-out attempts were made to regain Termoli through its cemetery and down the railway line by smashing a way through to annihilate the stubborn British raiders, they all failed. It was Paddy Mayne's belief that the enemy soldiers had insufficient morale to advance too far forward as they feared being cut off – a situation that they had faced several times on the retreat since Sicily. Consequently, their attack was abandoned when the threat to the town was greatest and the Germans were forced to withdraw with heavy casualties.

The Commando Brigadier was J.F. Durnford-Slater, a seasoned and well-respected senior commander and his brigade major was the calm and collected Brian Franks. Roy Farran, one of the veterans of 2nd SAS who saw some of the fiercest fighting at Termoli at first hand, and indeed throughout most of the war, was particularly impressed with Franks' calm approach when under fire during one of the most dangerous and prolonged bombardments. Soldiers of all sides, even hardened veterans, detest being under heavy shelling when they are powerless to strike back and only have the option to grit their teeth and get through as best they can.

Farran candidly described his own fears when trapped by this bout of particularly accurate and deadly enemy shell fire at Termoli: 'The building had been hit only a few minutes before by a shell which killed the staff captain. Brigadier Durnford-Slater, and especially the Brigade Major, Brian Franks, struck me as being incredibly cool amongst it all. When we were led out of the position in the windows of the hotel it was humiliating but I felt forced to duck at every shell. Brian Franks walked on as if nothing had happened!' Franks was no ordinary commander, as the SAS were soon to find out in their most deadly arena of combat, the treacherous forests of France against the murderous SS.

As the Allies broke out of the Normandy invasion beach-head in August 1944 and began to sweep through France, Franks played a leading part in one of the toughest SAS missions, Operation Loyton.

At the beginning of August, Franks, now a lieutenant colonel commanding 2nd SAS, was ordered to operate in the area between the Baccarat–St-Dié road and the

French–German border, with a force numbering well under a hundred men. His instructions were to cause the greatest harassment to the Germans by disrupting their transport, supply routes, vehicles and lines of communication. Another major task would be to gather as much intelligence as possible about the movement of enemy forces, especially any that could have tactical significance regarding the current main battle lines and ammunition dumps or fuel supplies. Locations of headquarters close to the front and any other opportunist targets that could be hit by air strikes brought in by radio were of particular importance.

Capt Druce and Lt Dill parachuted in as the initial reconnaissance party to meet the Maquis Resistance men and women and prepare the dropping zone for Franks and his main body of SAS. It was arranged for the main party to drop on the night of 31 August near St Remy, but a traitor among the Maquis had to be shot dead after trying to give the game away. As the raiders dropped from 1,100 ft this man fired his Sten gun in a bid to alert the Germans. Fortunately his plan failed, but Franks was not impressed and the incident did not bode well for the future chances of combined co-operation.

Loyton then got fully underway with Franks' SAS raiders killing enemy soldiers in ambushes, blowing up vehicles and cutting railway lines. Surprise was total as the enemy was caught unprepared initially, but this situation was not to last as the Germans organised themselves for a mass retaliation. Franks had originally intended to use the local Maquis Resistance fighters to work alongside his raiding parties, but now changed his mind as he realised that close liaison with them would have jeopardised the whole operation. From now onwards, he constantly shifted his camps and operated independently from bases that were secret and secure. Some of the other SAS groups were virtually wiped out by lapses in Maquis security, while other raiders found Resistance members to be brave and trustworthy and that their local knowledge was invaluable in saving lives. It was a lottery that Franks was not prepared to gamble on as his party was so deeply ensconced in enemy territory. Despite the considerable success of the operation, the SAS did not get away scot-free and some of Franks' men had to suffer the fury of the Germans in Gestapo cells, torture, degradation and even execution.

With plastic explosive mines, the raiders blew up two enemy troop trucks on 8 September, killing the German soldiers in them. They then entered the hamlet of La Chapellotte and found themselves face to face with a German patrol. A brisk gunfight ensued at point-blank range, with the crack shots of the SAS winning the day. The team sent the Germans scattering and then departed rapidly themselves to try to keep one step ahead of the inevitable retaliation. SS troops and Alsatian dogs later surrounded the raiders, but all somehow managed to slip away. Local Maquis played an invaluable role in locating any SAS men who had become separated from the main group during and after missions, collecting them and returning them to their units. The missions carried out as part of Operation Loyton during the first ten days of September were so successful that the Germans were forced to send more troops to north-eastern France in a vain bid to curtail SAS activities. Franks' bold scheme was to deceive the Germans into believing there were far more of his men present than the mere eighty-seven he actually had.

The success of Franks' plan is illustrated by a post-war report which reveals that two complete German divisions of top-quality fighting troops had been detached from the main battle to try to counter the devastating effects of the Loyton raiders, who were becoming an exceptionally painful thorn in the side of the German forces throughout the area. However, because of the large numbers of German troops sent to suppress the SAS, Franks' job became increasingly difficult. In effect, the SAS were paying the price for being so good at their tasks.

By 11 September the Loyton band were in danger of being surrounded, pinned down and eliminated by vastly superior enemy forces. It was a familiar story and one that the wily SAS commander fully expected and intended to avoid. The trick was knowing precisely the right time to call it a day and pull out. However, this time, the writing was firmly on the wall. It was time to depart – and quickly. In attempting to fight his way out of the unfolding trap, Franks detached one group under Lt Black to create a diversion to keep the encircling Germans busy while the rest escaped. Franks and the rest got away, but Black and his men were captured after putting up a titanic struggle. Lt Black, Sgt Terry-Hall, Cpls Iveson and Winder and Pts Lloyd, Crozier, Dowling and Salter became aware too late of the Wehrmacht and Gestapo units surrounding them.

The eight SAS men tried desperately to slip away but after a 4-hour gun battle, Black was wounded in the leg and finally the SAS men's ammunition ran out. German soldiers approached and after a fierce hand-to-hand battle, took them prisoner. The group was taken to the Gestapo prison at Strasbourg, where they were all interrogated and tortured. Lt Black and his comrades were then taken back to the St-Dié area and murdered in a wood nearby, joining a long list of soldiers who had become victims of the war crimes perpetrated by the Gestapo and SS.

Meanwhile, on the night of 19 September Lt Col Franks had received an air drop of reinforcements and six jeeps, which were equipped with either twin-barrelled quick-firing Vickers K machine-guns or a .5 Browning heavy machine-gun. Franks decided to use these vehicles to hit the Germans hard deep behind their lines, while other members of his group continued with intelligence-gathering patrols on foot.

On 23 September four jeeps, one commanded by Franks himself, were travelling through the Celles valley on a fighting patrol when they cunningly joined a German convoy and destroyed the leading truck and three staff cars in a welter of machine-gun fire. Then Franks and Dill drove across country towards Allarmont, coming under fire north-east of Celles. Franks' jeep overturned while trying to get into a position in which to engage the enemy and Dill drove smack into an ambush. There followed a fierce battle against more than eighty SS and Wehrmacht troops, during which the SAS men amazingly succeeded in fighting their way out on foot, still shooting as they melted into the countryside.

By the end of September, the pace of the main battle was slowing down as the Germans had succeeded in stabilising the front line mainly due to a brilliant improvised scheme by Gen Model. Although the SAS continued to harass the enemy at every opportunity, Franks found he was too close behind the lines for comfort and his men had, in any event, already used up all their explosives and most of their ammunition. It was time to bring Operation Loyton to an end.

On 9 October, Franks ordered his teams to make their way to the west and make contact with the USA Army. A special rendezvous was established for stragglers infiltrating back through the lines which was kept open until 12 October, by which time most of the Loyton survivors had returned. Sixty-three of Franks' 2nd SAS men passed safely through the German lines to meet the US Seventh Army, but thirty-one did not return – a high casualty rate. This outstanding SAS operation, under Franks' masterly control, had succeeded in bringing the battle to the very gates of Germany.

BILL STIRLING – THE GREAT SACRIFICE

Lt Col Bill Stirling, brother of SAS founder David, carried out one of the bravest and most honourable deeds in the Regiment's history during the Second World War. His act of courage and self-sacrifice was not on the battlefield and his opponents were those in higher command at British and Allied headquarters. The crunch came on the run up to Operation Overlord, the historic D-Day invasion of France designed to liberate the whole of Western Europe from Nazi domination.

Bill Stirling, the able and respected commanding officer of the 2nd SAS Regiment, had, since just before the Allied invasion of Sicily in 1943, fought a fierce running battle with the high command over the proposed use and alleged misuse of his SAS raiding parties in the Italian theatre of war. He was taking up the case already argued so passionately by famous brother David.

Just before the invasion of Sicily, Stirling wrote a strongly worded memo to senior headquarters staff at 15th Army Group, dated 1 July 1943, explaining the exciting scope of his command and how this potential was not being fulfilled to its greatest and most effective extent. Details noted in John Strawson's *A History of the SAS Regiment* record a familiar pattern of passionate argument that the SAS should be expanded and used to its fullest capabilities. This was tempered by a growing frustration with the planners' seemingly limited grasp of the tactical possibilities of behind-the-lines operations at this crucial stage in the war. In the memo Stirling stressed:

A very high degree of individual training will make it possible to work in far smaller parties than other troops where vital tasks exist and which cannot conveniently or economically be tackled by regular formations and, more particularly, which require action far behind the enemy's lines . . .

After a few months, should requirements appear for the disruption of Italian communications via Albania to Greece, a force of 300 men could work over hundreds of miles in up to 140 parties with shattering effects.

In Italy, jeep patrols brought in by gliders could fight their way to vital objectives with explosives by the ton. In concert with a major operation, mountainous areas could be infested with small parties, which if sufficiently numerous, will completely saturate local defences and paralyse communications . . .

Second SAS Regiment is prepared to accept rough, unreconnoitred landings which can easily be undertaken with imperceptible increases in dropping casualties and advantages too obvious to mention.

But, in arguing for the SAS to be used strategically in an integral role as part of the main plan, not in a subsidiary or diversionary way, bitter and undisguised opposition from the higher command staff soon crept in.

Towards the end of 1943 Italy's change of sides to the Allied cause provided a golden but fleeting opportunity for exploitation through widespread use of behind-the-lines SAS raiding parties. Lt Col Stirling again exchanged tough words with the top brass, this time with the staff at Supreme Allied Headquarters in Italy, who also seemed to have trouble in fully grasping the most effective role for the British Special Forces. The planners simply refused to allow Stirling's men to attack behind the lines in sufficient strength, as he argued they must.

Stirling wanted to parachute in a large number of fully supported and supplied SAS parties behind the lines which, he claimed could have had a major influence on the Salerno landings bridgehead, cutting rail supplies and German reinforcements in a decisive stranglehold. He especially wanted to drop the SAS into the triangle in Northern Italy enclosed by Florence, Bologna and Spezia where the teams would be able to use high explosives to do huge damage to the key focus of the railway system, which the Germans needed to rush reinforcements to the front. However, the planners in their wisdom stubbornly remained unconvinced and refused to allow operations on this scale.

The hierarchy partially relented and permitted a token mission to take place, but only after Stirling had applied further pressure. A handful of men were allowed to parachute in and managed to derail fourteen trains in the successful Operation Speedwell. It was clear proof of what might have been achieved. But Stirling knew that many more men would be needed to disrupt the network adequately and disable it for any length of time. Frustrations deepened considerably on Stirling's part, though strictly controlled at this stage by established military etiquette, but the powder-keg conflict simmered on with increasing intensity. It was soon to explode into major controversy with widespread and irrevocable repercussions as Allied intentions turned to the long-awaited invasion of mainland Europe.

Lt Col Stirling was provoked into launching his most blistering attack on the planners yet when they unveiled their top-secret scheme for the deployment of the SAS in France as part of the massive Second Front. These proposed missions were rightly perceived as near suicidal by Stirling and constituted the last straw that shattered his long-suffering patience with the red-tape bureaucrats. Allied planners insisted that the SAS troops should be parachuted in force into zones just behind the beach-heads, effectively as a disruptive element between the defending enemy infantry on the coastal areas and his large panzer tank reserves inland.

Stirling was furious, arguing that his men would be trapped and decimated in such a restricted area. They would also be unable to carry out their missions effectively or for very long periods without their essential mobility and flexibility in manoeuvre and supply. To anyone who knew anything about the workings of the SAS, it was sheer lunacy. Stirling dug in his heels and refused point blank to be swayed. The embattled colonel insisted that the proposed scheme would be a criminal waste of the special skills and capabilities of his elite troops, who should be used instead to create mayhem deep behind the enemy lines, destroying German supply routes, communications and advance headquarters, as his brother's raiders had so famously done in North Africa.

In the midst of this momentous debate about which fighting role was appropriate for the SAS, Lt Col Stirling wrote a despairing memo to the decision-makers, contained in the following extract from Bradford and Dillon's *Rogue Warrior of the SAS*. The frustration felt in Stirling's every fibre is almost palpable: 'We should be used as a stiffener to SOE [Special Operations Executive] and the Maquis. We did that kind of work well in Italy. I don't think the question before you is whether SAS troops are worthwhile or not, but under whose command they should come.'

Stirling doggedly stuck to his guns and finally won the argument over SAS deployment and ensured the preservation of the entire SAS – but at the cost of his own resignation. It is almost certain that he deliberately took this decision knowing full well that this was the only way to change drastically the course of events. Thankfully for the SAS forces then, and now, his noble gesture succeeded. However, it was a senseless waste that such an able and popular commander and superb tactician had to be lost at such a crucial time in the war due to bureaucratic intransigence. Stirling had narrowly failed to negotiate the tricky diplomatic tightrope so nimbly trod by his illustrious brother.

As events were to prove, it was a tactical victory that was absolutely vital for the future development of the SAS and the survival of so many of its brave raiders. Countless lives were saved by Stirling's selfless stand. All experts agree that if the short-sighted planners had had their way, hundreds of SAS officers and men would have been needlessly wiped out within weeks of the invasion in France, with the efforts of the Foreign SAS seriously diluted. It is no exaggeration to say that but for Stirling's courageous last stand, France could easily have become the graveyard where the SAS dream was buried for good.

Bill Stirling's Career and Influence on Others

Stirling's command had begun brightly in 1943 when he proudly took charge of the newly formed 2nd SAS in Algeria, setting up an intensive training base at Philippeville. The terrain was much more rugged and difficult to traverse in jeeps and trucks and on foot than the desert haunts of 1st SAS, and the enemy positions were static and well defended. Initially, therefore, the 2nd SAS raiders found this restricted typical SAS operations, but the unit used the breathing space to weld itself into a highly effective fighting force, growing in confidence and expertise with each successive operation.

Bill Stirling and brother David were cast in a similar mould, both possessing fiercely determined and independent characters. They also looked very much alike. Both were tall, slim, handsome, well educated, self-assured, immensely capable and had the utter loyalty and respect of the men serving under them. David Stirling's capture by the Germans in Tunisia, as the war in North Africa drew to a victorious close for the Allies, came as an enormous shock to the fighting soldiers of the SAS and, not least, to brother Bill, who now took up the torch to ensure the SAS continued to develop and grow in the way his brother had planned it should.

David Stirling's removal happened just as he hoped that the SAS would be the first unit from Eighth Army to link up with the American First Army, which had earlier landed in Algeria and was now trapping the remaining German forces in a gigantic pincer movement. David Stirling was sure that the kudos gained from this high-profile mission would help in the on-going crusade to persuade those in higher command that the SAS was an essential unit that deserved to be expanded. As John Strawson says in *A History of the SAS Regiment*, Stirling later explained that his motive was not simply to contact the American First Army, but to sow the seed for the formation of a full SAS Brigade. David Stirling said:

> My plan was to bring in my brother Bill's 2nd SAS Regiment and to divide down my own Regiment, which had grown beyond the official establishment of a full regiment into the nucleus of a third one.
>
> This would enable me to keep one regiment in each of the three main areas – the eastern Mediterranean, the central Mediterranean–Italy area and the future Second Front. I felt it was vital to get intervention and support from a more important formation than Middle East Headquarters. The first step in this plan seemed to be to acquire the sympathy of the 1st Army's top brass and to consult my brother Bill, who had recently arrived on the 1st Army front, as to the state of the

game at the War Office. I was conscious that the
reputation of the SAS would be greatly enhanced if it
could claim to be the first fighting unit to establish
contact between the Eighth (British) and (American)
1st armies.

David Stirling, ever the opportunist PR man where his
regimental brainchild was concerned, personally took out a
patrol to complete this link-up, but due to a combination of
sheer misfortune and the fact that the area chosen near the
Gabes Gap was not ideal raiding country, the scheme
backfired badly and resulted in his capture. From his prison
cell, via clandestine communication, Stirling nominated his
successor in command of 1st SAS, the legendary Paddy
Mayne, who Stirling said was 'exactly the man' the SAS
force needed as its new leader. The way events turned out
later in Italy, France, Belgium, Holland and Germany, this
proved to be an understatement.

Meanwhile, the 2nd SAS under Lt Col Bill Stirling, who
gained many recruits from No. 62 Commando, a raiding
unit recently sent out from Britain, had enough trained
men to unleash raids on Pantelleria, Lampedusa, Sicily
and Sardinia. But probably the hardest action in Italy for
a contingent of Bill Stirling's 2nd SAS men, in
conjunction with Paddy Mayne's temporarily renamed
Special Raiding Squadron (1st SAS) and some teak-tough
Commando units, was at Termoli on the eastern coast of
Italy, where the combined British Special Forces
successfully resisted concerted attacks by much stronger
and better-supported elite German units.

Maj Roy Farran, later to win lasting fame in Italy and
France, was part of Bill Stirling's 2nd SAS and played a key
role in the hard-fought Termoli action, now one of the
Regiment's prominent battle honours. In his book *Winged
Dagger* he describes the strenuous training programme,
instituted by Lt Col Stirling, which really sorted out the
men from the boys just as today's infamous selection
process is designed to do for the modern SAS. He said:

For the first ten days, my body ached so much that I could only listen with open mouth to the tales of the old hands in the mess, but gradually I became fit enough to be restored to my normal low intelligence. My seniority gave me a post as second-in-command to Sandy Scratchley, who was commanding a newly raised squadron then in training for a landing in Sicily.

About a fortnight before the Allied landings in Sicily, Bill Stirling revealed the exact nature of our task in a lecture in the operations hut. We were to land a short time ahead of the Highland Division, seize a certain lighthouse which was suspected of housing a number of machine guns so sighted as to be able to sweep the beaches on which the landings were to take place. He showed us an air photograph of the island on which the lighthouse was situated and left us to work out our plan.

He had a great knack for appreciating the crux of a problem and we readily agreed to his wise modifications. At the time, most of the unit was much more concerned with large parachute operations in northern Sicily, Sardinia and Italy, so that we were left very much to ourselves in our minor tasks.

The landing on Sicily was on the tip of Cape Passero. In the event, it was unopposed and the lighthouse was occupied without resistance. Italian morale collapsed rapidly with the sheer weight of the Allied bombardment.

When Stirling was given his alarming ultimatum about the use of the SAS in the D-Day behind-the-lines drops and the tension boiled over into outright rebellion and resignation, his men were stunned and extremely angry at the tragic outcome. The scent of mutiny was in the air. On Stirling's shock resignation, Maj Roy Farran said:

This was a serious situation for a volunteer unit since our main allegiance was to our Colonel, in whom we had the greatest confidence. I knew the full facts and contemplated resigning, since I fully supported Bill Stirling's views over our proper role.

If I had decided to go, almost all the regiment would have gone with me.

As it was, Bill Stirling took the broad view and asked me to stay under Brian Franks, whose behaviour I had so admired during the battle of Termoli. I was very keen to fight with the SAS in France and, as far as I was concerned, what Bill Stirling said went. I agreed to stay. I have never regretted it since, for Brian Franks proved to be one of the best commanding officers one could wish for and at least we knew that we were to be finally employed in exactly the way Bill Stirling had visualised.

As it turned out, when the SAS returned to the UK to reform, ready for the invasion in 1944, sanity had fully returned. The SAS Regiment was almost doubled in size by the HQ staff and the command structure placed under 21 Army Group, headed by Montgomery and the Supreme Allied Headquarters of Gen Eisenhower. As Lt Col Bill Stirling had so passionately predicted, in France, and later in Belgium and Holland, SAS parties properly deployed deep behind enemy lines successfully attacked and destroyed Nazi forces, communications, headquarters and gathered intelligence, operating with local Resistance fighters and finally in Germany engaged in countless crucial missions, including key reconnaissance, hit-and-run attacks and the capture of war criminals. The decision mainly to drop the SAS raiders deeply behind the significant invasion zones on the Normandy beach-head was completely and utterly vindicated.

History records that David Stirling was the famous founder of the SAS. However, it is no exaggeration to say that without the courageous stand of his brother Lt Col Bill Stirling the Regiment could easily have come to an untimely end in the fields and forests of France in 1944, crushed by panzers and overwhelming Nazi forces instead of blossoming into the world-leading force it is today.

ERIC BARKWORTH – SAS AVENGER

Maj Eric 'Bill' Barkworth was unorthodox, dedicated and many would say outstandingly gifted: Indeed, shortly before he died in November 1990, SAS founder David Stirling proudly described Maj Barkworth in a personal letter to me as an 'exceedingly efficient and adventurous intelligence officer'. One of Barkworth's memorable – and most poignant – achievements after the end of the war in Europe was in successfully locating the bodies of most of the SAS raiders who were tortured, murdered and secretly buried by the SS and Gestapo in France under Hitler's infamous Commando Order. He and his crack unit also managed to track down and bring to justice several of those responsible for the barbaric war crimes committed on captured SAS, who were acting legitimately as serving soldiers, in uniform and entitled to the benefits of the Hague Convention like any other captured soldiers.

Yet despite his undoubted attributes, many of Barkworth's former comrades have testified that he was undoubtedly eccentric, as many clever men often are, and that his highly individual methods sometimes rankled with and angered officers from other units. He could, however, always be relied on to get results, often under the most difficult circumstances and accompanied by intense pressure from those in higher command. One of his finest qualities was that he was extremely loyal to the soldiers who worked for him and to the fighting soldiers of the Regiment. He was a strong, confident character and like others in the SAS, notably Lt Cols Bill Stirling and Paddy Mayne, could at times become highly irritated with those in higher command when he perceived the best interests of the Regiment were not being served.

Barkworth was at times rude to his superiors, and even on occasion to full-blown generals and consistently had a scathing disdain for Army protocol. For instance, there were occasions when he would walk into an officers' mess improperly dressed without batting an eye, and he was not averse to bending, if not breaking, rules on occasion if it suited him. However, his exceptional ability and high value to the Regiment meant that such foibles were largely tolerated or ignored.

Barkworth's team's thoroughness and stamina in sifting a mountain of information that emanated from numerous intelligence sources and quickly getting this data out to the fighting units by covert radio messages ensured that casualties among the ranks of the behind-the-lines raiders, though at times desperately heavy, were kept to a minimum. Especially in the wide-ranging and highly complex operations in France after D-Day, many SAS soldiers, NCOs and officers owed their lives to Barkworth and his dedicated team of NCO intelligence operatives – and their counterparts in 1st SAS, who were engaged in similar vital work. Accurate intelligence was the very lifeblood of a Special Force such as the SAS, which was taking high risks on a daily basis. This applied equally in North Africa, Italy and later in France, Belgium, Holland and Germany itself and there was no one better than Barkworth at the unique and testing mind games demanded by operations deep behind enemy lines against a cunning and often ruthless foe.

After going out to the Middle East with the Commandos earlier in the war, Barkworth volunteered for the SAS, joining the 2nd SAS Intelligence unit at Philippeville in Algeria in 1943. He assembled around him a team consisting of a handful of experienced NCOs, one of whom was my late father, Jack Morgan, described by Barkworth in a report to the SAS Intelligence Troop in England in 1944 as 'of very great value to the Intelligence section'. He served at Barkworth's right hand throughout the key campaigns. Maj Barkworth's men were by this crucial point of the war turning out an enormous amount of vital and detailed work. Jack Morgan's SAS intelligence comrades included CSM Fred 'Dusty' Rhodes, Arthur Relf, Intelligence Assault Sgt Sid Lunt and a few others. The unit was not only elite, but also operated with a minimum number of personnel, largely because of security, which was extremely tight.

Jack Morgan had served previously in the RASC as a lorry

driver in the Western Desert from 1941. He was strafed and bombed on numerous occasions while driving ammunition trucks and troops to the major battles flowing back and forth, up and down the North African coastline as the British, Commonwealth and Allied forces and their German and Italian opponents battled for supremacy. The fate of the entire war literally hung in the balance as Rommel threatened not only to take the vital Middle East oilfields, but also to achieve a decisive link up with the German armies in Russia.

When Rommel overran the 'impregnable' British fortress of Tobruk in 1942, Jack Morgan refused to surrender and, with a handful of comrades as passengers, drove his truck off into the desert, leaving behind the pursuing tanks and planes and deliberately got 'lost'. It was a brave act of stubborn defiance and initiative, which undoubtedly had a bearing on his later selection for the SAS. Jack navigated the truck, without a map or compass and with only the stars and his gut instinct to assist him, hundreds of miles back to the British lines at Alamein, where he was given a rousing reception for his miraculous escape. A guardian angel must have been watching over him, however, as approaching the British lines, he unwittingly drove the truck clean through the unmarked minefield. Minutes later, when he had gone for provisions for his hungry and thirsty men, a lone Stuka came over, dropped a bomb on the truck and tragically killed all the friends he had brought back so far to supposed safety.

Following this escapade, Jack was invited to try for SAS selection, passed with flying colours and joined Barkworth's elite band. He served in the final victory in the North African campaign and then moved overseas once more to take part in the Italian campaign, which was to cost the British and Allied forces so dearly and provide some of the sternest tests for the SAS raiders.

As the detailed planning for the mass SAS drops in support of the D-Day invasion got underway at a secluded large house near Kilmarnock, Scotland, morale soared as victory was at last in sight. Each and every member of the team was made to feel that they were a key link in Barkworth's crack intelligence chain. In all campaigns, Barkworth operated on a high degree of skill, cunning, knowledge and, at times, sheer bluff – and he encouraged his SAS operatives to use any psychological weapons at their disposal when interrogating prisoners, barring, naturally, resorting to any physical violence. A perfect example of this is a true and previously unpublished story told to me by my late father, who was detailed to interrogate two very arrogant German prisoners captured in Italy.

One was an officer and the other a corporal and though both were obviously apprehensive at being questioned by an SAS NCO, with good reason bearing in mind that all German units had at this stage of the war been ordered to shoot any SAS personnel they captured on Hitler's specific orders, neither would give any information about themselves or their units. Jack said: 'I could see that they were determined not to give a thing away and their sheer arrogance annoyed me, so I called the guard over and told him quietly to take the corporal outside to another hut, then to return and let loose a long burst from his Sten gun just outside the window. This he did, returning and snapping a smart salute, barking the words "I've carried out your orders, corporal."' The effect on the German officer was electric! He sank to his knees, begging for his life, pleading with the SAS interrogator not to have him shot. Needless to say, there was no intention at all of executing him, but Cpl Morgan now got much more information out of the by now trembling officer than he had hoped for in the first place – all without harming a hair on his head. It was a classic case of the successful effect of Barkworth's clever mental ploys and the triumph of cunning over brute force. It was later speculated among the SAS operatives that the German officer was likely a relatively brave man who would probably have resisted harsh treatment, but who had been crushed into submission by the power of his own imagination. It was by no means the only occasion when clever psychological warfare brought dramatic results. The SAS intelligence men were carefully chosen to operate on their own initiative using their wits and imagination, attributes that were often frowned upon in many of the regular Army units.

My father often spoke of Maj Barkworth after the war with genuine admiration and affection, describing the impressive success rate of his intelligence unit, which was achieved by skill and dedication and a phenomenal work rate which some, unfortunately, could not keep up with and were therefore forced to drop out. But Barkworth was also by necessity a hard taskmaster. The amount of intelligence needed for the post-D-Day drops in France, particularly, was colossal and exceedingly stressful for the teams involved. Both SAS intelligence squads run by Barkworth (2nd SAS) and Maj Mike Blackman (1st SAS) did exceptional work considering the fact that not only were there vast numbers of missions operating in Europe with hundreds of the 1st and 2nd fighting SAS participating, but also those of the French and Belgian SAS contingents to take into account.

Another tragic chore for the SAS intelligence men was having to receive and collate the harrowing and alarming tales of torture and execution that began to emanate from France in the weeks and months after the invasion, especially where the notorious SS and Gestapo units were operating in force. Hitler's secret Commando Order to execute all captured SAS and Commandos was further confirmed in the spring of 1944 when a report describing the chilling situation was received from Lt Quentin Hughes of 2nd SAS after his capture in Italy.

Hughes and five other SAS raiders were parachuted into Italy as part of Operation Pomegranate to destroy German aircraft at San Egido. He and another officer reached the target and placed Lewes bombs on seven aircraft. Unfortunately, one of the bombs exploded prematurely killing the other officer and badly wounding Hughes, resulting in his capture. At first he was well treated and taken to hospital, but during interrogation was told that when he recovered he would be handed over to the Gestapo and shot as a saboteur.

Fortunately for Hughes, a senior German staff officer who was also a patient was a Special Forces veteran of the assault on Fort Eben Emael in Belgium at the beginning of the war and sympathised with his plight. He and another colleague used their influence to ensure that Hughes was not handed over to the Gestapo, arranging for his papers to be altered stating he was a legitimate prisoner of war. At the last minute, Hughes was sent by train to the main prisoner clearing camp at Mantua, but escaped and found his way back to British lines. Hughes immediately wrote a lucid report warning that SAS parachutists who were captured would automatically be executed and this was passed to Airborne headquarters, at that time well into the complex planning for the D-Day drops.

After the war, Maj Barkworth issued a report claiming that Hughes' significant warning was, however, ignored at the time. He said that reference to other men of the Regiment who had not returned, or been reported as casualties, was explained away by the fact that the enemy probably wished to keep the SAS confused about the success of their operations. He recorded ruefully: 'It was not until the dead bodies of murdered prisoners had been found in France and a copy of the Commando Order in Italy in the autumn of 1944 that these actions of the Germans were taken seriously; even then, it was only in March 1945 that Eisenhower, the Allied Supreme Commander, made a wireless proclamation.'

In fairness, having talked to several of the wartime fighting SAS on this matter, the SAS already knew how brutal some units of the German forces, especially the SS, could be to prisoners, civilians or indeed anyone who got in their way. The general consensus in hindsight is that even if a comprehensive, general warning had been issued on the brink of D-Day it would, in practice, have made little difference. The crucial behind-the-lines drops simply had to take place in a country at that time seething with

SS and Gestapo units hell bent on the destruction of the feared SAS raiders, who wreaked untold havoc in the rear of the German forces from day one.

Although my father never spoke a word about his SAS activities to anyone outside the family nor divulged any of the sensitive information that he knew and guarded loyally even years after the war had ended, he did talk occasionally at home with great sadness of the horrific treatment that was meted out to some of the men he knew well. It shocked, angered and sickened all the men of SAS Intelligence who had briefed the troops for their dangerous missions just days before they left, never to return. One brave officer, who I now know to have been Maj Reynolds, was so badly beaten after capture in a brutal attempt to extract information that his bones came through his body. Almost unbelievable cruelty was perpetrated on SAS troops who were legitimate combat soldiers. Another wounded and helpless 1st SAS officer was beaten to death with rifle butts by SS soldiers. A courageous member of the French Resistance caught hiding petrol for the SAS jeep patrols was doused in petrol and burned alive. There were many other similar atrocities.

Yet during the war and for some period afterwards, many veterans confirm that few people in Britain had heard of the SAS, let alone knew anything of their outstanding exploits in the desert and later great sacrifices in occupied Europe. Secrecy was high among the SAS combatants and generally scrupulously well kept and, in fact, my father said people often mistook his now famous Winged Dagger badge and beret for a similar Polish badge and headgear. In addition, after the war had ended most of the SAS records mysteriously 'disappeared' while being moved to another destination in the UK, adding to the mystique surrounding the Regiment.

But now, as the war drew to a close, the SAS had not forgotten their comrades who had simply disappeared in France and Western Europe in the dangerous missions after D-Day and desperately wanted to find out what had happened to them. This was especially true of

the most senior officers in the Regiment, among them Lt Col
Franks, who had commanded Operation Loyton, whose losses
had been particularly heavy with no trace found of the
missing SAS men. This mystery and several others were
eventually solved by Maj Barkworth and his specially selected
War Crimes Investigation Team which was sent to Germany
after the end of hostilities, as recorded in the excellently
researched *The Secret Hunters* by Anthony Kemp. Barkworth
successfully tracked down many of the war criminals
responsible for the atrocities perpetrated on the SAS and
located the remains of the missing SAS men in a complex
investigation.

Lt Col Brian Franks was instrumental in providing the
impetus for this secret search which continued for about
two years, even after the Regiment had officially ceased
to exist. At the end of a successful series of missions on
Operation Loyton in north-east France, there were thirty-
one SAS men who remained unaccounted for – a heavy
toll in SAS terms. Lt Col Franks was desperate to find out
what had happened to the men of his command who had
simply disappeared off the face of the earth. Solving the
puzzle was likely to be extremely complicated, if not
impossible. But he knew he had the perfect officer for the
job in the form of Maj Barkworth, who combined the
organisational skills of the military mind with the flair
and tenacity of a crack Scotland Yard detective.

Maj Barkworth was put in charge of the SAS War Crimes
Investigation Team, assisted by CSM Rhodes. The first
important lead came from the French, who were aware of the
existence of a mass grave at Gaggenau, a small town east of
the Rhine. Not far away there had been the Nazi camp of
Schirmeck where the French occupation authorities acting on
a tip-off had discovered a grave containing twenty-seven
bodies, both British and American. Barkworth asked Lt Col
Franks for formal permission to take a small team out to
Europe in search of more information. At the end of May
1945, Barkworth, Rhodes and four others left for the
continent, taking with them a jeep and a truck. They were

unaware that their quest would take many months and spread over an enormous distance.

SAS headquarters at Wivenhoe, in southern England, was still functioning at this time and communications were linked by high-powered radio operated by the Phantom signals unit, another secret war-time force. Barkworth was well equipped for foreign interrogations, being fluent in German and having excellent French. The men under him needed little motivation as they were looking for the bodies of their dead friends and comrades. The Gaggenau bodies were dug up once more and a pathologist inspected the remains. Even though the bodies were very badly decomposed, the SAS men realised to their horror that they could recognise and identify several by sight. Clothing and other items found on the bodies showed that these were indeed the Loyton men for which they were searching. Tags were found on the bodies of Maj Reynolds, Capt Whateley-Smith and a wristwatch, similar to those issued to all the fighting SAS. These were all uniquely numbered and this one corresponded with the watch issued to Lt Dill. Frenchman Roger Souchal, who had miraculously survived imprisonment at Schirmeck, told of horrific beatings meted out to Capt Whateley-Smith and Lt Dill at the Gestapo base at Saales. Two French priests also confirmed that Maj Reynolds was so badly beaten that his bones became visible through his skin.

The man the SAS team most wanted to catch was Oberwachtmeister Heinrich Neuschwanger who was alleged to have fired the shots at Gaggenau and was said to be primarily responsible for the beatings of prisoners at Schirmeck. In August 1945, Neuschwanger was tracked down, arrested and taken by Barkworth and Rhodes to the scene of his crimes. Rhodes described what happened and later admitted it was the only time in all his wartime service that he lost his temper with a prisoner. In Anthony Kemp's *The Secret Hunters*, he recalled:

In particular I remember that we brought Neuschwanger back to the scene of the crime and took him to the bomb crater [where the men were shot]. Our officer commanding, Major Bill Barkworth, was speaking to him and asked him what were his feelings about the murders that had taken place when the war was practically finished. He just stood there in a very arrogant sort of way.

Barkworth turned and looked at me and I looked at him thinking about the people that we knew personally – that's when my temper went.

So I knocked him to the bottom of the bomb crater, into about 18 inches of water that was in the bottom. But he was fortunate because he was coming out. The people that had gone in there before weren't.

Barkworth's SAS investigation team had many more successes, including tracking down the remains of six SAS murdered in the Moussey area. Sgt Davis had become separated from his patrol in woods in late August, was betrayed and captured and believed to be one of those interrogated at the Schirmeck camp. In the spring of 1945, a forest worker found a body subsequently identified as Davis. Davis had been shot, it is presumed for refusing to betray the whereabouts of his comrades at the main SAS camp. Sgt Fitzpatrick and Pts Elliott and Conway parachuted in on the night of 1 September 1944. Unfortunately, Elliott broke his thigh on landing and the others loyally did not leave him to his fate, the three of them hiding in a wood near a farm, where a French woman betrayed them. After arrest, the three were interrogated, brought back to the farm, shot and their bodies burnt. Two other murdered SAS found in the same area were both privates, Brown and Lewis. They were captured, taken to Schirmeck and then shot at the hamlet of Le Harcholet.

The case at St-Dié investigated by Barkworth accounted for another eight missing SAS personnel. The team found that Lt Black, Cpls Winder and Iveson, Sgt Terry-Hall and parachutists Salter, Lloyd, Dowling and Crosier were captured and imprisoned, again at Schirmeck and shot near St-Dié at the end of September 1944.

Investigations in the so-called La Grande Fosse case concerned the murder of a further eight SAS raiders. Members of a German armoured unit captured this group, commanded by Lt Dill, on 7 October. The men were handed over to the Gestapo at Saales where other captured SAS personnel joined them. Dill was later murdered at Gaggenau, as already described and the other ranks shot on 15 October in the area of woods known as La Grande Fosse. In many cases, the SAS men were found to have been shot in the back of the head at close range, execution-style.

By mid-November, the missing murdered SAS men had largely been tracked down and Maj Barkworth was able to submit his official report on his investigations just a month after the official disbandment of the Regiment. This was not the end of the story by a long way, however. The bodies of many SAS had been traced, but now the torturers and murderers of the British raiders had to be found and brought to justice. Barkworth's SAS investigation team now ranged far and wide over the British, American and French zones of occupation, scouring prison camps and numerous other sources, looking for the guilty parties. It was not unlike looking for a needle in a haystack, possibly at times even harder. Those responsible made it as difficult as possible to be identified and, when confronted, usually denied all responsibility of the crimes. So eyewitnesses had to be found to give reliable, accurate statements of what they had seen.

Of the main culprits, Neuschwanger, who had personally shot the SAS victims at the mass grave at Gaggenau, was traced and placed under the jurisdiction of British justice, found guilty and hanged. Barkworth and Rhodes were invited to witness his execution. In Kemp's *Secret Hunters*, Rhodes said: 'He was marched to the place where he was going to be hanged . . . right up to the moment that he was hung I don't think it worried him one little bit. I don't think he had any sorrow or remorse at all in him, that man, he was cruel.' Several of the German Kommando death squads who dealt with the Maquis and had been involved in the St-Dié murders of Loyton SAS victims were also sentenced to death. Others who were implicated received severe prison sentences. Some of the leading German personnel responsible for the orders that led to the deaths of the SAS men were brought to justice too, including Schneider, one of the main instigators, who was executed in January 1947.

Barkworth and his men had by this time spent nearly two years painstakingly tracking down the war criminals who had murdered scores of SAS raiders. The missing troops and officers had been accounted for and, where possible, given a decent burial. The team had scored a resounding, but poignant, triumph. Maj Barkworth emigrated to Australia after the war, married and started a successful business. He died in 1986.

Barkworth's lasting legacy is that Regimental honour had been restored after one of the most ferocious onslaughts on its soldiers in its history. More importantly, however, comrades tortured and executed in the most brutal circumstances imaginable had been justly avenged.

W.H. SMITH RETAIL LTD
BLUEWATER PARK
TELEPHONE NO: 01322 386843

VAT REG NO: 238 5548 36
Thank You For Shopping With Us
Cashier: Caroline Newton

	£
MORGAN,DAGGERS DRAWN	4.99
1 BAL DUE	4.99

CARD VOUCHER: CUSTOMER COPY

MASTERCARD		4.99
************8000	04/03	
CHANGE		0.00

PLEASE KEEP THIS COPY
FOR YOUR RECORDS

2628 006 52 4148 18:19 28FEB03

Save as you
spend with

WHSmith
CLUBCARD

It's **FREE** to join - ask for more details.

www.whsmith.co.uk
Customer Relations 0870 444 6 444
WHSmith Limited Registered no. 237811 England
Registered Office: Greenbridge Road, Swindon, Wiltshire SN3 3RX
VAT Reg no. 238 5548 36

Save as you

Unsung Heroes

Denis Bell

DENIS BELL – FIGHTING FIREBRAND

Three times wounded L/Cpl Denis Bell saw plenty of action throughout the Second World War in 1st SAS and SRS under the legendary Lt Col Paddy Mayne, and earlier in the 11th Scottish Commandos under Lt Col Geoffrey Keyes VC. He survived the costly major Commando raid at the Litani River in the Lebanon, and later served throughout all the SAS campaigns from the Western Desert to Sicily, Italy, France, Belgium, Holland, Germany and the final liberation of Norway. He was in action more or less constantly with the Commandos or the SAS from 1940 to 1945 and led a charmed life. His story is included in this book because it is so typical of the daring bravery shown time and again by so many SAS and SBS troopers, NCOs and officers, and it is a tribute to every one of them.

Many veterans and historians firmly believe that all SAS and SBS soldiers who took part in clandestine missions throughout the war were heroes in their own right and it is a fact that the hand-picked recruits from the cream of the regiments of the British Army faced perils way above the normal call of duty, as did other specialised units in all branches of the armed forces. But to go into action behind the lines in the first place, the SAS and SBS had to either parachute into usually dark and hostile drop zones with no reserve chute, assault beaches from landing craft under withering fire, or be dropped miles from hostile coasts by submarine to make their way to their targets in flimsy canoes or boats. Once at their destination, they often had to march many miles across rugged terrain, operate hundreds of miles behind the enemy lines for prolonged periods on foot or in jeeps, or caiques in the case of the SBS – and they all faced the additional peril of being tortured and shot if they were caught. Denis said: 'Later in the war, in Italy they had us all out on parade and told us about the discovery of Hitler's order that all SAS and Commandos captured should be executed. We were given the opportunity to return to our regiments with no honour lost, but no-one did and the reaction was just the same throughout the 2nd SAS.'

Denis Bell was born in the County Durham village of Butterknowle, near Barnard Castle, a typical, tough mining community. His parental upbringing was, as he readily admits, hard but fair and when the storm of war burst upon an ill-prepared Britain and France in 1939, Denis immediately volunteered for action. His father John Wilkinson Bell had served with the cavalry in France in the First World War and he was proud to see his son arrive home on his first leave in uniform and tin helmet, carrying the same sort of Lee Enfield rifle he himself had been issued with more than three decades before.

Denis originally joined the Royal Army Ordnance Corp, but found potato bashing and endless drill tiresome. He was young, determined and very fit and the frustrations of barrack room inaction left him wound up like a tightly coiled spring. This manifested itself early on in a comical, but potentially serious incident that could have got him thrown out of the Army, but which demonstrated that he possessed the flashpoint spark considered so vital an ingredient in potential recruits to the SAS. He recalled: 'This drill sergeant was swearing at us on the parade ground, calling us a "shower of Bs". I was furious and just stepped from the front rank and floored him. I was immediately arrested and got seven days confined to barracks. I was hauled before the CO and told him in all innocence that I'd had a religious upbringing and had never been spoken to like that before in my life. The CO just replied I was in the army now and things were like that and

I'd better get used to it!' Denis' religious leanings were literally to save his life later when he went into battle for the first time.

In mid-1940, Denis grabbed at the chance to join the 11th Scottish Commandos who were forming in Scotland ready to go overseas and, ironically, considering his later SAS service, one of the young officers was none other than Paddy Mayne. Geoffrey Keyes, of Rommel raid fame, was another outstanding and well-respected officer in the unit. Training took place on the remote Isle of Arran, near Largs in Scotland, and was so rigorous that many did not stay the course. One of the first tasks was to march three-quarters of the way across Scotland to weed out any weaklings. 'We took part in some of the first live firing assault courses on Arran, crawling under barbed wire with other troops blasting away with automatic weapons over us. You kept your heads down or you'd had it! We were set loose on the barren island without shelter and had to use our initiative to find something to eat. We caught and killed a sheep and one of the lads butchered it and we cooked it over an open fire. It is amazing what you will do if you are desperate, cold and hungry enough!'

Once fully trained, Denis and his comrades set sail for the Middle East and were ordered to assault Vichy French positions in the Lebanon at what became known as the Battle of the Litani River. Combined with a landward assault by Australian forces, the mission was to pre-empt a possible Axis expansion threatening the Middle East from an additional quarter. Due to a navigational error, many of the assault landing craft were set down on the wrong location at the heart of the enemy defences, which were much stronger than expected, covered by many interlocking machine-guns and other weapons. It was a debacle. The commanding officer Col Pedder and half the officers were wiped out and 120 men were killed and many more wounded out of a total force of nearly 400. Denis was hit in the arm and the bullet stopped just short of his heart, lodged in the prayer book he always kept in his top pocket – a miraculous escape. The Commandos gallantly took the enemy positions despite their heavy losses, and the Allied force of Australian troops advancing north through Palestine linked up to secure the situation, but the raid had been a salutary lesson.

Afterwards, a decision was taken to disband the Layforce group of Middle East Commando units, which included the 11th Scottish, as it was difficult to mount sufficiently effective amphibious operations for which they were designed, principally due to a shortage of suitable naval support.

The majority of the 11th Scottish Commando survivors were given the choice of joining the newly formed L Detachment SAS at Kabrit, near Cairo, the Long Range Desert Group or the Special Boat Section. Denis chose the SAS and underwent further arduous training.

Meanwhile, a party of 11th Scottish Commandos were training hard for a last, gallant mission that was to go down in history – the famous Rommel Raid. On 15 November 1941, to coincide with Gen Cunningham's major offensive of 18 November, a group of Commandos under Lt Col Geoffrey Keyes attempted to kill or abduct Rommel in his headquarters 250 miles behind the lines at Beda Littoria, near Benghazi. Tragically, Keyes was killed during the daring amphibious assault. Coincidentally, on 16 November, David Stirling and his raiders of L Detachment SAS set out on their first, equally famous, but disastrous parachute raid on the enemy airfields at Tmimi and Gazala.

From now onwards, perilous missions such as this were bread and butter to the highly trained ex-Commando men like Denis, but sabotage techniques and pinpoint accurate navigation in the featureless desert were brand-new skills that had to be learned – and quickly if the SAS men were to survive and prosper. During the next months in the desert, Denis got to know David Stirling well and often talked with the unassuming but brilliantly confident SAS commander, in the respectful relationship of lance corporal to commanding officer. Paddy Mayne, the towering sandy-haired former heavyweight boxing champion and rugby international was an inspiration, but also an education, to all the men. Denis said: 'Paddy was brave as a lion and so calm. But when he had taken a few drinks you had to watch out, he had a hell of a punch! But we would all have followed him to the ends of the earth.'

When the SAS were equipped with jeeps, heavily armed with Vickers K machine-guns in order to strike at will at targets along the desert independently of the LRDG, Denis took over the role as driver of one of the nimble, long-range vehicles, although the three-man crew would alternate roles as circumstances demanded. He took part in numerous raids, including the big jeep raid at Sidi Haneish, near Fuka, described earlier. 'Going into action is hard to describe unless you have experienced it,' Denis said. 'You get a prickly feeling at the back of the neck. It's something you never get used to – just like the first time you shoot a man and see him go down. But it was a case of either him or you. Raids like this were the reason why SAS training had to be so hard. Reactions had to be at a peak so that we could fight our way out of tight corners and you took it for granted that everyone could rely on everyone else. Stirling and Paddy thought everything out in detail before we did a mission. We didn't just blast our way in. Stealth, surprise and timing were crucial.'

With victory in the desert achieved at last in 1943, Denis and the temporarily renamed Special Raiding Squadron were at the forefront of landings in Sicily and Italy. At the seaborne raid of Augusta, Denis was involved in two memorable episodes, one a lucky hit that saved the day for his hard-pressed comrades and the other a terrifying mistake that made his blood turn to ice:

We had got ashore from the landing craft but were taking casualties from a machine-gun which was pouring down a withering fire from a well sited and well protected pill box above the beach. I spotted a two-inch mortar that a soldier near me had been carrying before he was killed and there were a couple of bombs nearby, so I thought why not have a go. I shouted 'Watch this lads, I'll put one right through the slit.' Aiming the small mortar manually and just pointing it in the general direction of the strong point, blow me if I didn't do just that with the first bomb! It got a great cheer and we were able to move off that part of the beach and get into the town proper. If I tried to do it again, I never could in a million years.'

Advancing up one of the main streets in the town with a file of SRS on either side of the street and tail end Charlies walking backwards and covering the rear, Denis got a chilling shock: 'It was tense, because there could have been plenty of enemy soldiers about ready to spring an ambush and I kept a hard grip on my Tommy gun. We were all keeping our eyes tightly peeled, when suddenly I looked into this doorway and glimpsed a soldier pointing a gun directly at me. I let fly with a heck of a burst and heard a great splintering of glass amongst the shattering din. Then some of my mates started laughing. I had shot my own reflection in a large mirror that had been in the hallway! It's better to be safe than sorry, but I got some ribbing for a while after that, I can tell you.'

It was also in Italy that a sniper came within an ace of killing the young lance corporal. Denis was observing enemy movements from behind a low wall when suddenly a bullet ricocheted with a deafening whine off the stone just millimetres from his head, sending fragments stinging into his cheek. The shot had come without warning from behind. 'The shock was tremendous, but a split second later I whirled round and saw the sniper hiding in a nearby tree – an Italian shouting "*Mama Mia*" as he fumbled to reload. But before he had chance to get off another shot, I drilled the blighter with my Tommy gun.'

Denis would confirm that the battle for Termoli was one of the toughest actions the SRS and 2nd SAS were involved in and, for a time, it was touch and go before the superior German forces were forced to withdraw. Termoli is not a happy memory for most SAS veterans, but they doggedly stuck it out and beat off crack troops equipped with tanks, artillery and took everything the Germans threw at them, albeit suffering some heavy losses.

When Denis returned to England to prepare with 1st SAS and 2nd SAS for the invasion of France, he married his sweetheart Alice and painted her name on his jeep for good luck. Although he made around thirty-five parachute drops in his long SAS career, the drop into France on Operation Haggard just after the D-Day invasion unsettled him for the very first time. 'We all knew it was going to be rough, especially if we got captured with so many SS troops and Gestapo about and several of my comrades were subsequently caught, tortured and shot, but that wasn't the reason for the tension. It was because I had something to lose now – a new wife and thoughts of our life ahead together. Before, I never thought about the danger for a second, but now this vital mission just had to be done and you had to put all thoughts of home and loved ones to the back of your mind, bite the bullet and get on with it.'

Strangely, thoughts of Alice saved Denis' life in a bizarre and inexplicable incident as he and another trooper crested a ridge, deep in France, on their way to reconnoitre a railway line that was to be blown up. Denis takes up the tale:

There appeared to be no-one about and no danger. We were alert and keeping our eyes peeled when suddenly I heard Alice's voice yell loudly in my ear 'Duck!' I flinched downwards instinctively and, just at that precise moment, a German Spandau machine-gun burst sliced through the air where my head had just been.

Both of us went to ground immediately and crawled into cover to work our way round and get the blighter, but when we got to where we judged he had been, he had legged it. He must have been on his own, or we'd have been for it. I can't explain this incident, I have never experienced premonitions or anything of that kind before or since. But it happened and I am still here to tell the tale.

On another occasion in France, Denis and another comrade were lying in wait near a road waiting for a convoy or suitable target to come by, when suddenly a group of German soldier cyclists came by – about as soft and tempting a target as they were ever likely to be presented with. The SAS pair opened up with Bren gun and Tommy gun and skittled the stunned soldiers with devastating bursts from their meagre remaining ammunition. But then, amazingly, every one of the German troopers got up unharmed and ran for cover. 'It was virtually impossible to miss, but we did and we felt very sheepish about it too,' said Denis. 'Nothing like that ever happened to me throughout the rest of the entire war, but strange things occur. Needless to say we didn't brag about it when we got back to our forest base camp.'

Throughout France and later in Belgium, Holland and Germany, Denis and his comrades came across some of the despicable atrocities perpetrated by the SS. Many good friends were captured and suffered appalling brutality, but the iron-like morale of the SAS held firm. 'When we came across the SS we just tried to kill the lot of them,' said Denis. 'They were bestial thugs, unlike the other German soldiers we fought who were hard opponents, but fair. They were simply inhuman and we gave them no quarter.'

It was in Germany, just after the incident when Paddy Mayne won his fourth DSO, that Denis was nearly killed once more, but this time inadvertently by one of his own comrades as he returned from a scouting patrol deep behind enemy lines. L/Cpl Bell, Capt Tim Iredale, Lt Grierson and Lt Surrey Dane were returning through a dense wood of conifer saplings when tragedy struck and they were mistaken for approaching enemy troops by one of their own men. Denis confirms that the correct password had been shouted out as they approached the main body of SAS, commanded by the legendary Mayne. But a burst of Bren gun fire suddenly rent the air and two officers were hit and very badly injured. The sentry had either misheard, or not heard, the password.

Iredale and Grierson needed urgent medical attention if they were to stand a chance of survival, although Denis and Surrey Dane had miraculously not been hit. Denis said:

> The man who had fired by tragic mistake was absolutely distraught. Because of the denseness of saplings, he couldn't see us properly as we approached. These things happen in war. Unfortunately, there was no doctor with our party and Paddy had a terrible decision to make. In the end, it was decided to drive a jeep under a white flag to the German lines to see if they could get urgent attention for the wounded officers. I doubt whether one of them would have survived anyway, he was in a very bad way.
>
> The soldier who had done the damage bravely volunteered to drive them in the hope that the Germans might have either cared for the wounded or allowed the party through to the British lines for treatment there. It was not long before the end of the war and there was a slim chance they would not be shot, so long as they could steer clear of the SS.

However, sadly, neither Denis or any of his close comrades saw or heard anything about the SAS trio again, although some accounts suggest they initially made it to the German lines, where a doctor pledged safe conduct for the wounded men. As with many incidents connected with the wartime SAS, what happened next is not clear. Whatever the outcome, however, the bravery of the SAS sentry, who was most at risk in the circumstances as he was uninjured and most likely to face brutal interrogation, possible torture and execution, was beyond doubt. The Germans would have been extremely keen to learn where the main body of SAS were in hiding so they could mount a raid. If the SAS man was captured, tortured and shot, he obviously gave nothing away for the group was not attacked.

After the surrender in Germany, Paddy Mayne and his triumphant SAS travelled to Norway to supervise the capitulation of the very large German forces there. For most it was a case of wine, women and song and some long awaited letting off of steam after the tense privations of the last few years. But Denis could not wait to return home to Britain and his young bride Alice. However, after the shock disbandment of the SAS just weeks later, Denis felt a furious resentment that all that the SAS had achieved after so much effort and suffering now appeared to count for nothing. When his medals later arrived from the War Office, he threw them in the dustbin in disgust, a decision he regretted deeply in later years. However, the SAS Association, which looks after the interests of veterans from conflicts from the Second World War to the present day, replaced them in latter years with an authentic replica set, after being informed about the situation by a friend of Denis'.

So, looking back, was it all worth it? Denis: 'I served with some of the finest soldiers this country has ever produced and we did make a difference to the end result, not just in the desert but in all theatres of war we were engaged in. If I had to do it all again, I honestly would not hesitate.'

Appendix I

Maps

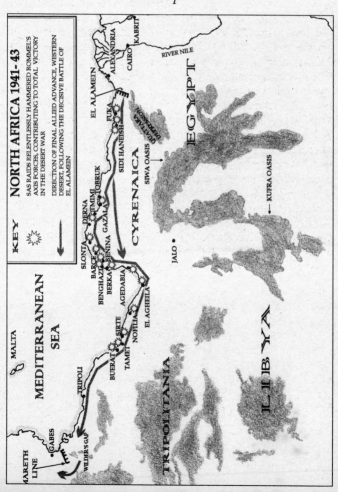

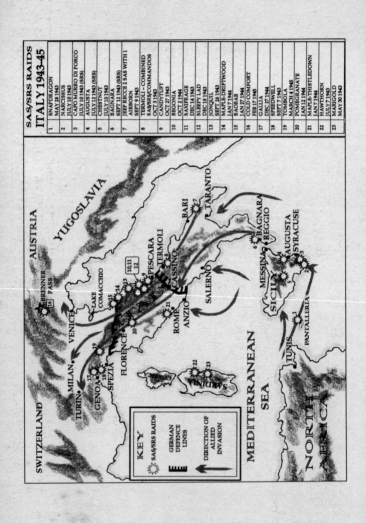

	SAS/SRS RAIDS ITALY 1943-45	
1	SNAPDRAGON	MAY 28 1943
2	NARCISSUS	JULY 10 1943
3	CAPO MURRO DI PORCO	JULY 10 1943 (SRS)
4	AUGUSTA	JULY 12 1943 (SRS)
5	CHESTNUT	JULY 10 1943
6	BAGNARA	JULY 10 1943
7	JBEP RBCCB 2 SAS WITH 1 AIRBORN	SEPT 12 1943 (SRS) SEPT 9 1943
8	TERMOLI – COMBINED SAS/SRS/COMMANDOS	OCT 3 1943
9	CANDYTUFT	OCT 27 1943
10	BIGONIA	OCT 2 1944
11	SAXIFRAGE	DEC 14 1943
12	SLEEPY LAD	DEC 18 1943
13	JONQUIL	SEPT 18 1943
14	MAPLE-DRIFTWOOD	JAN 7 1944
15	BAOBAB	JAN 27 1944
16	COLD COMFORT	FEB 17 1945
17	GALLIA	DEC 27 1944
18	SPEEDWELL	SEPT 7 1943
19	TOMBOLA	MARCH 4 1945
20	POMEGRANATE	JAN 12 1944
21	MAPLE-THISTLEDOWN	JAN 1944
22	HAWTHORN	JULY 7 1943
23	MARIGOLD	MAY 30 1943

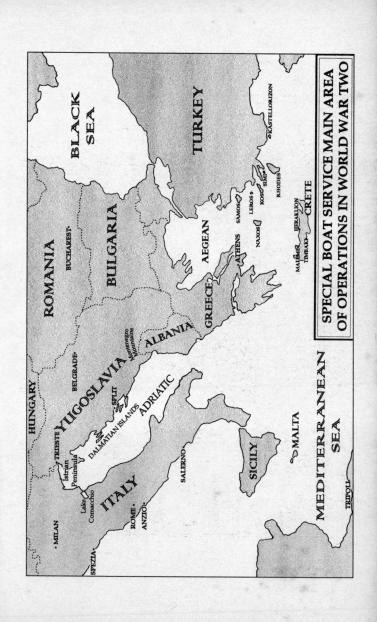

SPECIAL BOAT SERVICE MAIN AREA
OF OPERATIONS IN WORLD WAR TWO

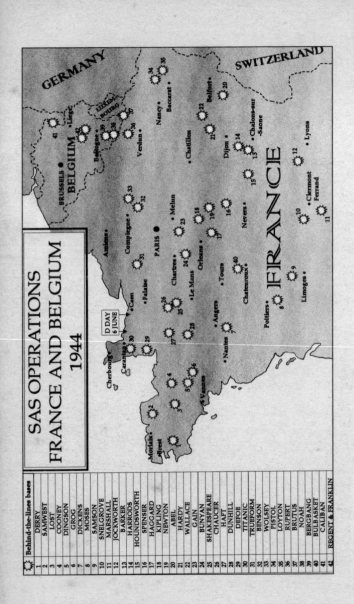

SAS OPERATIONS
FRANCE AND BELGIUM
1944

✿	Behind-the-lines bases
1	DERRY
2	SAMWEST
3	LOST
4	COONEY
5	DINGSON
6	GROG
7	DICKENS
8	MOSES
9	SAMSON
10	SNELGROVE
11	MARSHALL
12	JOCKWORTH
13	BARKER
14	HARRODS
15	HOUNDSWORTH
16	SPENSER
17	HAGGARD
18	KIPLING
19	NEWTON
20	ABEL
21	HARDY
22	WALLACE
23	GAIN
24	BUNYAN
25	SHAKESPEARE
26	CHAUCER
27	HAFT
28	DUNHILL
29	DEFOE
30	TITANIC
31	TRUEFORM
32	BENSON
33	WOLSEY
34	PISTOL
35	LOYTON
36	RUPERT
37	BRUTUS
38	NOAH
39	BERGBANG
40	BULBASKET
41	CALIBAN
42	REGENT & FRANKLIN

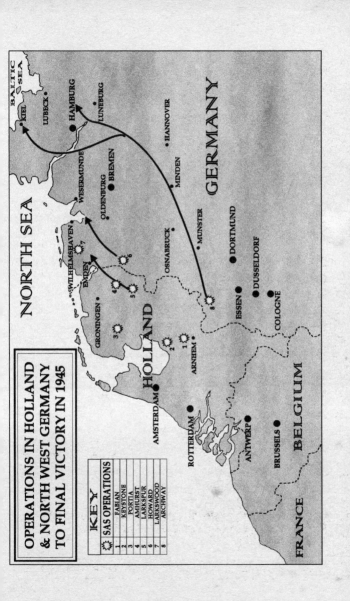

OPERATIONS IN HOLLAND & NORTH WEST GERMANY TO FINAL VICTORY IN 1945

KEY	
SAS OPERATIONS	
1	FABIAN
2	KEYSTONE
3	PORTIA
4	AMHURST
5	LARKSPUR
6	HOWARD
7	LARKSWOOD
8	ARCHWAY

NORTH SEA

BALTIC SEA

GERMANY

HOLLAND

BELGIUM

FRANCE

KIEL · LUBECK · HAMBURG · LUNEBURG · HANNOVER · WESERMUNDE · BREMEN · OLDENBURG · MINDEN · WILHELMSHAVEN · EMDEN · OSNABRUCK · MUNSTER · DORTMUND · GRONINGEN · DUSSELDORF · ESSEN · COLOGNE · AMSTERDAM · ARNHEM · ROTTERDAM · ANTWERP · BRUSSELS

Appendix II

Two of the Fearless Legends'
Official Citations

Lt Col Robert Blair Mayne, commanding officer of 1st SAS Regiment, was recommended for the third bar to his Distinguished Service Order in April 1945. The award of this decoration plus his foreign honours made Mayne the most decorated British soldier of the Second World War, barring the award of the ultimate honour, the Victoria Cross.

On Monday, April 9th, 1945 Lt Col Mayne was ordered by the General Officer Commanding Canadian 4 Armoured Division to lead his Regiment, then consisting of two armoured jeep squadrons, through the German lines.

His general axis of advance was North-east through the city of Oldenburg with the special task to clear a path for the Canadian armoured cars and tanks and to cause alarm and disorganisation behind the enemy lines.

As subsequent events proved, the task of Lt Col Mayne's forces was entirely and completely successful. This success, however, was solely due to the brilliant leadership of Lt Col Mayne who, by a single act of supreme bravery, drove the enemy from a strongly held key village, thereby breaking the crust of the enemy defences in the whole of this sector.

The following is a detailed account of the Colonel's individual action which called for unsurpassed heroism and cool, clear-sighted military knowledge.

Lt Col Mayne, on receiving a wireless message from the leading squadron reporting that it was heavily engaged by enemy fire and that the Squadron Commander had been killed, immediately drove forward to the scene of the action.

From the time of his arrival until the end of the action, Lt Col Mayne was in full view of the enemy and exposed to fire from small arms, machine-guns and sniper's rifles. On arrival, he summed up the situation in a matter of seconds and entered the nearest house alone and ensured that the enemy there had either withdrawn or been killed.

He then seized a Bren gun and magazines and, single handed, fired burst after burst into the second house killing and wounding all the enemy there and also opening fire on the woods.

He then ordered a jeep to come forward and take over his fire position, he himself returning to the forward section where he disposed the men to best advantage and ordered another jeep to come forward.

He got in the jeep and with another officer as rear gunner, drove past the position where the Squadron Commander had been killed a few minutes previously and continued to a point a hundred yards ahead where a further section of jeeps were halted by intense and accurate enemy fire.

This section had suffered casualties in killed and wounded owing to the heavy enemy fire and the survivors were unable at the time to influence the action in any way until the arrival of Lt Col Mayne.

The Colonel continued along the road, all the time engaging the enemy with fire from his own jeep. Having swept the area very thoroughly with close-range fire, he turned his jeep round and drove back down the road still in full view of the enemy.

By this time, the enemy had suffered heavy casualties and was starting to withdraw. Nevertheless, they maintained an accurate fire on the road and it appeared almost impossible to extricate the [SAS] wounded who were in the ditch near the forward jeep.

Any attempt at rescuing these men under these conditions appeared virtually suicidal owing to the highly concentrated and accurate fire of the Germans.

Though he fully realised the risk he was taking, Colonel Mayne turned his jeep round once again and returned to try and rescue these wounded. Then by superlative determination and by displaying gallantry of the very highest degree and in the face of intense enemy machine-gun fire, he lifted the wounded one by one into the jeep, turned round and drove back to the main body.

The entire enemy position had been wiped out. The majority of the enemy had been killed or wounded, leaving a very small remnant who were now in full retreat.

The Squadron, having suffered no further casualties, were able to continue their advance and drive deeper behind the enemy lines to complete their task of sabotage and destruction of the enemy.

Finally they reached a point, twenty miles ahead of the advance guard of the advancing Canadian Division, thus threatening the rear of the Germans, who finally withdrew.

From the time of the arrival of Colonel Mayne, his cool and determined action and his complete command of the situation, together with his unsurpassed gallantry, inspired all ranks. Not only did he save the lives of the wounded, but also completely defeated and destroyed the enemy.

Maj Anders Lassen of the SBS, who had already been awarded three Military Crosses earlier in the war, was recommended for the Victoria Cross posthumously in April 1945, having been killed in an heroic action aged only twenty-four.

In Italy on the night of the 8/9th April, 1945, Major Lassen was ordered to take out a night patrol of one officer and 17 other ranks to raid the north shore of Lake Comacchio.

His tasks were to cause as many casualties and as much confusion as possible, to give the impression of a major landing and to capture prisoners.

No previous reconnaissance was possible and the party found itself on a narrow road flanked on both sides by water.

Preceded by two scouts, Major Lassen led his men along the road towards the town. They were challenged approximately 800 yards from a position on the side of the road. An attempt to allay suspicion by answering that they were fishermen returning home failed, for when moving forward again to overpower the sentry, machine gun fire started from the position and also from two other blockhouses to the rear.

Major Lassen himself then attacked with grenades and annihilated the first position containing four Germans and two machine guns.

Ignoring the hail of bullets sweeping the road from the three enemy positions, an additional one having come into action from 300 yards down the road, he raced forward to engage the second position under covering fire from the remainder of the force.

Throwing in more grenades, he silenced this position, which was then overrun by his patrol. Two enemy were killed, two captured and two more machine guns silenced.

By this time, the [SBS] force had suffered casualties and its firepower was very considerably reduced. Still under a heavy cone of fire, Major Lassen rallied and reorganised his force and brought his fire to bear on the third position.

Moving forward himself, he flung in more grenades – which produced a cry of 'Kamerad'. He then went forward to within three or four yards of the position to order the enemy outside and to take their surrender.

While shouting to them to come out, he was hit by a burst of Spandau fire from the left of the position and fell mortally wounded, but even whilst falling he flung a grenade, wounding some of the occupants and enabling his patrol to dash in and capture this final position.

Major Lassen refused to be evacuated, as he said it would impede the withdrawal and endanger further lives and, as ammunition was nearly exhausted, the force had to withdraw.

By his magnificent leadership and complete disregard for his personal safety, Major Lassen had, in the face of overwhelming superiority, achieved his object. Three positions were wiped out, accounting for six machine guns, killing eight and wounding others of the enemy and two prisoners were taken.

The high sense of devotion to duty and the esteem in which he was held by the men he led, added to his own magnificent courage, enabled Major Lassen to carry out all the tasks he had been given with complete success.

Bibliography

Bradford, R. and Dillon, M. *Rogue Warrior of the SAS*, Murray, 1987

Cowles, Virginia. '*The Phantom Major*', *The Story of David Stirling and the SAS Regiment*, Collins, 1958

Farran, Roy. *Winged Dagger*, Collins, 1948

——. *Operation Tombola*, Arms & Armour Press, 1986

Fraser McLuskey, J. *Parachute Padre*, SCM Press, 1951

Geraghty, Tony. *This is the SAS*, Arms & Armour Press, 1982

Harrison, Derrick. *These Men are Dangerous*, Cassell, 1957

Hoe, Alan. *David Stirling*, Warner, 1994

Irving, David. *Rommel: The Trail of the Fox*, Weidenfeld & Nicolson, 1977

James (Pleydell), Malcolm. *Born of the Desert*, Collins, 1945 (reprinted with additional material by Greenhill Books, 1991, 2001)

Kemp, Anthony. *The Secret Hunters*, Michael O'Mara, 1986

Kennedy Shaw, W.B. *Long Range Desert Group*, Collins, 1945

Ladd, J.D. *SBS The Invisible Raiders*, Arms & Armour Press, 1983

Langley, Mike. *Anders Lassen VC, MC of the SAS*, New English Library, 1988

Lloyd Owen, David. *Providence Their Guide*, Harrap, 1980

Maclean, Fitzroy. *Eastern Approaches*, Jonathan Cape, 1949

Marrinan, Patrick. *Colonel Paddy*, Ulster Press, n.d.

Peniakoff, Vladimir. *Popski's Private Army*, Jonathan Cape, 1950

Pitt, Barrie. *Special Boat Squadron*, Century, 1983

Pleydell, see Malcolm James

Strawson, John. *A History of the SAS Regiment*, Secker and Warburg, 1984

Thompson, J. *War Behind Enemy Lines*, Sidgwick & Jackson in association with the Imperial War Museum, 1998

Warner, Philip. *The Special Air Service*, Kimber, 1971

Index

Agedabia 99, 156
airfields, attacks on 8–9,
    34, 97–101, 155,
    178, 207–8
  Fuka 41–4
  Rhodes and Crete 12, 64,
    162–7
  Sidi Haneish 13–15
Algeria 17, 74–6, 178,
    198, 204
Allott, Capt Ken 165–6
Almonds, Sgt Jim 99, 101
American Army 45, 128,
    132, 154, 179, 183
Appleyard, Maj Geoffrey
    62–3
areas of operations 226–9
Auchinleck, Gen Sir Claude
    5, 6, 8, 26, 27–8
Augusta (Sicily) 47,
    219–20

Barkworth, Maj Eric 19, 73,
    203–14
Belgium 21, 202, 222,
    228
Bell, L/Cpl Denis 34, 126,
    149, 215–24
Belsen 126, 133–6
Benghazi 11–12, 104–6,
    114, 118–19, 145,
    157

Bennett, RSM Bob 43, 57–8
Berge, George 10, 12, 103,
    162–3
Black, Lt James 193, 212
Blackman, Maj Mike 51,
    207
Bond, Maj Dick 49
Bond, James 109–11, 113
Bouerat harbour, raid on 11
Bradford, Capt Roy 145–8

Cairo 104, 114, 117
Calvert, Brig 'Mad Mike' 21,
    51
Campbell, Gen Jock 70–3
Canadian Army 21, 48–9,
    51
Castellerano 77–9
Celle massacre 133
Challenor, Sgt Harold
    'Tanky' 172
Channel Islands 62–3
Chatillon, Battle of 81–5
Churchill, Randolph 105,
    109
Churchill, Winston 3, 5,
    15, 103
Clarke, Cpl 81, 83
Clarke, Lt Col Dudley 3, 6
Comacchio 17, 65–8
Commando Order, Hitler's
    63, 138, 175–7, 179,

203, 207–8
reaction to 19, 206, 216
Cooper, Lt Col Johnny 98,
    102, 125–36, 178
Crete, raids on 63–4, 68,
    69–70, 162–5

D-Day 18–19, 145, 150,
    155–6, 207–8
Daniels, Sgt George 'Bebe'
    170–80, 182
decorations 230–4
Dill, Lt David 191, 211, 213
Dudgeon, Capt 171, 175–7
Duggan, Marine 165–7
Durnford-Slater, Brig J.F.
    190
DuVivier, Sgt Jeff 102, 145

El Alamein 31, 70, 73, 117
executions see Commando
    Order

Fairbairn, William 60–1
Fairbairn Sykes , William
    fighting knife 60–1
Farran, Maj Roy 58, 68–93,
    74–6, 200–2
Fenwick, Maj Ian 149–55
Fleming, Ian 109, 110
Fôret d'Orleans 150–5
Fôret St Jean 81–6
France, missions in 19–20,
    47–8, 68, 81–6,
    137–55, 157–60, 228
  Normandy invasion
    190–4, 202, 221–2
Franks, Lt Col Brian 18,

103, 187–94, 202,
    210
Fraser, Maj Bill 6, 102,
    155–60
Free French SAS 10–11, 12,
    16, 128, 152, 207
Fuka 13–15, 30–1, 44,
    114, 145, 219

Gabes 16, 128, 129, 131,
    200
Gaggenau 210–11, 213
Germany, missions in
    133–6, 229
Gestapo 19, 20, 193,
    207–9, 211
Goddard, Lt Monty 52–3
Greece 15, 65, 165–7, 227
  see also Crete
Greek Sacred Squadron 12,
    16
Greville-Bell, Capt Anthony
    172–4
Grierson, Lt R. 222–3

Hall, L/Cpl James 'Curly'
    139–40
Harrison, Capt Derrick 51,
    137–44
Harvey, Lt Ken 90, 91, 92
Haselden, Col John 118–19
Holland 21, 202, 222,
    229
Houndsworth base 47–8,
    52–4, 157
Hughes, Lt Quentin 207–8
Hull, L/Cpl William 'Billy'
    49–50, 54, 55–6

insignia 10–11, 15, 61, 209
intelligence 18, 49,
    110–11, 118–19, 157
  Eric Barkworth's 19,
    203–14
  faulty 149–50, 152
Iredale, Capt Tim 222–3
Italy, missions in 17, 21,
    76–81, 87–93,
    170–90, 220–1, 226
  see also Sicily

Jackson, Peter 78–9
Jalo oasis 9, 102
jeeps 12–15, 30–1, 49–50,
    76–9, 81–6, 138–44
Jellicoe, Lt Col Earl George
    12, 15, 16, 59, 64,
    68, 161–5

Keyes, Lt Col Geoffrey 40,
    41, 157, 158, 217
knife, Fairbairn-Sykes
    Commando 60–1
Kufra oasis 119, 121, 125

L Detachment 9, 16, 34,
    41, 95, 125, 155–6
  formed 6–8, 12, 103,
    113–14, 218
Lapraik, Maj John 15,
    167–9
Lassen, Maj Anders 17,
    59–68, 161, 232–4
Laybourn, Tpr Jimmy 91
Laycock, Maj Gen Sir Robert
    4, 63–8, 95
Layforce 6, 28, 95, 126, 218

Lee, Ramon 81, 83
Leigh, Lt David 83
Lewes, Lt 'Jock' John 4, 6,
    10, 25–6, 94–103
Lewes bomb 8, 29, 31, 44,
    98, 99, 155–6
Lilley, Sgt Bob 99, 100–2,
    113–17
Litani River, Battle of 40,
    215, 217–18
Long Range Desert Group
    (LRDG) 5, 9, 29, 99,
    100, 105
Lucy-sur-Yonne 145–8

McGinn, Sgt 'Maggie'
    145–7
McGonigal, Lt Eoin 6, 33, 98
Mackie, Capt Jim 82–3
Maclean, Fitzroy 15,
    103–13
McLeod, Brig R. 21, 158
Maleme airfield 64, 70
Malta 114, 162, 164–5
Maquis *see* French *under*
    resistance
Marble Arch 100, 101
March-Phillips, Gus 62
Mayne, Lt Col R.B. 'Paddy'
    6, 9, 11, 32–58, 102,
    148, 184–6
  commands 1st SAS 16
  and David Stirling
    39–40, 41
  decorations 38–9, 43,
    44–51, 230–2
  drinking vii–viii, 36, 40,
    57-8, 219

on raids 14, 33, 34,
41–3, 98–9, 119
Montgomery, FM Bernard
24, 119, 202
Morgan, Cpl Jack 73,
204–7, 209
Moss, Sgt 165–6
Moussey 212

Neuschwanger,
Oberwachtmeister
Heinrich 211–13
North Africa 6–17, 25–34,
40–4, 70–6, 94–125,
128–33, 155–60,
204–5
map 225
Norway 21–2, 41, 56,
179–80, 182, 224

Oldenburg 48–50, 54–5
Operations 16, 19, 20
Airthief 180–1
Gain 150
Haggard 221
Houndsworth 19, 145
Kipling 137
Loyton 190–4, 210–11,
213
Overlord 18, 155, 156
Pomegranate 207–8
Speedwell 170–86, 196
Tombola 21, 87–93
Wallace 48, 81–6
origins of SAS/SBS 1–8, 11,
15, 16, 161
Owen, Maj Gen David Lloyd
9, 38, 44

parachutes 4, 25–6
missions 29, 87–8, 97–9,
145, 150, 159,
170–2, 221
training 7, 28, 75–6,
95–7
Patterson, Maj Ian 168–9
Pedder, Col 40, 217
Persia 111–13
Philippeville base 17, 74–6,
178, 198, 204
Pinckney, Capt Philip 171,
180–3
Popski 178

red beret, origin of 11
regiments, formation of 16,
17, 21
Relf, Sgt Arthur 204
resistance
French 20, 48, 53, 85–6,
145–7, 154–5, 192
unreliability of 36,
81–2, 149–50, 152,
191
Italian 88–90
Yugoslav 103–4, 113
Reynolds, Maj Denis 209,
211
Rhodes, CSM Fred 'Dusty'
204, 210, 213
Rhodes 15, 165–7
Riccomini, Lt James 90,
92
Ritchie, Maj Gen Sir Neil 5,
9
Robinson, Sgt Tim 84–5,
172

Rommel, Erwin 4, 5, 40–1, 117, 155–60 205, 218
Rose, Sgt Maj 46
Russian Army 89–90, 93, 133

Sadler, Capt Mike 129–31
St Dié massacre 193, 212–13, 214
Sangro River 185
Sardinia, assault on 17
Sark 62–3
Schirmeck 211–13
Scott, Lt John 50, 51
Scratchley, Maj Sandy 74, 201
Seekings, Sgt Reg 42, 45, 47, 105, 135, 178, 183–6, 189
Sicily 17, 45–7, 125, 183, 200–2, 226
Sidi Haneish 13–15, 30–1, 219
Sillito, L/Sgt John 47, 117–25
Simi 65, 168
Skinner, Pte A. 47
Small Scale Raiding Force 16, 62, 64
Special Raiding Squadron (SRS) 17, 36, 45–7, 52, 64, 161–2, 185–90
SS troops 20, 85, 135, 139–44, 149, 190–4, 207–9
'sticky bomb' see Lewes bomb

Stirling, Lt Col David 4–5, 22, 23–32, 37–8, 43–4, 94–5, 127
capture 16, 31–2, 128–33
forms SAS/SBS 6–8, 11, 103–4
and Paddy Mayne 39–40, 41
on raids 14–15, 98–100, 218–19
Stirling, Lt Col William 'Bill' 16, 18, 174, 194–202
Stokes, Sgt 182
Surrey Dane, Lt 222–3
Sutherland, Col David 64, 165–7
Sutherland, Lt Col David 15
Syracuse 45, 46–7

Tait, Gp Capt J.B. 'Willie' 39
Tamet airfield, raid on 41–4, 99
Taxis, Sgt Freddie 130, 131
Termoli 17, 52, 79–81, 184–5, 188–90, 200, 220–1
Terry-Hall, Sgt Frank 193, 212
Tobruk 71–2, 73, 95, 114, 117, 118–19, 205
training 6–8, 10, 12, 28, 33, 74–6, 95–7, 178
pistol shooting 62, 65
SBS 162
survival 171, 182–3, 217

Tunisia 16, 128–33, 198

Villa Calvi/Rossi 89–93

weaponry 3–4, 7, 25, 45, 62
  Commando knife 60–1
  Vickers K machine-guns 13, 53, 137, 140–2, 146–7
Wedderburn, Lt 'Tojo' 172
Wellsted, Capt Ian 145–7
Western Desert 25–34, 40–4, 70–3, 94–125, 155–60, 204–5

Whateley-Smith, Capt Anthony 211
White, Sgt Frederick 'Chalky' 144–9
Wiseman, Capt Johnny 36–7, 47, 189
Woodhouse, Lt Col John 103

Young, Sgt Bob 84
Yugoslavia 15, 103–4, 113, 169

Zahidi, Gen 111–13